PROTESTANTISM, REVOLUTION AND
SCOTTISH POLITICAL THOUGHT

Scottish Religious Cultures *Historical Perspectives*

Series Editors: Scott R. Spurlock and Crawford Gribben

Religion has played a key formational role in the development of Scottish society shaping cultural norms, defining individual and corporate identities, and underpinning legal and political institutions. This series presents the very best scholarship on the role of religion as a formative and yet divisive force in Scottish society and highlights its positive and negative functions in the development of the nation's culture. The impact of the Scots diaspora on the wider world means that the subject has major significance far outwith Scotland.

Available titles

George Mackay Brown and the Scottish Catholic Imagination
Linden Bicket

Poor Relief and the Church in Scotland, 1560–1650
John McCallum

Jewish Orthodoxy in Scotland: Rabbi Dr Salis Daiches and Religious Leadership
Hannah Holtschneider

Modern Social Christianity in Scotland and Beyond: Essays in Honour of Stewart J. Brown
Edited by Andrew Kloes and Laura Mair

Scottish Presbyterianism: The Case of Dunblane and Stirling, 1690–1710
Andrew Muirhead

The Scots Afrikaners: Identity Politics and Intertwined Religious Cultures in Southern and Central Africa
Retief Müller

The Revival of Evangelicalism: Mission and Piety in the Victorian Church of Scotland
Andrew Michael Jones

Miracles of Healing: Psychotherapy and Religion in Twentieth-century Scotland
Gavin Miller

George Strachan of the Mearns: Seventeenth-century Orientalist
Tom McInally

Bantu Presbyterian Church of South Africa: A History of the Free Church of Scotland Mission
Graham A. Duncan

Dissent After Disruption: Church and State in Scotland, 1843–63
Ryan Mallon

Scottish Liturgical Traditions and Religious Politics: From Reformers to Jacobites, 1560–1764
Edited by Allan I. Macinnes, Patricia Barton and Kieran German

John Kennedy of Dingwall (1819–1884): Evangelicalism in the Scottish Highlands
Alasdair J. Macleod

Mission, Race and Colonialism in Malawi: Alexander Hetherwick of Blantyre
Kenneth R. Ross

Protestantism, Revolution and Scottish Political Thought: The European Context, 1637–1651
Karie Schultz

Civic Reformation and Religious Change in Sixteenth-century Scottish Towns
Timothy Slonosky

Forthcoming titles

The Dynamics of Dissent: Politics, Religion and the Law in Restoration Scotland
Neil McIntyre

William Guild and Moderate Divinity in Early Modern Scotland
Russell Newton

edinburghuniversitypress.com/series/src

PROTESTANTISM, REVOLUTION AND SCOTTISH POLITICAL THOUGHT

The European Context, 1637–1651

KARIE SCHULTZ

EDINBURGH
University Press

Edinburgh University Press is one of the leading university presses in the UK. We publish academic books and journals in our selected subject areas across the humanities and social sciences, combining cutting-edge scholarship with high editorial and production values to produce academic works of lasting importance. For more information visit our website: edinburghuniversitypress.com

© Karie Schultz, 2024, 2025

Edinburgh University Press Ltd
13 Infirmary Street
Edinburgh EH1 1LT

First published in hardback by Edinburgh University Press 2024

Typeset in 10/12 ITC New Baskerville by
Cheshire Typesetting Ltd, Cuddington, Cheshire

A CIP record for this book is available from the British Library

ISBN 978 1 4744 9311 6 (hardback)
ISBN 978 1 4744 9312 3 (paperback)
ISBN 978 1 4744 9313 0 (webready PDF)
ISBN 978 1 4744 9314 7 (epub)

The right of Karie Schultz to be identified as author of this work has been asserted in accordance with the Copyright, Designs and Patents Act 1988 and the Copyright and Related Rights Regulations 2003 (SI No. 2498).

Contents

Acknowledgements	vi
List of Abbreviations	viii
Introduction	1
1 The Godly Commonwealth in Early Modern Protestant Thought	24
2 *Adiaphora* and Ecclesiastical Reform	46
3 Royalist Political Thought	67
4 Church Government and the Commonwealth	93
5 Covenanter Political Thought	116
6 The Evolution of Resistance Theory	137
Conclusion	161
Bibliography	166
Index	191

Acknowledgements

There are a great many people to thank for their support as I developed this book over the past few years. I began this research during my PhD at Queen's University Belfast (2016–20), undertaken as part of a European Research Council project entitled 'War and the Supernatural in Early Modern Europe.' The project team included the Principal Investigator, Ian Campbell, in addition to Floris Verhaart, Todd Rester and Francesco Quatrini. I am extremely fortunate to have worked so closely with such a supportive group of scholars, while the seminars, workshops and conferences hosted by the project team greatly improved the research underlying this book. I am also grateful to members of our international advisory board – especially Sarah Mortimer and John McCafferty – for being so instrumental in shaping both this research and my academic career afterward. I would additionally like to thank Crawford Gribben for his exceptional mentorship during my time at Queen's, as well as the examiners of my doctoral thesis, Scott Dixon and John Coffey; their insightful comments ultimately informed how I approached this book (though they are in no way responsible for its faults!).

I wrote most of this book during a nine-month fellowship that I held at the British School at Rome (2020–21). It was not easy to conduct extensive research on Scottish history while locked down at the research institute during the height of Covid-19. I am exceedingly grateful for the encouragement and support that I received from Chris Wickham (the interim Director of the BSR at that time) and Leslie Brubaker, as well as for the friendship of William Aslet, Maria Harvey, Georgios Markou, Max Fletcher, and Zoe Farrell. It would have been impossible to complete this work while applying for postdoctoral fellowships without their camaraderie and good humour. I am also thankful for the friendship of Jan Machielsen, both for keeping me sane during the height of Covid and for his knowledge as I forayed from the research underlying this book to new work on Scottish Catholicism. May we all meet again in Rome soon.

Although I began this research at Queen's University Belfast, I completed it during my Leverhulme Early Career Fellowship at the University of St Andrews (2021–24). Multiple academics at the institution have helped me through the book-writing process and the trials of the ECR world. My mentor, Amy Blakeway, has selflessly given much of her time to always be at hand with words of wisdom. Roger Mason, Emily Michelson, and Richard Whatmore have also provided unparalleled encouragement, direction, and a great sense of community during all stages of my fellowship.

Lastly, I must thank the friends and family who have supported me through the highs and lows of academia (and who made sure that I ate and slept while finishing this project). I will forever be grateful for the friendship of Claire McNulty, Lauren Rose Browne, and Harrison Perkins as we all completed our PhDs together at Queen's. It certainly made the process far more enjoyable. To Grace Marie Wierenga and Haley Frye, you may both live an ocean away, but your support has always been close at hand. But above all else, to my parents, my sister Stephanie, and my partner Adam, thank you for supporting me to your utmost (even though none of you will read beyond the title of this book!). I hope you know that it has only been made possible because of you.

Karie Schultz
3 August 2023
University of St Andrews

Abbreviations

AUL	Aberdeen University Library
CUP	Cambridge University Press
EHR	*English Historical Review*
EUL	Edinburgh University Library
EUP	Edinburgh University Press
GUL	Glasgow University Library
MUP	Manchester University Press
NCL	New College Library, University of Edinburgh
NLS	National Library of Scotland
NRS	National Records of Scotland
OUP	Oxford University Press
RPS	*Records of the Parliaments of Scotland to 1707* [http://www.rps.ac.uk]
SHR	*Scottish Historical Review*
StAUL	St Andrews University Library
TRHS	*Transactions of the Royal Historical Society*

Introduction

On 28 February 1638, a group of Scots gathered at Greyfriars Kirk in Edinburgh to sign one of the most revolutionary documents in their kingdom's history: the National Covenant. Those who subscribed registered their opposition to the series of unpopular ecclesiastical reforms imposed by King Charles I (1600–1649) and Archbishop William Laud (1573–1645) that aligned the kirk more closely with the Church of England.[1] These reforms included the Book of Canons (1636), a set of controversial church laws which stipulated that clergy and laity who denied the king's supremacy over all ecclesiastical matters would be excommunicated.[2] Ministers also had to recite (rather than extemporise) prayers from the new Book of Common Prayer (1637) that Charles imposed through his royal prerogative, often against the wishes of Scottish ministers. On 23 July 1637, hostility to the prayer book erupted into popular riots, ones which reportedly began at St Giles' Cathedral but which soon engulfed other areas of the kingdom. The drafting of the National Covenant thus reflected gradually increasing tensions regarding the king's intervention in the kirk and his attempts to align its worship practices with those of the English church. However, the Covenant equally represented opposition to Charles's apparently arbitrary rule through the royal prerogative, forcing Scots to confront challenging political questions about the purpose of the commonwealth, constitutional limits on the king's sovereignty, and the legitimacy of resistance to magistrates as they entered a decade of violent, devastating warfare.

Scholars have long recognised the revolutionary nature of the Covenanting movement, especially the ways in which it altered Scotland's religious and political landscape after 1638.[3] To appeal to as many Scots as possible, the Covenanting leadership strategically fashioned the Covenant as an ambiguous document, enabling its supporters to ascribe their own personal meanings and motivations to the act of subscription.[4] As a result, previously marginalised individuals increased their engagement in the political process by subscribing, petitioning, rioting and oath-taking.[5] While the Covenant did unify a large portion of Scottish society behind a shared commitment to defending the 'true religion' against Charles's innovations, acceptance was far from universal. Following the drafting of the Covenant, the Tables (the Covenanters' provisional government in Edinburgh comprising nobles, gentry, burgesses and clergy) sent commissioners on a subscription campaign. Copies of the Covenant circulated widely, and ministers mobilised to provide their support from the pulpit. Nevertheless, strong pockets of anti-Covenanting sentiment emerged, while those who refused to subscribe cited an array of theological, legal and political reasons for their opposition. Such rifts within Scottish society intensified as armed conflict with the king arose, first during the Bishops' Wars (1639–1640), followed by the Wars of the Three Kingdoms (1639–1653). To raise finances, personnel and general support for their war effort, the Covenanting leadership created an increasingly coercive (yet ultimately unsuccessful) state predicated upon the maintenance of religious orthodoxy across society. Nevertheless, great diversity persisted within Scottish intellectual culture as royalists and Covenanters alike adapted cutting-edge political and religious ideas advanced by early modern Protestant intellectuals across continental Europe to their own conflicts.

This book examines the intellectual culture underlying the Scottish Revolution (1637–1651), focusing specifically on the relationship between ecclesiological ideas (those about the abstract nature of the church) and political ones (those about civil government and the commonwealth). It takes a distinctly cross-confessional and transnational approach, assessing how royalists and Covenanters combined Lutheran, Reformed and Catholic scholastic ideas from continental Europe with distinctly Scottish approaches to kingship and the kirk. In doing so, this book uses Covenanted Scotland as a case study to reconsider broader historiographical debates about the relationship between religion and politics in the early modern period. It demonstrates that political concepts traditionally associated with the modern state – such as consent of the governed, parliamentary sovereignty or the election of magistrates – did not emerge only when Scottish intellectuals marginalised their religious concerns in a process of secularisation. Instead, these political ideas played a significant role in how Scots solved a crisis about proper worship, defended the compatibility of civil and ecclesiastical governments, and promoted their preferred religious settlement for the British Isles. By focusing on Covenanted Scotland, a location frequently overlooked in histories of early modern political thought, this book provides a critical new perspective on how ecclesiological debates informed the advancement of those political ideas commonly associated with secularisation and modernisation.

Protestantism and Revolution in Early Modern Europe

This book makes two key historiographical interventions, one within the history of early modern religion and politics, and the other within the history of Scottish intellectual culture. First, scholars have long debated whether Protestantism (and especially Calvinism) constituted a revolutionary ideology responsible for the development of modernity. In the wake of the Protestant reformations, a series of destructive wars raged across continental Europe, including but not limited to the Peasants' War (1524–1525) in the German-speaking lands, the two Schmalkaldic Wars

(1546–1547, 1552–1555) in the Holy Roman Empire, the French Wars of Religion (1562–1598), the Dutch Revolt (ca. 1566–1648) and the Thirty Years' War (1618–1648) across central Europe. Some scholars – such as Roland Bainton, James Turner Johnson and Michael Walzer – claimed that Calvinist theology distinctively contributed to the outbreak of these conflicts by motivating the 'elect' to wage crusades against heretics and infidels.[6] As a result, early modern Reformed intellectuals replaced traditional just war theory with a radically different conception of holy war.[7] As Bainton argued, Calvinists believed that, 'The Church consisted approximately of the elect . . . with a commission to establish holy commonwealths, whether by persuasion or constraint of the ungodly.'[8] Calvinists thus viewed warfare as a divinely sanctioned crusade to extirpate the ungodly.

Walzer took Bainton's thesis a step further when considering the case of the English Puritans, agreeing that they advanced a new theory of holy war as 'a certain sort of war, very different from the just war or the constitutional act of resistance.'[9] The Puritans abandoned the idea that a just war existed between two parties of equal moral standing. Instead, as the elect, they stood on the side of the godly in a war against evil. This conception of godly versus wicked characterised medieval interpretations of holy war thought, a tradition that Puritan writers revived 'to form the basis of a conception of the English civil wars radically different from that of lawyers and Parliamentarians.'[10] English Puritans thus believed that God would aid their holy cause, and that their ungodly and wicked enemies deserved unsparing prosecution. Walzer simplistically equated the term 'crusade' with 'revolution', arguing that, 'Behind both crusade and revolution lay the idea of contention for a cause.'[11] This led him to conclude that English Puritans waged a crusade in the 1640s to create a revolutionary new political order, one in which they triumphed over depravity and established a holy commonwealth.

This emphasis on Calvinism's unique, revolutionary character prompted other scholars to seek alternative, non-religious causes for political change. For example, Quentin Skinner downplayed the uniqueness of Calvinism in producing a distinctive theory of resistance that had revolutionary implications. Instead, he claimed that

> The revolutions of sixteenth-century Europe were, of course, largely conducted by professed Calvinists, but the theories in terms of which they sought to explain and justify their actions were not, at least in their main outlines, specifically Calvinist at all.[12]

Furthermore, Protestants paradoxically contributed to the emergence of the modern state through the secularisation of their political thought. Faced with prolonged warfare across Europe, early modern intellectuals began to reject religious ideology, conceiving instead of a secular end for the state that would better ensure temporal peace. According to Skinner, for a number of political theorists, 'if there were to be any prospect of achieving civic peace, the powers of the State would have to be divorced from the duty to uphold any particular faith.'[13] As a result, 'the religious upheavals of the Reformation made a paradoxical yet vital contribution to the crystallising of the modern, secularised concept of the State.'[14] Political theorists ultimately ceased to view participation in politics as a duty to God, one that might oblige subjects to resist an ungodly civil magistrate on behalf of the true religion.[15] Instead, politics came to serve a secular rather than religious end: the physical safety and material security of the people. As Ian Campbell summarised, 'The liberal historiography of the modern secular state has often depicted Calvinist theories of resistance and revolution as providing an escape path from religious conflict towards a secular doctrine of popular sovereignty.'[16] Within this historiographical tradition, Protestants made a critical contribution to sixteenth- and seventeenth-century revolutions by drastically reconsidering the end of politics, developing secular justifications for warfare and prioritising popular sovereignty.

Scholars have also examined these broader tensions about religious and secular justifications for warfare, especially the unique role of Calvinism, during the Wars of the Three Kingdoms (albeit often from an English perspective). For example, Christopher Hill intentionally sought non-religious explanations for the English Revolution by 'leaving Puritanism aside'.[17] He argued that the civil wars in England were more revolutionary than religious wars occurring elsewhere in Europe because they had multiple non-religious causes – long-standing economic grievances and deeply rooted social tensions – that fomented a broad, populist uprising. Puritanism thus provided the perfect social conditions in which class struggles might erupt into civil war, but faith alone did not motivate English subjects to take up arms. As Skinner summarised, in England, the civil war thus appeared as a revolution 'recognisably modern in the sense of being secular in its premises and populist in its vindication of government by, as well as for, the people.'[18]

John Morrill resisted this materialistic interpretation, emphasising predominantly religious justifications for the wars instead. He maintained that, although the civil war constituted 'a *defensive* political operation, a defence of existing liberties against an arbitrary king, it was an *aggressive* religious operation, a challenge to the whole of the existing structure and practice.'[19] As a result, it 'was not the first European revolution: it was the last of the Wars of Religion.'[20] Morrill later reassessed his approach, recognising criticism that he 'created a monocausal explanation of the civil war', one that 'put religious causes on a pedestal'.[21] Nevertheless, he maintained that the king's opponents more readily embraced religious language to defend resistance, and that they appeared hesitant to advance legal or constitutional arguments.[22] Scholars have since moved away from this strict dichotomy between religious war and political revolution, focusing instead on the complex combination of short-term factors (economic, constitutional, personal and religious) that culminated in armed conflict throughout the 1640s.[23] But the tension between religious justifications for warfare (such as defence of the true religion or the necessity of holy war to eradicate idolatry) and apparently secular legal-constitutional ones (such as popular sovereignty, the election of magistrates and parliamentary limits on monarchical authority) persists within the intellectual history of the period.

Scotland's Revolution, 1637–1651

Despite the wealth of debate about the relationship between Protestantism and revolution (both in early modern Europe and in the English civil wars), Scotland has rarely factored into these conversations. Following the advent of 'British history' or a 'three kingdoms' approach – one that accounts for the deeply interconnected nature of developments across England, Scotland, Ireland and Wales – historians have reconsidered Scotland's crucial role in these conflicts.[24] Although there are many strengths to this approach, Glenn Burgess has rightly noted that, 'The study of English political discourse is well developed; but that is not true of Scottish ... there is little to check the potential capacity of "British" history to distort our picture of Scottish political thought.'[25] Indeed, the Covenanters' justifications for war have often been interpreted as more monolithically religious (akin to holy war theories) than the legal-constitutional reasoning of their English contemporaries. For example, Morrill argued that the Covenanters' aggressive attempts to advance Presbyterianism across the British Isles during the Anglo-Scottish wars of 1639–51 resulted in 'wars of religion in a purer sense' for the Scots than for the English.[26] Burgess likewise claimed that the Covenanters advanced a pure theory of holy war, one that contrasted the justifications of English clergymen who defended the wars on legal grounds 'because of their acceptance of widespread conventions condemning the use of force for religious purposes.'[27] By contrast, the Covenanters exemplified a '"pure" theory of religious war' that their English contemporaries were reluctant to adopt.[28] Similarly, Edward Vallance maintained that, 'In contrast with the largely secular case for resistance put forward by Parliamentarian authors, Scottish covenanters developed an essentially religious justification for rebellion', one based upon the covenantal obligation to defend the true religion.[29] Drawing upon a limited number of printed works from Scotland, frequently only Samuel Rutherford's *Lex, Rex* (1644), these studies suggest that Scottish society primarily comprised proponents of holy war, resulting in a skewed or oversimplified interpretation of the kingdom's diverse intellectual culture.

Certainly, it cannot be denied that religion significantly motivated the Covenanters to resist their king, while they were more likely to emphasise the importance of being a nation covenanted with God in defence of their military action. Following Scotland's Protestant Reformation in 1560, Scots experienced decades of controversial royal intervention in the church as they struggled to forge their own religious orthodoxy. Throughout the 1590s, King James VI slowly dismantled Presbyterianism, a form of hierarchical church government based upon elders, presbyteries, synods and the General Assembly. He believed that Presbyterianism threatened absolute monarchy because it allowed ecclesiastical authorities to operate independently of royal oversight, even holding the king accountable to church censure like any other subject. James favoured instituting episcopacy instead, a polity that gave him greater control over individual parishes through his direct appointment of bishops. The Union of Crowns in 1603 wrought additional challenges for the kirk. Pursuing a policy of 'ecclesiastical convergence', or at the very least seeking greater uniformity between the Churches of England and Scotland, James instituted highly unpopular ceremonies in his northern kingdom.[30] For example, the divisive Five Articles of Perth (1618) mandated kneeling at communion, confirmation by bishops and the observance of holy days, practices that characterised the Church of England and (for Scottish sceptics) threatened to reintroduce 'popery' into the Reformed kirk.[31]

When Charles I succeeded to the throne in 1625, he inherited a plethora of escalating religious tensions while pursuing his own unpopular ecclesiastical policies (notably without his father's political acumen or willingness to compromise). Charles effectively excluded the Scottish parliament from its historical role in reforming the church when he imposed the Book of Canons and Book of Common Prayer through his royal prerogative. His heavy-handed approach resulted in widespread civil unrest preceding the National Covenant, and eventually in the armed conflicts of the Bishops' Wars. Following the start of civil war in England in 1642, the Covenanters actively sought to export Presbyterianism across the British Isles (not just secure its safety at home) when they allied with the English parliamentarians in the Solemn League and Covenant (1643). Although the English viewed this treaty as a military alliance, the Covenanters sought 'to bring the Churches of God in the three kingdoms to the nearest conjunction and uniformity in religion, confession of faith, form of church-government, directory for worship and catechising.'[32] The Covenanters also worked towards a Presbyterian settlement for England by sending commissioners to the Westminster Assembly (1643–1653), the body of divines appointed to restructure the Church of England. Here, they promoted a Scottish brand of Presbyterianism to an English audience, although scholars have contested their level of uniformity, influence and success.[33]

In the latter half of the 1640s, religion remained a dominant concern, albeit one that fractured any initial unity of the Covenanting movement. Although the desire to establish Presbyterianism beyond Scotland's borders persisted, Covenanters diverged regarding whether they should guarantee this settlement through prolonged warfare against the king, or whether they should compromise with Charles to counter the growing threat posed by the English Independents. After Charles escaped captivity and fled to the Isle of Wight in 1647, a small group of moderate Covenanter nobles joined him in a secret military alliance known as the Engagement. The king agreed to establish Presbyterianism in England for three years, but he refused to subscribe the Covenant himself or compel his English subjects to do so against their consciences. The question of whether the Covenanters should accept such limited terms divided them into Engagers (those who supported the alliance) and anti-Engagers (those who opposed it). After the defeat of the Engagers' army in August 1648, individuals who had dissented from the alliance formed the 'Kirk Party', purging both Parliament and the General Assembly of all former Engagers and royalists. Although the most ardent supporters of Presbyterianism retained positions of political and religious prominence in the late 1640s, their justifications of resistance to the king did have its limitations. The Scots denounced Charles's execution at the hands of the Rump Parliament in January 1649, swiftly proclaimed Charles II as the new king and crowned him in 1651 on the condition that he swear the Covenants and accept their terms in the Treaty of Breda (1650). Although Charles II reluctantly endorsed Presbyterianism, he still struggled to secure the Scots' committed allegiance.[34] As the events of the 1640s demonstrate, militant defence of the true religion and the active promulgation of Presbyterianism beyond Scotland's borders did significantly motivate the Covenanters' political and military decisions.

Nevertheless, many Scots (especially nobles) resisted for alternative reasons. Allan Macinnes has shown that multiple political, economic, religious and social grievances converged to produce explosive levels of discontent with Charles's reign.[35] Many Scots resented the absentee kingship that made Charles both geographically and culturally detached from his northern kingdom. The nobility, in particular, disliked the king's landholding and taxation policies, while others resented the perceived decrease in their political clout within his court.[36] Indeed, Maurice Lee rightly observed that, 'Religious discontent by itself would not have provoked the alliance among the people who counted in Scotland', one that included nobles, lawyers, ministers, and burgesses of the burghs.[37] Additionally, not all Scots who resisted the king ardently sought a Presbyterian settlement across the three kingdoms. Instead, the National Covenant became 'a revolutionary enterprise binding the Scottish people by social compact to justify and consolidate revolt against Britannic monarchy', a revolution that had many complex causes beyond religion.[38] Scots' desire to preserve their traditions and customs from English encroachment, their frustration with the king's seemingly arbitrary rule against the laws of the land, and their religious grievances all converged to generate a desire for military resistance.

On these grounds, historians of early modern Scotland have argued that the kingdom underwent its own revolution between 1637 and 1651, one that differed in nature from that in England. For example, David Stevenson pioneered an interpretation of the Scottish Revolution as 'essentially conservative', focused on restoration rather than progressive, forward-looking change.[39] Yet the Scots' involvement in the civil wars 'amounted to more than a mere *coup d'état*, resulting in both a substantial shift of power from the monarch to Parliament, and in the abolition of the clergy as one of the parliamentary Estates.[40] As a result, Scotland's revolution presaged 'a major change in the character of the government of the country brought about by violence'.[41] But unlike the English Revolution, these political changes had religious underpinnings while 'the quarrel between state and society was primarily religious in form'.[42] Other scholars have taken a different perspective on the idea of the 'Scottish Revolution'. Most recently, Laura Stewart convincingly reassessed Stevenson's institutional focus on the parliamentary Estates and his conservative view of restoration. Instead, she demonstrated 'the ways in which different social groups engaged with the construction and representation of political processes distinctive to Scotland.'[43] The changes that the National Covenant wrought extended beyond civic institutions and comprised widespread social and cultural developments. The interpretive vagueness and the strategic ambiguity of the Covenant itself generated 'political and ideological contests over the meaning of authority', created new spaces for debate and drew 'subordinate groupings, including women as well as men, into politics'.[44] Ultimately, the Scottish Revolution 'brought about the establishment of a confessional state predicated on a powerful, but unstable, alliance between secular and ecclesiastical authority', one that required the Covenanting leadership to pursue an unprecedented 'harnessing of human and material resources'.[45]

Nevertheless, there has been no sustained analysis of how the ideas about church and state debated by royalists and Covenanters contributed to (or challenged) the revolutionary nature of this period. While the conflicts in Scotland between 1637 and 1651 did not result in religious plurality or the emergence of radical new political groups (as in England), they did significantly alter how Scots on all sides of the conflict thought about their governing institutions. As a result, this book offers a comprehensive approach to Scottish intellectual culture by examining the relationship between the political and ecclesiological ideas underlying the kingdom's 'Revolution'. To do so, it shifts the focus away from the British Isles and towards the transnational, cross-confessional context in which Scots developed their ideas. The wars that embroiled the British archipelago in the 1640s were neither new nor unprecedented within the wider Protestant world. Developments in Scotland resembled those in other kingdoms, principalities, territories and city-states across post-Reformation Europe. As Scots debated languages of political and religious legitimacy, they reflected upon wider problems about the relationships between law and gospel, church and state, reason and revelation, and subjects and princes that confronted Protestants globally as they struggled 'above all else with the legacy of the Reformation'.[46]

The international dimension to Scottish intellectual culture is unsurprising given the kingdom's vast connections to the world beyond Britain in the seventeenth century. The migration of Scottish exiles, diplomats and merchants all established Scotland's position within Europe.⁴⁷ Scottish soldiers also fought in overseas conflicts, such as the Thirty Years War, where they contributed to the international Protestant cause.⁴⁸ The kingdom's intellectual culture was equally outward looking in its focus. Scottish students often studied at universities overseas, predominantly in the Low Countries and the German-speaking lands, where they forged vital academic and confessional networks.⁴⁹ Regents at Scotland's five universities – St Andrews, Glasgow, Edinburgh, King's College Aberdeen and Marischal College Aberdeen – also instructed their students about the ethical, philosophical and theological debates taking place in Europe while integrating the latest pedagogical trends into their curriculum.⁵⁰

By situating Scottish political and ecclesiological thought within the broader intellectual trends developing on the continent, this analysis challenges the narrative that the Covenanters waged a 'holy war' that they justified as a defence of the true religion, often at the expense of legal-constitutional arguments. Nor were their legitimisations of resistance for religious purposes unusual within wider Protestant intellectual circles. They certainly turned to scripture for examples of civil polities and warfare, but they joined their scriptural exegesis with a high respect for human rationality and agency over political life. Crucially, when advocating for a Presbyterian settlement for all three kingdoms, the Covenanting leadership needed to show that this form of church government could coexist peacefully with (rather than challenge) existing civic institutions. Politics and ecclesiology therefore went hand in hand and provided Scots with interconnected ways of thinking about the legitimacy of waging war. The primary aim of this book is therefore to examine how Scots engaged with and adapted classical, Lutheran, Calvinist and Catholic scholastic ideas to their own context. In doing so, it sheds critical light on the great diversity of intellectual traditions within Covenanted Scotland that laid foundations for the political, cultural and social changes of the kingdom's revolution.

Royalists and Covenanters: Diverging Intellectual Traditions

Apart from situating Scottish intellectual culture in a cross-confessional European context, this book makes a second historiographical intervention: examining Covenanter ideas alongside those of their royalist contemporaries. When embarking on their subscription campaign in 1638, Covenanter commissioners frequently encountered written and physical hostility. They even had to employ tactics of coercion to ensure conformity to their agenda, such as deposing or exiling their opposition. But most scholarship on Scottish political thought has focused on the Covenanters' intellectual output, or on the ideas that their predecessors produced during the Scottish Reformation. For example, Roger Mason and J. H. Burns pioneered the study of Scottish political thought during the sixteenth and seventeenth centuries in its 'British' context while still accounting for distinctively Scottish elements, such as models of elective kingship.[51] Others examined treatments of law, history and custom in the works of key Scottish intellectuals – George Buchanan (1506–1582), John Knox (ca. 1514–1572), James VI (1566–1625) and Andrew Melville (1545–1622) – all of whom contributed to unique Scottish intellectual traditions about the nature of monarchy and Presbyterianism.[52] The study of Covenanting political theory in the 1640s is equally well studied.[53] Biographies of individual Covenanters, such as Samuel Rutherford (1600–1661), Robert Baillie (1602–1662), Archibald Campbell, Marquis of Argyll (1607–1661) and James Graham, Marquis of Montrose (1612–1650), have highlighted their similarity to Reformed intellectuals beyond Scotland's borders.[54]

However, the political and ecclesiological concerns of those who refused subscription of the Covenant, or those who militarily supported the king, have not received the same level of analysis. Scholars traditionally restricted anti-Covenanting sentiment to the so-called 'conservative north' of Scotland, or to Episcopalians who favoured strong monarchical authority over the church.[55] But recent scholarship has begun to uncover the diversity and complexity of Scottish royalism as a movement.[56] Resistance to the Covenant was far more widespread than has previously been acknowledged, extending to the universities, the merchant classes and the burghs. Those who resisted also articulated a range of political, legal and theological justifications for their opposition. Recent scholarship has therefore done much to emphasise the diverse nature of Scottish royalism, although it has focused predominantly on the writings of individual royalists, or on the nature of the movement in precise settings (such as the universities or specific cities). There has been little analysis of the intellectual resistance that royalists posed to the Covenanting leadership as a whole, not just during the National Covenant debates but throughout the 1640s.

The marginalisation of Scottish royalists in studies of political thought and intellectual culture has likely occurred for a few reasons. First, people's loyalties and allegiances frequently shifted during the Wars of the Three Kingdoms, making it difficult to determine who truly counted as a 'royalist'. The Covenanters' coercive subscription campaign, coupled with their tendency to purge or depose their opposition from positions of political and religious prominence, resulted in malleable allegiances throughout this period. Some Scots who initially resisted the Covenanters changed their position under duress or for their own welfare, such as Donald Mackay, Lord Reay (1591–1649) who 'spent much of 1638 and 1639 fluctuating between his preference for the royalist cause and adopting an expedient attitude toward the National Covenant'.[57] Scottish royalism thus comprised individuals who supported Charles unwaveringly, in addition to others who changed their allegiances frequently throughout the civil wars. A significant middle group also emerged, one that included 'a majority of the population, who initially put peace and quiet above principle'.[58] While it is becoming increasingly difficult to define precisely what being a 'Covenanter' meant, it is equally challenging to describe 'royalism' as a commitment to a single set of ideological principles.

Additionally, many Scottish royalists had personal and pragmatic reasons for their allegiances rather than an expressed interest in any specific theory of political power. While the Covenanting leadership actively engaged in a propaganda campaign to defend the National Covenant and the Solemn League and Covenant south of the border, royalists more often referenced kinship, personal friendship or the desire to protect a *status-quo* political order that sustained noble power. As Barry Robertson observed, 'Royalist nobles were much more likely to expound their instinctive loyalty to Charles I and their adherence to the hierarchical order of society.'[59] Similarly, Nicole Greenspan noted that not all royalists supported the king 'out of coherent, rational political or constitutional views of the nature of political authority'.[60] As a result, fewer royalist writings on political theory exist than for the Covenanters, contributing to an overemphasis on the homogeneity of Scottish intellectual culture after 1637.

However, the scarcity of royalist writings on political thought partially reflects the concept of inherited versus invented loyalties as opposed to a complete disinterest in such theories. In response to the Covenanters' arguments in favour of resistance, royalists frequently articulated some version of the divine right theory of kingship. According to this theory, God directly appointed rulers to act as His regents on earth. Any individual who resisted the king therefore resisted the hand of God and transgressed their divinely mandated duty of obedience. Although this theory had roots in medieval and post-Reformation thought, James VI developed it in a Scottish context specifically to counter Buchanan's defence of limited, elective monarchy.[61] While scholars have debated whether the divine right theory of kingship made monarchy fully absolute, or whether kings remained limited by divine and natural law, many royalists across the British Isles defended their obedience with reference to this inherited position, one that reflected an organic, hierarchical order within political society.[62] By contrast, Covenanter leaders worked much harder to create an alternative theory of the civil state that overturned existing norms about obedience and legitimised subjects taking up arms for religion. Consequently, they produced more material defending their cause to persuade and mobilise the English and Scottish publics on their behalf.[63] As a result, the smaller number of royalist writings does not necessarily prove their disinterest in abstract theories of political power.

Additionally, the Whig historiographical tradition long portrayed the divine right theory of kingship (and the royalists who advanced it) as antiquated or conservative impediments to the progressive establishment of constitutionalism and modern liberalism. But royalists were not backwards-looking individuals who hindered their more progressive parliamentarian and Covenanter contemporaries from championing constitutional monarchy and the rule of law.[64] The royalist movement was just as intellectually complex and comprised individuals from many professions and social backgrounds, such as ministers, civic leaders, burgesses of the burghs, professors and nobles. Scottish royalism thus became a potent force throughout the kingdom, one that represented the reception of competing, yet equally important, Protestant and Roman Catholic intellectual traditions within Scotland – a story that Covenanter writings alone cannot tell.

Method and Terminology

In some ways, this book departs from current scholarly trends in the study of early modern Scotland that emphasise popular engagement with religion and politics and a movement away from the intellectual 'elite'. As a result, a few methodological points deserve express consideration to articulate both the scope and limitations of this study. First, as a comparative survey of Scottish political and ecclesiological ideas, this book does focus predominantly on the writings of a core set of intellectual elite. This group comprises royalist and Covenanter intellectuals who received a university education, and who authored works that clearly articulated political and ecclesiological ideas in response to the conflicts after 1637. These individuals were frequently well-known to their contemporaries and held positions within Scotland's religious, educational or civic institutions. Admittedly, some of these authors did not fully represent the interests or views of most Scots, while they tended to ally with a 'radical mainstream of gentry and burgesses' to coordinate the war effort.[65] Recent scholarship has consequently shifted the focus away from the elite leadership, focusing instead on broader engagement with the Covenant among members of the wider population.

However, the main purpose of this book is to offer an analysis of the ideas that lay at the core of the cultural, religious and political developments of the Scottish Revolution. This examination therefore depends upon the writings of individuals who advanced concrete theories about politics and ecclesiology, generally the Covenanter and royalist leadership. Where possible, I have supplemented their writings with manuscripts, sermons, popular pamphlets and works by lesser-known authors. I do not suggest that all Scots adhered to the ideas that I will discuss, or that these were the only reasons behind Scots' allegiances in this period. Indeed, many Scots were wholly unconcerned with abstract ideas about monarchy, political power or church government. Instead, many were more affected by popular religious practices that determined the everyday structures under which they lived.[66] Yet we should not discount the importance of texts which claimed to represent the ideological basis of the royalist or Covenanting movements, or ones that served as propaganda to mobilise the Scottish public, even if these works did not result in a steadfast commitment to one ideological programme of reform among the wider population.

Additionally, this book does not address the popular reception of political and ecclesiological ideas within Scotland through engagement with print culture. We know that print and pamphleteering significantly shaped public opinion during the Wars of the Three Kingdoms, creating additional spaces for public debate and ushering in new forms of political and societal association.[67] Protestations, petitions, oaths and pamphlets all contributed to the formation of the public sphere and enabled broader engagement with the political process, especially in Covenanted Scotland.[68] Printed works demonstrate the ideas that Covenanter and royalists authors tried to disseminate on a larger social basis, both to defend their actions to opponents, and to sway public opinion in their favour. Nevertheless, this book focuses on reinterpreting royalist and Covenanter thought within a new, transnational and cross-confessional context, rather than investigating its dissemination and reception within Scottish society at large.

In conducting this study, I also acknowledge the limitations of the terms 'royalists' and 'Covenanters', two oppositional categories that are notoriously difficult to define. Being a Covenanter or a royalist meant different things to different people in this period, while not everyone who opposed or supported the king shared the same ideological convictions. The book begins with the controversies surrounding the prayer book in 1637 and concludes with the crowning of King Charles II in 1651. Any study of how people thought during these years must account for how some strengthened their commitment to the cause, some backtracked on previously held opinions and others changed their ideas entirely. I have attempted to capture the diversity of beliefs encompassed by the labels 'royalist' and 'Covenanter', in addition to how these beliefs changed over time, to prevent portraying either movement as intellectually uniform or static. But given my focus on a broad range of political and ecclesiological ideas – especially those useful for rethinking broader questions about the relationship between Protestantism and revolution in the early modern period – I cannot comprehensively account for all reasons underlying political allegiances, such as the financial, pragmatic and personal.

This book examines the reception of cross-confessional political and ecclesiological ideas in Covenanted Scotland. Some might object to how I have labelled 'Roman Catholic', 'Reformed', and 'Lutheran' as separate intellectual traditions given their various areas of overlap, especially in political thought. I have carefully chosen not to categorise patristic or medieval theologians, such as St Augustine (354–430) or Thomas Aquinas (1225–1274), as Roman Catholic authors, for seventeenth-century intellectuals treated pre-Reformation authors as part of the shared intellectual tradition of Western Christendom. Their writings did not carry the same political connotations as sixteenth- and seventeenth-century Catholic orders (like the Jesuits) who were known to the Reformed for their supposedly subversive political teachings. Scots drew upon pre-Reformation authors without contemporary political baggage, enabling them to claim the wider Christian tradition as support for their own positions. However, it is noteworthy that Reformed Scots did favourably, respectfully and accurately deploy many political arguments advanced by their Catholic scholastic contemporaries, authors with whom they warred over such theological matters as papal legitimacy and idolatrous forms of worship. Despite the vehement anti-Catholic hostility that permeated popular discourse, Scots did not cite these authors solely as a polemical strategy to discredit the arguments of their enemies as 'Jesuitical' or 'popish'. Instead, they gained valuable intellectual insights from the political and legal ideas advanced by their Catholic scholastic contemporaries, which had not yet been developed fully within Protestant circles.

As the Reformed attempted to forge their own orthodoxy throughout the seventeenth century, it is unsurprising that they turned toward pre-existing ideas developed by Catholic authors. As I will argue throughout this book, distinctive ways of thinking about politics characterised Catholic and Protestant intellectual traditions, ones that reflected the different priorities of early modern authors. For example, when faced with imperial expansion in the Americas, Catholics in the School of Salamanca clarified ideas about the natural law, the *ius gentium* (law of nations) and the origins of political authority in a way that Reformed authors did not. By contrast, Reformed theologians primarily discussed the legitimacy of resistance, self-defence and protection of the true religion as they responded to persecution and religious warfare. Catholic scholastic thought therefore provided Reformed authors with new methods for discussing the civil state and political power in ways that emphasised human rationality and agency over the natural world. By analysing the reception of Catholic scholastic ideas in Covenanted Scotland (including how these were directed toward a distinctly Protestant ecclesiological purpose), it is possible to provide a more complex picture of the cross-confessional nature of Protestant intellectual culture.

In doing so, this book reflects upon and incorporates the latest trends within intellectual history as scholars seek new ways of thinking about the relationship between political and religious ideas. Although highly persuasive, Skinner's argument that early modern political thought increasingly gained independence from the trappings of religion 'closed off a series of crucial questions about the relationship between the two'.[69] But scholars are breaking down this religious and political divide by seeking the inherent connections between the two categories of thought. This methodological approach has constituted a so-called 'religious turn' in the discipline, whereby faith and religious ideas are considered just as seriously as apparently 'secular' political ones.[70] Scholars have taken this approach in various directions. For example, John Coffey, Kevin Killeen, Eric Nelson and David Henreckson have all examined how early modern individuals drew upon scripture, specific theological categories or biblical narratives to supplement their political or philosophical ideas.[71] Others, such as Sarah

Mortimer and Annabel Brett, have reassessed how Protestants and Roman Catholics thought about divine and natural law to inform their views about the end of politics, the purpose of human societies and state formation.[72] Nicholas Tyacke demonstrated the inherent connections between political process and theology when he claimed that the rise of Arminianism provoked a counter-revolutionary reaction among English Calvinists that placed religion at the forefront of political change.[73] Jacqueline Rose also assessed the relationship between ecclesiology and politics, showing how debates about the nature of the church enabled English intellectuals to promote toleration after the Restoration in 1660.[74] This book thus applies a similar methodology to Scotland, assessing the intrinsic connections between theological ideas and political ones to better understand the various facets of the kingdom's intellectual culture in the early modern period.

Chapter Outline

This book is organised thematically into six chapters. Chapter 1 examines ideas about the godly commonwealth in early modern Protestant thought to provide an intellectual framework for Scottish political and ecclesiological debates after 1637. It first analyses early Protestant reformers' views on the two kingdoms (temporal and spiritual) and the magistrate's duty over religion, arguing that two general approaches emerged. On the one hand, the temporal kingdom might be a place for the maintenance of peace and order, meaning that civil government existed to coercively restrain sin and wickedness. On the other hand, the temporal kingdom might have an overtly religious end to advance God's glory. The civil magistrate therefore had a duty to punish spiritual crimes – such as heresy and blasphemy – and defend the godly commonwealth. The chapter investigates the reception of these strands within Scottish thought after the Reformation of 1560, especially in the context of Presbyterianism. It argues that royalists and Covenanters began from this shared intellectual framework but, as later chapters demonstrate, they derived substantially different ideas about the purpose of politics, the duties of civil magistrates and the responsibilities of Christian subjects that ultimately informed their political allegiances. This chapter therefore lays foundations as an intellectual framework for the rest of the book, analysing the varying interpretations of the 'godly commonwealth' that Scots later deconstructed and applied to their own context.

Chapter 2 examines the initial theological debates that emerged regarding the legitimacy of Charles's ecclesiastical reforms in the lead up to the National Covenant. It focuses specifically on ideas about *adiaphora* (matters indifferent to God) and the royal supremacy, two ecclesiological debates that also provided a model for kingship in the state. It argues that, by restricting the scope of *adiaphora* and limiting the ceremonies that could be determined according to the king's will, Covenanters paved the way for equally limiting his civil sovereignty. They instead located authority for church reform in Parliament, laying foundations for their theories of limited monarchy. Conversely, royalists developed a much larger category of *adiaphora* that provided the king (rather than Parliament) with greater authority over church reform, an authority that also extended to the state. This chapter thus demonstrates how debates about *adiaphora* and the royal supremacy surrounding the National Covenant were not just theological ones, for they raised important political questions about the nature of monarchy itself that royalists and Covenanters would develop in the years following.

Chapter 3 examines how royalists began to answer such questions about the nature of monarchy by turning toward their political thought. It demonstrates how their interpretation of *adiaphora* informed their emphasis on temporal peace secured through absolute monarchy. It compares the wide range of arguments that royalists drew from nature, scripture and Roman Catholic legal theory to defend the king's civil authority. It argues that they embraced a strand of Protestant political thought that prioritised government's coercive nature, the necessity of obedience, and the maintenance of civil order. They favoured civil stability over religious division, giving God greater direct agency over political affairs and making the Christian's duty one of obedience alone. Royalist political ideas, although centred on the need to maintain temporal peace, ultimately reflected their broader theological concerns about the king's absolute authority over the church.

Chapter 4 shifts the focus to another point of intersection between ecclesiology and political thought: debates about church government. It examines how royalists criticised Presbyterianism as a fundamental threat to absolute monarchy, specifically through reference to Roman Catholic debates about the papal deposing power and conciliarism. It then discusses how Covenanters responded by legitimising Presbyterianism as the only form of church government mandated by scripture (*jure divino*), and by articulating the scriptural warrants for excommunication. It argues that ideas about church government (especially Presbyterianism) deeply informed how royalists and Covenanters thought about Scotland's civic institutions, including whether civil government should be altered to complement the structure of the church.

Chapter 5 then analyses how Covenanters responded to the range of royalist criticisms discussed in the previous chapters, ones that emphasised the king's regulation of the church, the need for absolute monarchy and temporal peace in the state, and the politically subversive nature of Presbyterianism. It does so by examining the political ideas that Covenanter intellectuals advanced to defend limited monarchy (based upon increased parliamentary sovereignty) as the best form of government. It focuses primarily on how they merged Catholic scholastic political thought with a uniquely Reformed approach to the theological and political covenant. It argues that, unlike many of their royalist contemporaries, Covenanters drew upon a different view of the commonwealth, whereby God delegated power to subjects so they could make and unmake their own governments through rational political participation. In doing so, God gave Christians an active duty to contribute to the formation of the godly commonwealth, even with the force of arms.

The sixth and final chapter examines the breakdown and radicalisation of Covenanting political theory (and especially their defences of resistance) following the Engagement controversy (1647). It analyses how divisions that emerged within Scottish society – and especially in the General Assembly and Parliament – during the Engagement, the Act of Classes (1649), the execution of Charles I (1649) and the coronation of Charles II (1651) forced Covenanters to rethink the legitimacy of resistance by inferior magistrates and the nature of a godly nation covenanted with God. It also examines how Covenanters grappled with the unexpected, radical outcomes of their political theories in response the strengthening power of the English Independents. Ultimately, it suggests that these events constituted an intellectual breakdown of the Covenanting movement, resulting in a radicalisation of theories of resistance and ideas about the meaning of the 'godly commonwealth'.

Together, these chapters provide a picture of intellectual life during the Scottish Revolution that focuses specifically on how royalists and Covenanters thought about the relationship between human agency and divine sovereignty, the purpose of politics, and the duties of Christian subjects and magistrates. They also reinsert ecclesiology into a place of importance within the development of early modern political theory, highlighting the many intrinsic connections between various debates about church and state. Ultimately, this book is a history of religious and political ideas in Covenanted Scotland that seeks to fulfil three primary aims. First, it provides a more comprehensive overview of Scottish intellectual culture by focusing on both royalist and Covenanter ideas, examining how Scots on both sides of the conflict thought about church and state. Second, it internationalises Scottish political thought by examining how Catholic scholastic ideas, as well as Lutheran and Reformed intellectual traditions, enabled royalists and Covenanters to clarify the relationship between church and state in new ways. Lastly, it urges us to reconsider the positions of Calvinism, Lutheranism and Catholicism in secularisation narratives by giving greater focus to the importance of ecclesiology for the development of early modern political thought. The Covenanters were not simple holy war advocates who argued for defence of the true religion and the extirpation of idolatry and heresy. Nor were they forerunners of modern secularism through their emphasis on legal-constitutional justifications for warfare, including ideas about elective kingship and parliamentary sovereignty. Although scholars have been inclined to separate these two types of argument (with one leading to holy war and the other leading to political revolution), this book shows how they could emerge conjointly without prioritisation of one over the other. Instead, an ecclesiological crisis about the nature of the Reformed church in Scotland – one which demanded fundamental reconsideration of the king's civil and ecclesiastical power – contributed significantly to the expression of apparently 'secular' political theories underlying the modern state. It is only by recognising these intrinsic connections between political ideas and ecclesiological ones that we can truly understand the diverse intellectual culture of the Scottish Revolution.

Notes

1. Leonie James, *'This Great Firebrand': William Laud and Scotland, 1617–1645* (Woodbridge: Boydell, 2017), 98–107; Alan R. MacDonald, 'James VI and I, the Church of Scotland, and British Ecclesiastical Convergence,' *Historical Journal* 48, no. 4 (2005): 885–903; John Morrill, 'A British Patriarchy? Ecclesiastical Imperialism Under the Early Stuarts,' in *Religion, Culture and Society in Early Modern Britain*, eds Anthony Fletcher and Peter Roberts (Cambridge: CUP, 1994), 209–37.
2. William Laud, 'Canons and Constitvtions Ecclesiasticall, Gathered and put in forme, for the Government of the Church of Scotland,' in *The Works of the Most Reverend Father in God, William Laud, D. D.* (Oxford: John Henry Parker, 1853), 5: 586.
3. Laura A. M. Stewart, *Rethinking the Scottish Revolution: Covenanted Scotland, 1637–1651* (Oxford: OUP, 2016); Allan I. Macinnes, *The British Revolution, 1629–1660* (Basingstoke: Palgrave Macmillan, 2005), 111–19; David Stevenson, *The Scottish Revolution, 1637–1644: The Triumph of the Covenanters*, 2nd ed. (Edinburgh: John Donald, 2003); David Stevenson, *Revolution and Counter-Revolution in Scotland, 1644–1651* (London: Royal Historical Society, 1977).
4. Chris R. Langley, introduction to *The National Covenant in Scotland, 1638–1689*, ed. Chris R. Langley (Woodbridge: Boydell, 2020), 2–3.
5. Stewart, *Rethinking the Scottish Revolution*, 4.
6. James T. Johnson, *Ideology, Reason, and the Limitation of War: Religious and Secular Concepts, 1200–1740* (Princeton, NJ: Princeton University Press, 1975), 81–146; Michael Walzer, *The Revolution of the Saints: A Study in the Origins of Radical Politics* (London: Harvard University Press, 1965); Roland H. Bainton, *Christian Attitudes towards War and Peace: A Historical Survey and Critical Re-Evaluation* (New York: Abingdon, 1960), 143–51.
7. For an overview of this historiography, see Ian Campbell, introduction to *Protestant Politics Beyond Calvin: Reformed Theologians on War in the Sixteenth and Seventeenth Centuries*, ed. Ian Campbell and Floris Verhaart (London: Routledge, 2022), 2–9.
8. Bainton, *Christian Attitudes towards War and Peace*, 143.
9. Michael Walzer, 'War and Revolution in Puritan Thought,' *Political Studies* 12, no. 2 (1964): 227.
10. Walzer, 'War and Revolution,' 224.
11. Walzer, *Revolution of the Saints*, 270. For a critique of Walzer's terminology, see Johnson, *Ideology, Reason, and the Limitation of War*, 134–46.
12. Quentin Skinner, 'The Origins of the Calvinist Theory of Revolution,' in

After the Reformation: Essays in Honor of J.H. Hexter, ed. Barbara C. Malament (Manchester: MUP, 1980), 325.
13. Quentin Skinner, *The Foundations of Modern Political Thought* (Cambridge: CUP, 1978), 2: 352.
14. Skinner, *Foundations of Modern Political Thought*, 352.
15. Campbell, introduction to *Protestant Politics*, 4.
16. Campbell, introduction to *Protestant Politics*, 2.
17. Christopher Hill, *The Intellectual Origins of the English Revolution – Revisited* (Oxford: OUP, 1997), 7.
18. Skinner, 'Origins of the Calvinist Theory,' 309.
19. John Morrill, *The Nature of the English Revolution* (London: Longman, 1993), 14.
20. John Morrill, 'The Religious Context of the English Civil War,' *Transactions of the Royal Historical Society* 34 (1984): 178.
21. Morrill, *Nature of the English Revolution*, 38.
22. Morrill, *Nature of the English Revolution*, 39.
23. Glenn Burgess, 'Religion and the Historiography of the English Civil War,' in *England's Wars of Religion, Revisited*, eds Charles W. A. Prior and Glenn Burgess (Farnham: Ashgate, 2011), 1–25.
24. Kirsteen M. MacKenzie, *The Solemn League and Covenant of the Three Kingdoms and the Cromwellian Union, 1643–1664* (London: Routledge, 2018); John Morrill, ed., *The Scottish National Covenant in Its British Context* (Edinburgh: EUP, 1990); Conrad Russell, 'The British Problem and the English Civil War,' *History* 72, no. 236 (1987): 395–415; J. G. A. Pocock, 'The Limits and Divisions of British History: In Search of the Unknown Subject,' *American Historical Review* 87, no. 2 (1982): 311–36.
25. Glenn Burgess, 'Scottish or British? Politics and Political Thought in Scotland, c. 1500–1707,' *Historical Journal* 41, no. 2 (1998): 580.
26. Morrill, *Nature of the English Revolution*, 35.
27. Glenn Burgess, 'Was the English Civil War a War of Religion? The Evidence of Political Propaganda,' *Huntington Library Quarterly* 61, no. 2 (1998): 197.
28. Burgess, 'Was the English Civil War a War of Religion?', 195.
29. Edward Vallance, 'Preaching to the Converted: Religious Justifications for the English Civil War,' *Huntington Library Quarterly* 65, no. 3/4 (2002): 401.
30. MacDonald, 'James VI and I,' 885–903; Morrill, 'A British Patriarchy?,' 209–37.
31. Laura A. M. Stewart, 'The Political Repercussions of the Five Articles of Perth: A Reassessment of James VI and I's Religious Policies in Scotland,' *The Sixteenth Century Journal* 38, no. 4 (2007): 1,013–36; Laura A. M. Stewart, '"Brothers in truth": Propaganda, Public Opinion and the Perth Articles Debate in Scotland,' in *James VI and I: Ideas, Authority, and Government*, ed. Ralph Houlbrooke (London: Routledge, 2006), 151–68; John D. Ford, 'Conformity in Conscience: The Structure of the Perth Articles Debate in Scotland, 1618–1638,' *Journal of Ecclesiastical History* 46, no. 2 (1995): 256–77.
32. 'The Solemn League and Covenant,' in *The Covenants and the Covenanters: Covenants, Sermons, and Documents of the Covenanted Reformation*, ed. James Kerr (Edinburgh: R. W. Hunter, 1895), 132.
33. Chad Van Dixhoorn, 'Scottish Influence on the Westminster Assembly: A Study of the Synod's Summoning Ordinance and the Solemn League and Covenant,' *Scottish Church History* 37, no. 1 (2007): 55–88.

34. Nicole Greenspan, 'Charles II, Exile, and the Problem of Allegiance,' *Historical Journal* 54, no. 1 (2011): 93–102.
35. Allan I. Macinnes, *Charles I and the Making of the Covenanting Movement, 1625–1641* (Edinburgh: John Donald, 1991).
36. Maurice Lee, Jr, 'Scotland and the "General Crisis" of the Seventeenth Century,' *SHR* 63, no. 176 (1984): 146–51.
37. Maurice Lee, Jr, 'Scotland, the Union and the Idea of a "General Crisis",' in Mason, *Scots and Britons: Scottish Political Thought and the Union of 1603*, ed. Roger A. Mason (Cambridge: CUP, 1994), 51.
38. Macinnes, *British Revolution*, 114.
39. Stevenson, *Revolution and Counter-Revolution*, 232.
40. Stevenson, *Scottish Revolution*, 316.
41. Stevenson, *Scottish Revolution*, 316.
42. Stevenson, *Scottish Revolution*, 326.
43. Stewart, *Rethinking the Scottish Revolution*, 4.
44. Stewart, *Rethinking the Scottish Revolution*, 26.
45. Stewart, *Rethinking the Scottish Revolution*, 9.
46. Glenn Burgess, *British Political Thought, 1500–1660: The Politics of the Post Reformation* (Basingstoke: Palgrave Macmillan, 2009), xiv.
47. Neil McIntyre and Alison Cathcart, eds, *Scotland and the Wider World: Essays in Honour of Allan I. Macinnes* (Woodbridge: Boydell, 2022); David Worthington, *British and Irish Emigrants and Exiles in Europe, 1603–1688* (Leiden: Brill, 2010); Steve Murdoch, *Network North: Scottish Kin, Commercial and Covert Associations in Northern Europe, 1603–1746* (Leiden: Brill, 2006); Alexia Grosjean and Steve Murdoch, eds, *Scottish Communities Abroad in the Early Modern Period* (Leiden: Brill, 2005); Alexia Grosjean, *An Unofficial Alliance: Scotland and Sweden, 1569–1654* (Leiden: Brill, 2003).
48. Steve Murdoch, *Britain, Denmark-Norway and the House of Stuart, 1603–1660: A Diplomatic and Military Alliance* (East Linton: Tuckwell Press, 2003); David Worthington, *Scots in Habsburg Service, 1618–1648* (Leiden: Brill, 2003).
49. Esther Mijers, '"Addicted to Puritanism": Philosophical and Theological Relations between Scotland and the United Provinces in the First Half of the Seventeenth Century,' *History of Universities* 29, no. 2 (2017): 69–95; James K. Cameron, 'Some Scottish Students and Teachers at the University of Leiden in the Late 16th and Early 17th Centuries,' in *Scotland and the Low Countries, 1124–1994*, ed. Grant G. Simpson (East Linton: Tuckwell Press, 1996), 122–35.
50. Karie Schultz, 'Protestant Intellectual Culture and Political Ideas in the Scottish Universities, ca. 1600–50,' *Journal of the History of Ideas* 83, no. 1 (2022): 41–62; Alexander Broadie, ed. *Scottish Philosophy in the Seventeenth Century* (Oxford: OUP, 2020); Steven J. Reid, 'Reformed Scholasticism, Proto-Empiricism and the Intellectual "Long Reformation" in Scotland: The Philosophy of the "Aberdeen Doctors," c.1619–c.1641,' in *Scotland's Long Reformation: New Perspectives on Scottish Religion, c.1500–c.1660*, ed. John McCallum (Leiden: Brill, 2016), 149–78; Giovanni Gellera, 'The Reception of Descartes in the Seventeenth-Century Scottish Universities: Metaphysics and Natural Philosophy (1650–1680),' *Journal of Scottish Philosophy* 13, no. 3 (2015): 179–201.
51. Roger A. Mason and Martin S. Smith, eds *A Dialogue on the Law of Kingship among the Scots: A Critical Edition and Translation of George Buchanan's De Iure Regni apud Scotos Dialogus* (London: Routledge, 2004); J. H. Burns, *The True Law*

of Kingship: Concepts of Monarchy in Early-Modern Scotland (Oxford: Clarendon Press, 1996); Roger A. Mason, 'Imagining Scotland: Scottish Political Thought and the Problem of Britain, 1560–1650,' in Mason, *Scots and Britons*, 3–14.

52. Roger A. Mason and Steven J. Reid, eds, *Andrew Melville (1545–1622): Writings, Reception, and Reputation* (Farnham: Ashgate, 2014); Caroline Erskine and Roger A. Mason, eds, *George Buchanan: Political Thought in Early Modern Britain and Europe* (London: Routledge, 2012); Steven Reid, *Humanism and Calvinism: Andrew Melville and the Universities of Scotland, 1560–1625* (Farnham: Ashgate, 2011).

53. Ian Michael Smart, 'The Political Ideas of the Scottish Covenanters. 1638–88,' *History of Political Thought* 1, no. 2 (1980): 167–93.

54. Simon J. G. Burton, 'The Scholastic and Conciliar Roots of Samuel Rutherford's Political Philosophy: The Influence of Jean Gerson, Jacques Almain and John Mair,' in Broadie, *Scottish Philosophy*, 208–25; Alexander D. Campbell, *The Life and Works of Robert Baillie (1602–1662): Politics, Religion and Record-Keeping in the British Civil Wars* (Woodbridge: Boydell, 2017); Allan I. Macinnes, *The British Confederate: Archibald Campbell, Marquess of Argyll, c. 1607–1661* (Edinburgh: John Donald, 2011); Shaun Alberto De Freitas, 'Law and Federal-Republicanism: Samuel Rutherford's Quest for a Constitutional Model' (PhD diss., University of the Free State, 2014); John Coffey, *Politics, Religion and the British Revolutions: The Mind of Samuel Rutherford* (Cambridge: CUP, 1997); Mason, *Scots and Britons*, chs 10 and 11; John J. Scally, 'The Political Career of James, Third Marquis and First Duke of Hamilton (1606–1649) to 1643' (PhD diss., University of Cambridge, 1992); Edward J. Cowan, *Montrose: For Covenant and King* (London: Weidenfeld and Nicolson, 1977).

55. Gordon Donaldson, 'Scotland's Conservative North in the Sixteenth and Seventeenth Centuries,' *TRHS* 16 (1966): 65–79.

56. Langley, *National Covenant*, chs 3, 7, and 8; Andrew Lind, '"You may take my head from my shoulders, but not my heart from my soveraigne": Understanding Scottish Royalist Allegiance During the British Civil Wars, 1639–1651,' in *Loyalty to the Monarchy in Late Medieval and Early Modern Britain, c. 1400–1688*, eds Matthew Ward and Matthew Hefferan (Cham: Palgrave, 2020), 211–30; Andrew Lind, '"Bad and Evill Patriotts"?: Royalism in Scotland During the British Civil Wars, c. 1638–1651' (PhD diss., University of Glasgow, 2020); Salvatore Cipriano, 'The Scottish Universities and Opposition to the National Covenant, 1638,' *SHR* 97, no. 1 (2018): 12–37.

57. Barry Robertson, *Royalists at War in Scotland and Ireland, 1638–1650* (London: Routledge, 2016), 43; See also: Keith M. Brown, 'Courtiers and Cavaliers: Service, Anglicisation and Loyalty among the Royalist Nobility,' in Morrill, *Scottish National Covenant in its British Context*, 155–92.

58. Barbara Donagan, 'Varieties of Royalism,' in *Royalists and Royalism during the English Civil Wars*, eds Jason McElligott and David L. Smith (Cambridge: CUP, 2007), 66.

59. Robertson, *Royalists at War*, 35.

60. For the difficulties of defining a 'royalist', see Greenspan, 'Charles II,' 77–8.

61. James VI, *Basilikon doron. Devided into three bookes* (Edinburgh, 1599); James VI, *The True Lawe of Free Monarchies* (Edinburgh, 1598). See also: James VI and I, *King James VI and I: Political Writings*, ed. Johann P. Sommerville (Cambridge: CUP, 1995).

62. Glenn Burgess, 'The Divine Right of Kings Reconsidered,' *EHR* 107, no. 425 (1992): 837–61; James Daly, 'Cosmic Harmony and Political Thinking in Early Stuart England,' *Transactions of the American Philosophical Society* 69, no. 7 (1979): 1–41; Francis Oakley, *Omnipotence, Covenant and Order: An Excursion in the History of Ideas from Abelard to Leibniz* (Ithaca, NY: Cornell University Press, 1984); John Neville Figgis, *The Divine Right of Kings*, 2nd ed. (Cambridge: CUP, 1914).
63. Sarah Waurechen, 'Covenanter Propaganda and Conceptualizations of the Public during the Bishops' Wars, 1638–1640,' *Historical Journal* 52, no. 1 (2009): 63–86.
64. For recent favourable treatments of English and Scottish royalism, see Anthony Milton, *Laudian and Royalist Polemic in Seventeenth-Century England: The Career and Writings of Peter Heylyn* (Manchester: MUP, 2017); Jason McElligott and David L. Smith, eds, *Royalists and Royalism During the English Civil Wars* (Cambridge: CUP, 2007); Jason McElligott, *Royalism, Print and Censorship in Revolutionary England* (Woodbridge: Boydell, 2007); Jerome de Groot, *Royalist Identities* (Basingstoke: Palgrave Macmillan, 2004); David L. Smith, *Constitutional Royalism and the Search for Settlement, c. 1640–1649* (Cambridge: CUP, 1994); David Stevenson, 'The "Letter on Sovereign Power" and the Influence of Jean Bodin on Political Thought in Scotland,' *SHR* 61, no. 171 (1982): 25–43.
65. Macinnes, *Charles I*, 183.
66. Chris R. Langley, *Worship, Civil War and Community, 1638–1660* (London: Routledge, 2016); Margo Todd, *The Culture of Protestantism in Early Modern Scotland* (New Haven, CT: Yale University Press, 2002); Michael F. Graham, *The Uses of Reform: 'Godly Discipline' and Popular Behaviour in Scotland and Beyond, 1560–1610* (Leiden: Brill, 1996).
67. Noah Millstone, *Manuscript Circulation and the Invention of Politics in Early Stuart England* (Cambridge: CUP, 2016); Jason Peacey, *Print and Public Politics in the English Revolution* (Cambridge: CUP, 2013); Jason Peacey, *Politicians and Pamphleteers: Propaganda during the English Civil Wars and Interregnum* (Burlington, VT: Ashgate, 2004); Joad Raymond, *Pamphlets and Pamphleteering in Early Modern Britain* (Cambridge: CUP, 2003).
68. Karin Bowie, *Public Opinion in Early Modern Scotland. c. 1560–1707* (Cambridge: CUP, 2020); Stewart, *Rethinking the Scottish Revolution*, 29–38.
69. Sarah Mortimer, *Reformation, Resistance, and Reason of State (1517–1625)* (Oxford: OUP, 2021), 11.
70. John Coffey, 'Quentin Skinner and the Religious Dimension of Early Modern Political Thought,' in *Seeing Things Their Way: Intellectual History and the Return of Religion*, eds Alister Chapman, John Coffey and Brad S. Gregory (South Bend, IN: University of Notre Dame Press, 2009), 46–74.
71. David P. Henreckson, *The Immortal Commonwealth: Covenant, Community, and Political Resistance in Early Reformed Thought* (Cambridge; CUP, 2019); Kevin Killeen, *The Political Bible in Early Modern England* (Cambridge: CUP, 2017); John Coffey, 'England's Exodus: The Civil War as a War of Deliverance,' in Prior and Burgess, *England's Wars of Religion, Revisited*, 254–80; Eric Nelson, *The Hebrew Republic: Jewish Sources and the Transformation of European Political Thought* (Cambridge, MA: Harvard University Press, 2010).
72. Mortimer, *Reformation*, especially chs 3, 4 and 5; Annabel Brett, *Changes of State: Nature and the Limits of the City in Early Modern Natural Law* (Princeton, NJ: Princeton University Press, 2011).

73. Nicholas Tyacke, *Anti-Calvinists: The Rise of English Arminianism, c. 1590–1640* (Oxford: Clarendon, 1990); Nicholas Tyacke, 'Puritanism, Arminianism and Counter-Revolution,' in *The Origins of the English Civil War*, ed. Conrad Russell (London: Palgrave Macmillan, 1973), 119–43. See also: Peter Lake, 'Introduction: Puritanism, Arminianism and Nicholas Tyacke,' in *Religious Politics in Post-Reformation England*, eds Kenneth Fincham and Peter Lake (Woodbridge: Boydell, 2006), 1–15.
74. Jacqueline Rose, 'The Debate over Authority: *Adiaphora*, the Civil Magistrate, and the Settlement of Religion,' in *'Settling the Peace of the Church': 1662 Revisited*, ed. N. H. Keeble (Oxford: OUP, 2014), 29–56.

CHAPTER ONE

The Godly Commonwealth in Early Modern Protestant Thought

The Protestant reformations of the sixteenth century resulted in sweeping religious changes across Europe, ones that necessitated new ways of thinking about the end of politics. The earliest reformers needed to convince civil magistrates to advance and protect the new faith across their lands while proving that Protestantism complemented their political power, rather than threatened it. Following their rejection of papal authority, they also needed to develop a new working partnership between civil and ecclesiastical authorities to govern the church. Early modern Protestants thus developed a distinctive set of ideas about political life to achieve these aims and began to think differently about the purpose of politics than their Roman Catholic predecessors.[1] Catholics had traditionally viewed political life as a place for human beings to attain flourishing in the Aristotelian sense of *eudaimonia*, achieved by living in societies, exercising reason and striving after civic virtue. The temporal world thus had a natural end, one that did not concern the active or militant defence of the true religion. Equally, the church operated as a wholly independent institution governed by the pope without the interference of temporal magistrates. As Sarah Mortimer has shown, a distinct strand of thought emerged among Catholic conciliarists in the beginning of the sixteenth century, according to which political power derived from natural law rather than from God's direct grant.[2] By contrast, the earliest Protestant reformers 'dissolve[d] existing distinctions between natural and spiritual, temporal and ecclesiastical', conceiving instead of politics as essential for the advancement of God's glory and the upholding of divine law.[3] The end of politics therefore comprised the creation of a 'godly commonwealth' through multiple methods, such as social disciplining, the confessionalisation of education and the use of the civil sword to punish spiritual crimes.

However, Protestants diverged regarding the exact roles that the church and civic institutions should play in creating this godly commonwealth. More specifically, they questioned the remit of the *cura religionis*, or the civil magistrate's responsibility to care for religion by defending the church's confessional purity. This chapter explores how the earliest Protestant reformers conceived of the end of politics and the practical attainment of the godly commonwealth, resulting in a body of political and ecclesiological ideas that informed how royalists and Covenanters thought about their own context after 1637. It first outlines major developments in continental European Protestant thought (both Lutheran and Reformed) regarding two-kingdoms theology, and especially the magistrate's *cura religionis*. It argues that two general strands of thought emerged, both of which permeated royalist and Covenanter discourse. On the one hand, the temporal kingdom might have a purpose limited to the preservation of peace and order among sinful human beings. The civil magistrate thus wielded the civil sword only to punish transgressions of the natural law. On the other hand, the temporal kingdom might exist for the advancement of the true religion, meaning that the civil magistrate had an additional duty to prosecute spiritual crimes, such as blasphemy and heresy. After outlining the development of these two intellectual traditions, this chapter examines the reception and articulation of these ideas about the end of politics within the Scottish context following the kingdom's own reformation in 1560, demonstrating how they also reflected some Scots' distinctly Presbyterian concerns. Subsequent chapters then analyse how Scots inherited and developed these ideas about the meaning of the 'godly commonwealth' as they reassessed the nature of political power, the crown's involvement in the church and the legitimacy of resistance after 1637.

Two-Kingdoms Theology and the *Cura Religionis*

Within early modern Protestant thought, the idea of the 'godly commonwealth' emerged alongside developments in two-kingdoms theology. According to the latter doctrine, the world consisted of two realms or kingdoms (the temporal and the spiritual), each of which had different ends, authorities and jurisdictions.[4] The temporal kingdom, governed by civil law and secular magistrates, dealt with worldly concerns relevant to all people, including both Christians and non-Christians. Although sinfulness and wickedness prevailed, human beings operated according to reason, while they obeyed laws that preserved peace and order. By contrast, the spiritual kingdom involved matters of faith relevant to Christians alone, such as salvation, redemption and eternal life. Although the temporal kingdom had a distinctly worldly focus, it was not secular. God ruled all civic and ecclesiastical institutions as their creator, while Christ governed both kingdoms as the 'king of kings'. God's grace also infused each: the temporal with common grace (available to all human beings) and the spiritual with special grace (available only to Christians).

This paradigm of the two kingdoms was not unique to Protestantism. Roman Catholics had their own interpretations of the natural and supernatural spheres represented by civil rulers and the pope respectively, while patristic and medieval precedents also existed for these categories.[5] However, Protestants did construct a new working relationship between civil magistrates and the church in the absence of papal power. Ideally, authorities of both kingdoms would cooperate harmoniously to establish a godly commonwealth. In practice, this rarely happened, leading Protestant intellectuals to develop different theories about the relationship between the temporal and the spiritual, or between the church and the state. This section examines the key distinctions that emerged within sixteenth-century Protestant thought regarding the purpose of politics (articulated through the language of the two kingdoms), as well as the magistrate's responsibility with respect to religion.

A key starting point is the work of Martin Luther (1483–1546), the former Augustinian monk who (rather unintentionally) initiated the Protestant Reformation when he rejected the offering of indulgences in his famous *Ninety-Five Theses* (1517). Luther was a theologian first and foremost, not a political theorist, and he did not author any comprehensive works on politics during his lifetime. Instead, his ideas about the two kingdoms and the nature of civil power appeared in a series of works that he wrote at disparate stages throughout his life. He also developed and changed his political ideas in response to moments of political and religious exigency, such as the Peasants' War that took place in southwestern Germany between 1524 and 1525. In his initial writings on politics and civil government, Luther had two primary aims. First, he needed to theoretically empower civil magistrates to reform churches throughout their lands and protect newly converted communities. Second, to promote civil stability and prevent anarchy, he needed to challenge the politically subversive doctrines of the Anabaptists, a group of radical Protestants who believed that Christian liberty, combined with the positive transformations that the Holy Spirit brought about in the soul, negated the need for any laws or civil government among the 'saints'.

To these ends, Luther authored *On Secular Authority* (1523), one of his earliest, clearest and most comprehensive treatments of the two kingdoms (*Zwei Reiche*) and the nature of political power.[6] He wrote the treatise after George the Bearded, the Roman Catholic Duke of Saxony (1471–1539) prohibited the purchase of his vernacular translation of the New Testament on 7 November 1522. Luther took an exceptionally hostile stance toward civil rulers in this work as he attempted to theoretically protect the church from the interference of an ungodly, heretical magistrate opposed to reformation.[7] As a result, he distinguished sharply between the jurisdictions of temporal and spiritual authorities, unlike later generations of Protestant reformers who narrowed this gap (or dismissed it entirely) in favour of explicitly Christian commonwealths headed by godly princes. Nevertheless, this work remains one of Luther's most cogent articulations of ideas about civil government and the duties of magistrates.

Luther began by outlining the difference between the two kingdoms. As he explained, spiritual government 'fashions true Christians and just persons through the Holy Spirit under Christ.'[8] By contrast, secular or worldly government 'holds the Unchristian and wicked in check and forces them to keep the peace outwardly and be still.'[9] Different types of law prevailed in each kingdom. In particular, temporal government included 'laws that extend no further than the body' and that existed to regulate 'good and outward, earthly matters'.[10] Civil rulers must not create laws to direct the soul (which God alone ruled), meaning that government existed exclusively to restrain non-Christians and evildoers from committing wicked acts contrary to natural law. As a result, Luther argued that, '[C]are must be taken to keep these two governments distinct, and both must be allowed to continue [their work], the one to make [people] just, the other to create outward peace and prevent evildoing.'[11]

However, Luther recognised that spiritual and temporal governments depended upon one another in practice. If only civil government existed, human beings could never be made just without the aid of the Holy Spirit. If only spiritual government existed, sin and wickedness would run rampant, for the number of non-Christians in a political society far exceeded that of true Christians.[12] Additionally, all human beings, regardless of their spiritual status, required civil laws and secular magistrates to hold them accountable to natural law. Christians and non-Christians lived together in the temporal kingdom where good and evil mixed inextricably. Some people might masquerade as Christians, claiming freedom from all law and punishment while covertly pursuing wickedness.[13] For Luther, the Anabaptists provided an example of individuals who claimed to live as Christians guided by the Holy Spirit, but who risked anarchy by denouncing the need for civil government on the grounds of Christian liberty. As Luther maintained, measures for restraining non-Christians from committing evil acts and transgressing natural law thus benefitted every member of society, even Christians.

As a former Augustinian monk, Luther advanced a view of politics that resembled St Augustine's paradigm of the City of Man and the City of God, including the latter's emphasis on the coercive nature of civil government. For Augustine, God ordained political authorities primarily to control wayward human beings and mitigate the negative effects of sin.[14] Peaceful societies could not exist if people acted upon their depraved instincts freely without restraint. Luther embraced this Augustinian interpretation of human nature, rejecting the belief that humans were naturally sociable creatures who might attain civic virtue by participating in politics. Instead, such a positive view of human nature drawn from classical philosophy erroneously promoted the idea 'that there might be a kind of human excellence outside of God's earned gift'.[15] Luther's affinity for this Augustinian interpretation of human depravity equally informed his perspective on the coercive end of civil government. As he argued, the secular magistrate served as the father of the political community and as God's vicegerent on earth, tasked with the responsibility 'to preserve peace, punish sin, and restrain the wicked'.[16] The magistrate used the sword only to punish crimes against the second table of the Decalogue (or the Ten Commandments). The commandments of the second table governed human relationships by prohibiting stealing, murdering, bearing false witness or committing adultery. The civil punishment of spiritual crimes – such as blasphemy and heresy – fell beyond the magistrate's remit. As Luther argued, the power to restrain heresy 'by the use of outward means' did not apply to civil magistrates, and it was only 'for bishops to do that; that task has been assigned to them and not to rulers.'[17] He concluded that, 'The use of force can never prevent heresy. Preventing it requires a different sort of skill; this is not a battle that can be fought with a sword.'[18] Luther thus emphasised the separation (rather than the cooperation) of the two kingdoms, restricting the civil magistrate's authority to the maintenance of external peace between Christians and non-Christians.

However, Luther did increasingly justify the civil magistrate's authority over spiritual crimes later in his life. During the Peasants' War, Luther suggested that civil magistrates might use the sword to suppress blasphemy and heresy, as a way to secure the greater end of temporal peace.[19] He criticised the rebellious peasants for breaking the peace (a far worse evil than the injustices they faced), and for justifying their rebellion based upon the authority of scripture and the language of Christian liberty. Luther therefore encouraged the nobility to act quickly and harshly to suppress the rebellion.[20] Nevertheless, some scholars have argued that Luther remained overwhelmingly opposed to magisterial involvement in punishing spiritual crimes, and that the exceptional circumstances of the Peasants' War caused him to take an uncharacteristic, highly pragmatic approach. The civil suppression of blasphemy remained a last resort or emergency measure, not a precedent or standard for normal rule.[21]

Some scholars have also argued that Luther's conception of the temporal kingdom as a place for restraining human wickedness resulted in a 'secular' sphere, one that existed independently of the church and that operated under the remit of natural law alone.[22] According to this perspective, Luther's apparently strict separation of church and state produced a political passivity or 'quietism' in his thought that caused later generations of Lutherans to acquiesce to authoritarian political structures.[23] However, this unpopular interpretation does not accurately portray Luther's emphasis on the Christian subject's duty in politics. Indeed, Luther did conceive of a restricted or limited end for political life, especially in *On Secular Authority*. As Mortimer observed, he sometimes discussed politics in such a way that 'worldly rule seemed to be little more than a mechanism for dealing with depraved and corrupt human beings, indispensable but of little positive value.'[24] But crucially, Luther did not believe that Christians should live in simple, passive resignation to civil government, or that politics had no benefit beside the coercive maintenance of peace. While he acknowledged that government existed first and foremost to restrain sin, he also argued that Christians must participate fully in politics to advance God's glory. As Romans 13 demonstrated, God commanded Christians to submit to all civil authorities, both to serve their non-Christian neighbours and to exemplify godly behaviour. He maintained that Christians should pay taxes, obey all laws and honour those in authority.[25] By respecting their temporal rulers, Christians could 'serve and help them, and do what they can to uphold their power, so that they may continue their work', such as restraining sin.[26] When Christians undertook these political actions, they engaged in works of love toward their neighbours, ones that they might not personally require but which ultimately glorified God.

As is clear, Luther never developed a systematic political theory of his own, while his ideas about obedience, the punishment of spiritual crimes and magisterial involvement in the church evolved in response to specific moments of need. Yet he did lay important foundations for thinking about the ends and authorities of the two kingdoms that his successors and contemporaries developed more fully when they extended the magistrate's power over religion and paved the way for theories of resistance on religious grounds.[27] As John Witte has shown, a series of sixteenth-century Lutheran jurists, such as Johannes Eisermann (ca. 1485–1558) and Johann Oldendorp (ca. 1486–1567), innovated upon Luther's initial paradigm of the two kingdoms but 'tended to emphasize their cooperation' rather than their distinctions.[28] They also broadened the magistrate's jurisdiction to include the punishment of spiritual crimes committed against the first table of the Decalogue, such as blasphemy, idolatry or heresy. They therefore contributed to the emergence of an alternative strand of Protestant thought about politics: magistrates had an obligation to defend all Ten Commandments, including those pertaining to divine worship, thereby playing a critical role in the formation of an orthodox, godly commonwealth.

Such an approach to the civil magistrate's *cura religionis* appeared in the work of Luther's contemporary, close friend and university colleague Philip Melanchthon (1497–1560). In 1521, Melanchthon authored *Loci Communes*, a work of systematic theology in which he elaborated upon points of Christian doctrine following the structure of Paul's Epistle to the Romans. In doing so, he also systematised Luther's disparate political ideas into a more comprehensive, teachable format. Melanchthon discussed multiple points of theology, such as free will, the nature of sin, grace and faith, and the distinction between law and the gospel. He also elaborated upon the end of politics, outlining the specific duties that civil magistrates and subjects must perform to sustain the Christian commonwealth. As he argued, God ordained all civil governments to secure the common good. Christians could actively contribute to this common good by serving their neighbours, teaching others about Christian doctrine and advancing God's glory through their exemplary behaviour.[29] In this sense, Melanchthon's view of how humans should participate in politics resembled that of Luther: Christians must demonstrate the fruits of their good faith outwardly by acting in a godly manner toward the non-Christians in their communities.

But Melanchthon also expanded the civil magistrate's responsibilities to include the external care of the church. He maintained that magistrates had a duty to foster godliness and holiness among their subjects, describing the civil ruler as the one 'from whose neck hang the two tables of the Mosaic law'.[30] Rulers therefore acted as guardians or custodians of both tables, meaning that they protected the peace and glory of God as pertained to outward morals. This was an end superior to the simple maintenance of peace and order. For this reason, Melanchthon concluded that

> kings, princes, and rulers in our present age must inspect the churches ... that the worship of idols be prohibited and the teaching of false opinions which are in conflict with the Gospel not be encouraged or spread by any kind of people.[31]

The civil magistrate's duty ultimately included rooting out corruptive influences within the Christian commonwealth to maintain religious orthodoxy, while government existed not just for the coercive restraint of sinful human nature but for the direct advancement of God's glory.

These ideas about the two kingdoms, the formation of the godly commonwealth and the *cura religionis* were not an exclusively Lutheran conversation. Scholars disagree about the extent to which two-kingdoms theology (and the apparent separation of church and state) constituted an exclusively Lutheran paradigm, or whether it became a defining feature of Reformed thought too.[32] Nevertheless, similar ideas about the purpose of politics and the *cura religionis* (especially those articulated by Melanchthon) did permeate Reformed discourse.[33] For example, the view that subjects had a divinely mandated duty to obey civil authorities and contribute to the godly commonwealth appeared in the writings of John Calvin (1509–1564), the leading reformer based in Geneva. Calvin developed his own distinction between the temporal and spiritual kingdoms in Book IV, Chapter 20 of the *Institutes of the Christian Religion* (1536), one that suggested greater overlap between the two realms than Luther initially allowed. According to Calvin's framework, the spiritual kingdom pertained to the eternal kingdom of Christ and comprised matters of the conscience and the soul. The temporal kingdom pertained to bodily concerns (food, clothing, shelter, external behaviour and human relationships). Although he argued that 'the spiritual kingdom of Christ and civil government are things far removed from one another', civil government had the dual purpose of providing for bodily necessities and upholding the true religion in a Christian commonwealth.[34] As he stated, civil government existed to 'mould our conduct to civil justice, reconcile us one to another, and uphold and defend the common peace and tranquillity.'[35] Equally, it helped to 'foster and protect the external worship of God' by defending 'pure doctrine ... and the good condition of the Church'.[36]

Like Luther, Calvin expressed concerns about the Anabaptists' belief that civic institutions (such as courts, laws and magistrates) obstructed

Christian liberty and must be fully removed. On the contrary, civil government usefully restricted the spread of idolatry and blasphemy while instilling morality, decency and righteous conduct among the people. However, the civil sword did not affect human relationships with God, for it could not regulate the conscience, piety or spiritual discipline. As Calvin explained,

> I approve a political order that makes it its business to prevent true religion, which is contained in the law of God, from being besmirched and violated with impunity by public and manifest sacrilege. But in doing so, I no more allow men to make laws about religion and the worship of God allowing to their fancy as I did before.[37]

Like Melanchthon, Calvin incorporated language of the two tables to define the scope of the *cura religionis*, claiming that, 'The magistrate's competence extends to both Tables of the Decalogue.'[38] But his ideas about the *cura religionis* also changed throughout his lifetime. Although Calvin initially emphasised the worldly aims of civil government in the *Institutes*, such as the punishment of moral transgressions and actions that threatened temporal peace, he later 'began to emphasize government's obligation to promote and defend the true religion, and he increasingly turned toward the Old Testament as a norm for politics.'[39] Calvin thus raised important questions about the two kingdoms, the end of politics and the magistrate's *cura religionis* that later generations of Reformed authors adapted to understand the range of religious conflicts emerging throughout the sixteenth and seventeenth centuries.

The earliest Protestant reformers (such as Luther, Melanchthon and Calvin) thus presented interpretations of politics that differed from their Roman Catholic predecessors, providing the civil magistrate (rather than the pope) with distinct responsibilities over both religion and temporal affairs. But their theories about the formation of the godly commonwealth only worked if the magistrate ruled according to the true religion in a mono-confessional state. The multitude of religious wars that arose across Europe, such as the French Wars of Religion, the Dutch Revolt or the Thirty Years War, demonstrated that rulers rarely did so in practice. Later generations of Protestants thus had to reconsider how subjects should respond to tyrannical or ungodly rulers who threatened their lives, liberties and faith. They accordingly developed more comprehensive bodies of political thought based upon these initial theories, often in response to religious persecution at the hands of hostile civil magistrates. In particular, they had to consider what actions subjects or inferior magistrates might lawfully take against a supreme magistrate who failed in their *cura religionis* and began to actively persecute the faith.

For example, on 15 May 1548, Holy Roman Emperor Charles V (1500–1558) ordered the Augsburg Interim, an imperial decree intended to contain the spread of Lutheranism and restore religious peace. This decree commanded Protestants in the Holy Roman Empire to readopt the doctrines, practices and ceremonies of Roman Catholicism, including adherence to the seven sacraments. Lutheran pastors in the city of Magdeburg objected through the *Magdeburg Confession* (1550), an early expression of a Lutheran theory of resistance that incorporated Melanchthon's categories of the *cura religionis* and the godly commonwealth.[40] The first part of the *Confession* articulated and defended key points of Lutheran doctrine, while the second half legitimised resistance by inferior magistrates. It specifically considered whether inferior magistrates could use force against a superior who compelled their subjects into idolatry. Here, 'inferior magistrates' referred to those individuals who held positions of authority above the people, but who were also subject to a higher ruler. Examples might include princes under the rule of an emperor, or nobles under the authority of a king. Drawing upon Romans 13, the Magdeburg pastors argued that God ordained civil magistrates to honour good works and prevent evil ones.[41] Subjects therefore owed obedience only to a magistrate who fulfilled this end by contributing to the advancement and flourishing of the true religion. If a magistrate devolved into tyranny by persecuting and seeking to extinguish true worshippers, God commanded inferior magistrates to resist for their own protection, and for that of their subjects.[42] Magistrates thus existed both for the sake of the church and for the advancement of God's glory, while rulers could be held accountable for fulfilling the *cura religionis* by their inferiors.

The notion that inferior magistrates should protect the people from the tyranny of a superior also became standard within Reformed thought, especially among such canonical authors as Theodore Beza (1519–1605), the Marian exiles, and Philippe de Mornay (1549–1623), the probable author of the pseudonymous French Huguenot resistance tract *Vindiciae, contra tyrannos* (1579).[43] When faced with religious persecution, these authors developed their own theories of resistance, ones that reflected core tenets of the *Magdeburg Confession*. They similarly emphasised that civil magistrates existed both for the common good of humankind and for the promulgation of the true religion. If a ruler issued commandments contrary to either the natural law or the divine law, inferior magistrates had a divinely mandated duty to resist and institute a new superior who would rule appropriately. While the reception of these ideas about resistance within the Scottish context will be examined in Chapter 6, the theories of resistance that Covenanters came to advance – based upon defence of the true religion and protection of the godly commonwealth – reflected these important sixteenth-century Lutheran and Reformed precedents. Reformed authors thus established clear criteria for legitimising resistance: God commanded magistrates to protect the true religion against idolatry and contribute to the outward flourishing of the church. If they failed to do so, their duty devolved to their inferiors, even if this required the force of arms.

As this section has demonstrated, the earliest Protestant reformers understood the end of politics to include the preservation of temporal peace and the advancement of God's glory, though they disagreed about the relative importance of these two ends. Politics became a divinely mandated means of protecting the true religion, and political participation was less about free choice and a natural inclination for societal associations than it had been for Roman Catholics. Throughout the sixteenth century, the temporal kingdom (concerned primarily with the body and human relationships) became increasingly synonymous with the godly commonwealth, while Christian subjects and magistrates had distinct duties to fulfil. Yet the apparent uniformity of Protestant thought about the end of politics should not be overstated. Some reformers (like Luther) capitalised on an Augustinian conception of human depravity and the coercive nature of government. This approach resulted in a limited or restricted purpose for civil government: the preservation of temporal peace and order above all else. The magistrate had a duty to enforce the commands in the Decalogue that governed human relationships, but not necessarily to enforce the commands regulating true worship (unless these directly threatened civil stability). Other reformers gave the magistrate far greater control over religion – especially over the civil punishment of spiritual crimes – as the defender of both tables of the Decalogue. Despite the broad consensus among the earliest reformers that subjects should advance God's glory in their political communities through obedience to lawful magistrates, the religious wars of the sixteenth and seventeenth centuries forced later of generations of Protestants (including Scots) to debate the exact nature of how God called subjects and magistrates to participate in political life.

The Godly Commonwealth and the Scottish Reformation (1560)

Following their own Reformation in 1560, Scottish Protestants engaged with the same conversations about the end of politics, the *cura religionis* and the formation of the godly commonwealth that preoccupied their contemporaries in Europe. This international context for developing ideas about the godly commonwealth – ones based heavily upon divinely mandated duties for subjects and magistrates in political life – provided an essential intellectual framework for Scottish discourse about the two kingdoms. But Scots had their own unique concerns, including the need to intellectually defend Presbyterianism by securing the church's independence from royal interference. Yet in the years following 1560, the earliest Scottish reformers expressed significant ambiguity on the relationship between the two kingdoms, raising a host of problems about the godly prince's involvement in the church that continually surfaced under the reigns of James and Charles. This section examines how these ideas developed in a Scottish context between the Reformation of 1560 and the drafting of the National Covenant, focusing specifically on the ways in which Scots embraced or departed from earlier European intellectual traditions.

Scholars have already observed the pre-eminence of two-kingdoms thought in early modern Scotland, focusing specifically on the doctrine's implications for church-state relations in a Presbyterian context. For example, Alan MacDonald defined the two-kingdoms theory in Scotland as, 'The idea pressed by those in the Church who did not want the king as embodiment of the secular kingdom to interfere in the internal affairs of the Church, the embodiment of the spiritual kingdom.'[44] Others have argued that Reformed Scots were ideologically divided 'between those who believed that there was one kingdom, in which the king dominated both political and religious spheres, or two, in which church and state were under separate jurisdictions.'[45] Keith Brown also highlighted the jurisdictional context, describing the temporal and spiritual as 'two spheres of influence to be presided over by a working partnership of magistrates and ministers'.[46] These definitions, while accurate, primarily reflect the institutional implications of two-kingdoms theology for the relationship between church and state. But the doctrine raised additional questions about the duties that God required magistrates and subjects to perform in political life, an implication overlooked in current analyses of two-kingdoms theology within Scotland.

One problem with viewing Scottish approaches to the two kingdoms in isolation is the tendency to treat Presbyterians as especially theocratic in their desire to subordinate the king to ecclesiastical authorities and exclude him from headship over church affairs. The stereotype of Scottish Presbyterians as theocrats is pervasive. According to Gordon Donaldson, the two-kingdoms doctrine allowed Presbyterian ministers to advance a theocratic agenda, one that restricted the civil magistrate's authority over what was said in the pulpits and held rulers accountable to church censure.[47] Francis Lyall similarly maintained that Scottish ministers claimed 'the right to tell the civil arm how to exercise its own particular authority in accordance with the Word of God. This threatened theocracy.'[48] As a result, civil magistrates resisted Presbyterianism after 1560, deeming it politically subversive. By contrast, James Kirk resisted the idea that Scottish Presbyterians were inherently theocratic, arguing that they kept the two kingdoms theoretically distinct, and that each could be subject to separate authorities without the domination of either.[49] Indeed, for early modern Scots, theocracy would have implied the direct rule of the state by ecclesiastical authorities (such as priests), which was certainly not their aim.

By taking account of broader continental European Protestant ideas about the ends and authorities of the two kingdoms, it becomes clear that Scots were no more theocratic than many of their contemporaries in their attempts to fashion a godly commonwealth and resist royal authority in the church. Instead, they had a great respect for the separate ends and authorities of the two kingdoms, a paradigm that significantly reflected contemporary conversations about the doctrine in Europe. It was not unusual for the earliest Protestant reformers to limit the civil magistrate's involvement in ecclesiastical affairs, making their *cura religionis* pertinent to external matters of the church alone. Scottish Presbyterians equally reiterated separate ends for temporal and spiritual authorities, while confirming that the king should defend both tables of the Decalogue (in accordance with those standards for godly rule developing across Europe). They therefore did not view Presbyterianism as imposing church rule upon the state but as protecting the spiritual purity of the kirk from potentially idolatrous influences. Like most of their Protestant contemporaries in Europe, they believed that subjects and magistrates alike must contribute to the flourishing of the true religion, but they did not subordinate the state wholly to the church in a theocracy. Instead, they sought to keep the two kingdoms distinct, even excluding bishops from Parliament through the abolition of the clerical Estate in 1640.

Much of the debate that took place in Scotland during the 1630s and 1640s about the duty of the 'godly magistrate' (and Charles's failure to act as one) harkened back to the kingdom's post-Reformation history. As a result, the rest of this chapter discusses the precedents for and evolution of Scottish ideas about the two kingdoms and the end of politics after 1560. Early descriptions of the two kingdoms in a specifically Presbyterian context appeared in the *Second Book of Discipline*, presented to the General Assembly in 1578 and approved in 1581.[50] The *First Book of Discipline* (1560) had initially provided loose guidelines for church polity based upon those developed in Geneva, but the Scots abandoned the book's plans for polity and religious education. Following the forced abdication of Mary, Queen of Scots (1542–1587), the *Second Book* advanced a stricter Presbyterian model for the kirk using two-kingdoms language. It began with the assertion that God ordained both civil and ecclesiastical governments to create godly subjects and to advance the glory of God. These two governments had 'one authority, one ground, one finall cause, but are different in the manner, and forme of execution'.[51] Civil authorities held the power of the sword to punish temporal crimes, while ecclesiastical authorities possessed the power of the keys to execute spiritual discipline and excommunication.[52] The temporal and spiritual governments shared the same source of power and aimed to glorify God, but they had distinct tools to achieve their respective ends.

Indeed, the *Second Book* did subordinate the king to the spiritual discipline of ecclesiastical authorities, just like any other member of the church. It clarified that, '[A]s the ministers and others of the ecclesiasticall estate are subject to the magistrate civill, so ought the person of the magistrate be subject to the kirk spiritually, and in ecclesiasticall government.'[53] Yet the book did not fully exclude civil magistrates from their responsibility over the church either. It assigned them a specific set of duties that included a mixture of civil and ecclesiastical affairs: punishing vice, executing justice, maintaining the liberty of the church and preserving civic peace. It also affirmed the growing consensus among Protestant reformers that the civil magistrate 'ought to assist, maintaine and fortifie the iurisdiction of the kirk.'[54] But the *cura religionis* pertained exclusively to the church's outward defence. As the book recorded, 'The magistrate neither ought to preach, minister the sacraments, nor execute the censures of the kirk ... but command the ministers to observe the rule commanded in the word, and punish the transgressors by civill meanes.'[55] As Kirk has shown, this perspective on the two kingdoms, in addition to the role of the godly magistrate, reflected the same ideas contained within *De Regno Christi*, the work of the German Protestant reformer Martin Bucer (1491–1551). As he concluded, the *Second Book* provided 'a succinct summary of earlier strands of thought' about the Christian magistrate's office, introducing very little that was new or original.[56] The *Second Book* thus articulated similar ideas to those that had emerged on the continent about the symbiotic cooperation between magistrate and church to advance the godly commonwealth, while ensuring that the Presbyterian church could be insulated from royal oversight. It did subject the king to spiritual discipline if he had gone astray (like any individual), but it did not assert the interference of ecclesiastical authorities within civic institutions or government (as in a theocracy).

Scholars have equally pointed to Andrew Melville (1545–1622) as an essential Scottish reformer who developed a circle of Presbyterians committed to rejecting the king's authority over the church and to securing its independence. In 1596, he reportedly delivered a speech to King James VI in which he declared that there were

> two kings and two kingdoms in Scotland: there is King James, the head of this commonwealth, and there is Christ Jesus, the King of the church, whose subject James the Sixth is, and of whose kingdom he is not a king, nor a lord, nor a head, but a member.[57]

Scholars have often referenced this statement as evidence of Melville's strict separation of civil and ecclesiastical authority, although similar ideas about the two kingdoms appeared in his other works.[58] As Steven Reid noted, this 1596 statement has become a 'form of lazy shorthand' for describing Melville's belief in a two-kingdoms theory, characterised by the 'forthright rejection of the idea of royal supremacy over the church and adherence instead to the strict separation of the temporal and spiritual spheres of government.'[59] But Melville's articulation is crucial for demonstrating the lack of theocratic aims among Scotland's Presbyterians. As John Coffey has observed, 'The Melvillian concern to distinguish the spheres of church and state entailed a rejection of theocracy, if by that we mean rule by clerics.'[60] Nevertheless, Melville's appeal to the two kingdoms reflected his concerns about securing the church's independence from royal interference, while it reflected broader Protestant beliefs that the *cura religionis* extended only to the outward affairs of the church, rather than to its internal governance.

Together, the rejection of royal control over the kirk found in the *Second Book of Discipline* and in Melville's thought, which equally restricted the church from interfering within temporal affairs, contributed to a uniquely Scottish approach to the two kingdoms after 1560. Yet the core foundations of this theory, especially the assumption that the king should actively protect the true religion while keeping the two kingdoms as distinct as possible, reflected the broader consensus emerging among continental European Protestants. The earliest Scottish reformers may not have desired direct church rule over the state, but they did want to specify the nature of the 'godly magistrate' as one who ruled harmoniously in accordance with the will of the church. Less studied, however, is the same language of the two kingdoms, the magistrate's *cura religionis* and the two tables of the Decalogue within royalist and Covenanter discourse. The two-kingdoms paradigm was not the intellectual remit of Scottish Presbyterians alone. Instead, it functioned as a shared intellectual framework for how Scots thought about and contested the structure of their world, albeit one that resulted in drastically different ideas about the nature of political power after 1638.

The idea that the Covenanters (in particular) strove after theocracy derives, in part, from the criticisms waged against them by Scottish Episcopalians, or by supporters of monarchical authority. For example, Scots who favoured episcopacy, or those who simply supported royal authority over the church, used language of the two kingdoms to accuse the Covenanters of conflating their ends and authorities. For example, in 1639, the royalist author John Corbet (1603–1641) drew upon such terminology to criticise the Covenanters for seeking church rule over the state. Corbet had served as a minister in the Church of Scotland from 1637 until he was deposed from the ministry in 1639 for refusing to recognise the authority of the 1638 General Assembly. He fled to Ireland under the patronage of Thomas Wentworth where he wrote *The Ungirding of the Scottish Armour* (1639). In this treatise, Corbet denounced the Covenanters for resisting the king's authority over the church. He argued that the king held absolute power as the supreme judge and sword-bearer, claiming that the Covenanters did not honour him as the one whom God endowed as judge and executioner. Instead, they fell 'head-long in another point of poperie in making the generall assemblie an infallible Iudge, at whose determination ye sweare to stand, in judgment and practice.'[61]

More importantly, Corbet accused the Covenanters of usurping the king's *cura religionis* as the defender of the true religion. He relied upon the interpretation of the civil magistrate as the only individual whom God tasked with preserving both tables of the Decalogue, the very perspective on royal authority over religion common within Protestant intellectual circles. As he asked the Covenanters,

> Will you have king and subject of equall power, about the observation and preservation of the Tables? You are bound to keep the commandements of God, as well as your king; but the king is bound to do more,

to wit, to be carefull, that all his subjects keep them, and to punish transgressours.[62]

Corbet continued that subjects must 'keep the Tables themselves, but they have no authority to command others.'[63] Only magistrates could compel obedience among the people. Crucially, this meant that ministers could not force the king into spiritual obedience through the force of arms. Instead, Christian subjects could only employ spiritual weapons in the temporal kingdom. As Corbet argued, 'Gods law commands not to defend his right by armes: the weapons of our warfare are spirituall, and not carnall: patience, faith, with other graces, are our armour.'[64] If subjects repressed or resisted their superiors, they would take God's place. Corbet thus drew upon the same paradigm of the two kingdoms, including the magistrate's duty to defend both tables of the Decalogue, to safeguard royal power against a potential encroachment of the church.

Another royalist, John Forbes of Corse (1593–1648) – professor of divinity at King's College, Aberdeen and the eventual leader of the so-called 'Aberdeen Doctors' (discussed in Chapter 2) – also drew upon this two-kingdoms distinction to defend royal intervention in church reform. Yet he emphasised the king's duty to preserve peace and order above religious division. In 1629 (prior to the drafting of the National Covenant and outbreak of war with the king), Forbes published *Irenicum Amatoribus Veritatis et Pacis in Ecclesia Scoticana*, in which he defended James's imposition of the Five Articles of Perth and the lawfulness of episcopacy. He was primarily concerned that Scottish Protestants were sowing division over inconsequential matters of doctrine and worship. As a result, he argued that civil magistrates had a duty to preserve peace and order above all else, while their protection of the true religion was only secondary. As Forbes stated:

> The chief duty of the magistrate is to procure and conserve the public peace and tranquillity. Which of course, he never did more happily, than when he was truly a God-fearing and religious man, who ... promoted the preaching of true and sincere faith, perished all lies and superstitions with all their ungodliness and idolatry, and defended the Church of God.[65]

For Forbes, it would certainly be beneficial if magistrates possessed godly character and ruled harmoniously alongside the church. But their primary obligation comprised the preservation of temporal peace. Forbes's perspective thus resembled that advanced by Luther earlier in his life, according to which politics tended toward the maintenance of peace rather than toward the active formation of a uniform, godly commonwealth, especially one that resulted in intra-confessional conflict.

While some royalists drew upon ideas about the two kingdoms to promote temporal peace and defend royal authority against what they perceived as ecclesiastical encroachment on the state, Covenanters used the same paradigm in a different way. For example, Samuel Rutherford (ca. 1600–1661) outlined his own theory of the two kingdoms, one that reflected the perspective taken by both Melanchthon and Calvin, to defend Presbyterian church government. Born in Roxburghshire around 1600, Rutherford attended the University of Edinburgh, where he graduated with an MA in 1621. He served as a minister in Kirkcudbrightshire from 1627 until he was exiled to Aberdeen in 1636. He then attended the Glasgow Assembly in 1638 and was appointed professor of divinity at St Andrews. He remained in this position until 1643, at which time he began serving as a Scottish commissioner to the Westminster Assembly.

During his stay in London, he confronted the English Independents, who placed ecclesiastical authority in local congregations, and the Erastians, who located ecclesiastical authority in the civil magistrate. To challenge these two perspectives, Rutherford published *The divine right of church government and excommunication* (1646), in which he argued that Christ established Presbyterianism as the only acceptable form of church polity. In doing so, he had to confront the concerns of English theologians who believed that Presbyterianism threatened civil stability by limiting the king's lawful power over the church. In a section specifically dedicated to whether the civil magistrate should have ecclesiastical powers, Rutherford clearly described the separate ends and authorities of the two kingdoms. As he argued, the two kingdoms reflected the twofold character of human nature, consisting of an inward spiritual part (the conscience and the soul), and a visible, physical part that engaged in external acts of worship.[66] This distinction of body and soul reflected the spiritual and temporal structure of the world. As Rutherford argued, two types of governors existed:

> one over man in relation to his conscience and walking with God, and his brethren as members of a spiritual society, called a pastor or teacher; another in relation to his civill actions of peace and justice to his brother, as he is a member of a civill society, called a magistrate.[67]

Despite acknowledging that these two powers 'are both supream in their owne sphere', Rutherford claimed that there was a 'mutuall and reciprocall subjection of each to other' because ministers existed as civil subjects while they also cared for magistrates' souls.[68]

Rutherford's distinction between the two kingdoms was far from unusual and reflected pre-existing bodies of thought. He argued that magistrates must not interfere in the spiritual kingdom by preaching or administering the sacraments, for obedience to the true religion could never be enforced with the king's carnal weapons.[69] The king's power resided only in the external punishment of spiritual crimes, such as heresy and blasphemy, rather than in the internal governance of the conscience or soul. Like Melville, Rutherford also expressed distinctly Presbyterian concerns about royal authority over the church when he maintained that the king held the same status in the church as any other individual. As he claimed, 'Magistrates are no more gods and nursefathers in the church, then all christians are gods and nursefathers of the church.'[70] Instead, 'the Magistrate punisheth heresies and false doctrine as they disturb the peace of the civill state; therefore his power is civill.'[71] The magistrate's duty thus included defending the church by eradicating heresy and false doctrine, but only insofar as these threatened temporal peace. Only the church (through its spiritual weapons) could punish crimes against the first table of the Decalogue, ones which were scandalous and offensive to God. Rutherford therefore exhibited a similar perspective on the magistrate's *cura religionis* as his Protestant contemporaries in Europe, yet he continued to articulate these views with reference to distinct Presbyterian concerns about royal supremacy and the king's role over religious reform.

George Gillespie (1613–1648), one of the Covenanters' youngest and most prolific leaders, also discussed the similarities and differences between the ends and authorities of the two kingdoms. In 1646, he served as a Scottish commissioner to the Westminster Assembly where he wrote *Aaron's rod blossoming: or, the divine ordinance of church-government vindicated.* Like early Protestant reformers in continental Europe, Gillespie argued that civil power resulted from divine law and God's grace, not just from natural law. God appointed both civil and ecclesiastical powers for the good of human beings and the glory of God, making both 'mutually aiding and auxiliary, each to other. Magistracy strengthens the ministry, and the ministry strengthens magistracy.'[72] Referencing Luther, Gillespie distinguished between the two types of power. He argued:

> The effects of the civil power are civil laws, civil punishments, civil rewards. The effects of the ecclesiastical power, are determinations of controversies of faith, canons concerning order and decency in the church, ordination or deposition of church-officers, suspension from the sacrament, and excommunication.[73]

While Gillespie preserved separate ends for civil and ecclesiastical authorities, he granted magistrates the power of the sword to punish crimes external to the church. As he stated, 'The subordinate end of the civil power is, that all publike sins committed presumptuously against the moral law, may be exemplarly punished, and that peace, justice, and good order may be preserved and maintained in the Commonwealth.'[74] The civil magistrate therefore had a duty to protect the true religion, as Rutherford and earlier Protestant reformers had also argued, primarily to create a peacefully ordered commonwealth that provided good soil for the promulgation of the gospel.

However, Gillespie recognised that critics might see his emphasis on the magistrate as defender of both tables of the Decalogue as conflicting with separate powers for civil and ecclesiastical authorities. He attempted to resolve this tension when he argued that

Magistrates are appointed, not onely for civil policy, but for the conservation and purgation of Religion . . . The magistrate himself may not assume the administration of the keys, nor the dispensing of church-censures; he can but punish the external man with external punishments.[75]

For Gillespie, the idea of the two kingdoms was not only a way to reject the royal supremacy and secure independence of the church. Rather, like early Protestant reformers in Europe, he was equally interested in defining the magistrate's *cura religionis* to advance the godly commonwealth, the primary end of politics.

Rutherford and Gillespie thus conformed to the general Reformed consensus emerging in continental Europe that all political societies were Christian ones, and that magistrates must use the power of the sword to create perfect conditions for God's glory and the gospel to spread. They concurred that politics existed for a spiritual end, not just a natural one. But to this perspective, they added a uniquely Presbyterian interest in refuting royal supremacy and challenging the need for a temporal head of the church. Language of the two kingdoms, and the respective duties of subjects and magistrates with regard to upholding both tables of the Decalogue, thus remained paramount in Scottish discourse after 1560 as Scots grappled with the meaning of their own reformation history and debated the nature of their national church.

Conclusion

This chapter has examined Protestant ideas about the end of politics, including the meaning of the *cura religionis*, through the writings of early sixteenth- and seventeenth-century reformers, both in Scotland and elsewhere in Europe. It has demonstrated the emergence of two different strands of thought. On the one hand, politics might exist exclusively for the coercive restraint of human wickedness and sinfulness. The civil magistrate's primary duty included only worldly matters related to the second table of the Decalogue, such as executing justice to preserve peace. On the other hand, politics might be a divinely mandated duty to advance God's glory and protect the true religion, giving the civil magistrate a wider-ranging *cura religionis* that extended to punishing crimes against the first table. Scots equally took part in broader conversations about the end of politics and the godly commonwealth, adapting these traditions to their own debates after 1560 to defend or denounce the Presbyterian rejection of royal authority over the church.

Scholars have already shown that seventeenth-century Scots believed that civil and ecclesiastical authorities should cooperate to advance the true religion after 1560.[76] However, as this chapter has argued, debates about the relationships between the two kingdoms were not exclusively about institutional church-state relations. They raised important questions about the purpose of politics in general, such as whether rulers must prioritise temporal peace or the advancement of God's glory. How Protestants viewed the aim of politics equally affected the priorities they pursued, such as the preservation of civil stability above all else, or the active promulgation of religion through the force of arms, even if this action resulted in religious division. A broad consensus thus emerged among early modern Protestants, both in Scotland and continental Europe, that the aim of politics included securing a Christian commonwealth and advancing God's glory. Yet little agreement existed regarding how exactly magistrates and subjects might achieve this goal in practice, and what methods they might employ for its attainment. The following chapters will break down the ways in which Scots exploited these nuanced distinctions within Protestant thought about the two kingdoms after 1637 to defend their own allegiances as best fulfilling God's commandments for subjects in political life.

Notes

1. Henreckson, *Immortal Commonwealth* (see introduction, n. 71); John Coffey, 'The Language of Liberty in Calvinist Political Thought,' in *Freedom and the Construction of Europe: Volume 1, Religious and Constitutional Liberties*, eds Quentin Skinner and Martin van Gelderen (Cambridge: CUP, 2013), 296–316; Carlos M. N. Eire, *War against the Idols: The Reformation of Worship from Erasmus to Calvin* (Cambridge: CUP, 1986), ch. 8.
2. Mortimer, *Reformation*, ch. 3 (see introduction, n. 69).
3. Mortimer, *Reformation*, 63.
4. John Witte, Jr, *Law and Protestantism: The Legal Teachings of the Lutheran Reformation* (Cambridge: CUP, 2002), 5–9.
5. Jonathon D. Beeke, *Duplex Regnum Christi: Christ's Twofold Kingdom in Reformed Theology* (Leiden: Brill, 2021), 25–39; Matthew J. Tuininga, *Calvin's Political Theology and the Public Engagement of the Church: Christ's Two Kingdoms* (Cambridge: CUP, 2017), 24–32.
6. Martin Luther, *Von weltlicher uberkeyt wie weyt man yhr gehorsam schuldig sey* ([Augsburg], 1523). The English translation referenced here is: Martin Luther, 'On Secular Authority: How Far Does the Obedience Owed to it Extend? [*Von Weltlicher Oberkeit*],' in *Luther and Calvin on Secular Authority*, ed. and trans. Harro Höpfl (Cambridge: CUP, 1991), 3–43.
7. Höpfl, introduction to *Luther and Calvin*, x.
8. Luther, 'On Secular Authority,' 11.
9. Luther, 'On Secular Authority,' 11.
10. Luther, 'On Secular Authority,' 23.
11. Luther, 'On Secular Authority,' 12.
12. Luther, 'On Secular Authority,' 12.
13. Luther, 'On Secular Authority,' 11.
14. Augustine, *The City of God against the Pagans*, ed. and trans. R. W. Dyson (Cambridge: CUP, 1998), bk xix, chs 14–17. See also: Paul J. Weithman, 'Augustine and Aquinas on Original Sin and the Function of Political Authority,'

Journal of the History of Philosophy 30, no. 3 (1992): 354, 355–60; John Neville Figgis, *The Political Aspects of S. Augustine's 'City of God'* (London: Longmans, Green and Co., 1921).
15. Ian Campbell and Floris Verhaart, eds, *Protestant Politics Beyond Calvin: Reformed Theologians on War in the Sixteenth and Seventeenth Centuries* (London: Routledge, 2022), 12.
16. Luther, 'On Secular Authority,' 13.
17. Luther, 'On Secular Authority,' 30.
18. Luther, 'On Secular Authority,' 30.
19. Mortimer, *Reformation*, 71; David M. Whitford, '*Cura Religionis* or Two Kingdoms: The Late Luther on Religion and the State in the Lectures on Genesis,' *Church History* 73, no. 1 (2004): 41–62; James M. Estes, 'Luther on the Role of Secular Authority in the Reformation,' *Lutheran Quarterly* 17, no. 2 (2003): 199–225.
20. Martin Luther, 'Against the Robbing and Murdering Hordes of Peasants (1525)' in *The Essential Luther*, ed. and trans. Tryntje Helfferich (Cambridge: Hackett, 2018), 163–8.
21. Whitford, '*Cura Religionis*,' 62.
22. For a summary of this historiographical approach, see Beeke, *Duplex Regnum*, 2–6; William Wright, *Martin Luther's Understanding of God's Two Kingdoms: A Response to the Challenge of Skepticism* (Grand Rapids, MI: Baker Academic, 2010), 17–43.
23. Reinhold Niebuhr, *Christ and Culture* (New York: Harper & Row, 1975); Reinhold Niebuhr, *The Nature and Destiny of Man: A Christian Interpretation, vol. 2: Human Destiny* (New York: Charles Scribner's Sons, 1964); Karl Barth, *Eine Schweizer Stimme: 1938–1945* (Zürich: Evangelischer Verlag, 1948); Ernst Troeltsch, *The Social Teaching of the Christian Churches*, 2 vols., trans. Olive Wyon (London: George Allen & Unwin, 1931).
24. Mortimer, *Reformation*, 68.
25. Luther, 'On Secular Authority,' 14.
26. Luther, 'On Secular Authority,' 14.
27. Eire, *War against the Idols*, 285–7.
28. Witte, *Law and Protestantism*, 9.
29. Philip Melanchthon, 'Locus 20: Civil Rulers and the Validity of Governmental Matters,' in *Loci Communes, 1543*, trans. Jacob A. O. Preus (St Louis: Concordia Publishing House, 1992), 212.
30. Melanchthon, 'Locus 20,' 224.
31. Melanchthon, 'Locus 20,' 225.
32. Beeke, *Duplex Regnum*, 7–12; David Van Drunen, *Natural Law and the Two Kingdoms: A Study in the Development of Reformed Social Thought* (Grand Rapids, MI: Eerdmans, 2010), especially ch. 2.
33. Christoph Strohm, 'Melanchthon-Rezeption in der Ethik des frühen Calvinismus,' in *Melanchthon und der Calvinismus*, eds Günter Frank and Herman J. Selderhuis (Stuttgart: Frommann-Holzboog, 2005), 135–57.
34. John Calvin, 'On Civil Government [*Institutio Christianae Religionis*, Book IV, chapter 20]' in *Luther and Calvin*, 48.
35. Calvin, 'On Civil Government,' 49.
36. Calvin, 'On Civil Government,' 49.
37. Calvin, 'On Civil Government,' 50–1.
38. Calvin, 'On Civil Government,' 58.

39. Tuininga, *Calvin's Political Theology*, 254.
40. Nicolaus von Amsdorff, *Confessio et Apologia Pastorum & reliquorum ministrorum Ecclesiae Magdeburgensis* (Magdeburg, 1550).
41. Ibid., sig. [F3r–v].
42. Ibid., sig. [F4v–G1v].
43. Stephanus Junius Brutus, *Vindiciae, contra tyrannos: sive, de Principis in Populum, Populique in Principem, legitima potestate* (Edinburgh, 1579); Theodore Beza, *De jure magistratuum* (Lyon, 1574); Christopher Goodman, *How superior powers oght to be obeyd of their subjects* (Geneva, 1558); John Knox, *The First Blast of the Trumpet against the Montrous Regiment of Women* (Geneva, 1558); John Ponet, *A shorte treatise of politike pouuer and of the true obedience which subiectes owe to kynges and other civile governours* (Strasbourg, 1556); See also: Cynthia Grant Shoenberger, 'The Development of the Lutheran Theory of Resistance: 1523–1530,' *The Sixteenth Century Journal* 8, no. 1 (1977): 61–76; Richard Benert, 'Inferior Magistrates in Sixteenth-Century Political and Legal Thought' (PhD diss., University of Minnesota, 1967).
44. Alan R. MacDonald, 'Church and State in Scotland from the Reformation to the Covenanting Revolution,' in *A Companion to the Reformation in Scotland, c. 1525–1638*, ed. William Ian P. Hazlett (Leiden: Brill, 2022), 617.
45. Kirsty F. McAlister and Roland J. Tanner, 'The First Estate: Parliament and the Church,' in *The History of the Scottish Parliament: Volume 3: Parliament in Context, 1235–1707*, eds Keith M. Brown and Alan R. MacDonald (Edinburgh: EUP, 2010), 49.
46. Keith M. Brown, 'In Search of the Godly Magistrate in Reformation Scotland,' *Journal of Ecclesiastical History* 40, no. 4 (1989): 555.
47. Gordon Donaldson, *Scottish Church History* (Edinburgh: Scottish Academic Press, 1985), 234–6.
48. Francis Lyall, *Church and State in Scotland: Developing Law* (Abingdon: Routledge, 2016), 12.
49. James Kirk, *Patterns of Reform. Continuity and Change in the Reformation Kirk* (Edinburgh: T. & T. Clark, 1989), 242–9.
50. David G. Mullan, 'Revolution, Consensus, and Controversy: Reformation Thought in Scotland,' in Hazlett, *Companion to the Reformation in Scotland*, 157–9.
51. Church of Scotland, 'The Second Booke of Discipline,' in *The Doctrine and Discipline of the Kirke of Scotland* (London, 1641), 78.
52. Church of Scotland, 'The Second Booke of Discipline,' 79.
53. Church of Scotland, 'The Second Booke of Discipline,' 78.
54. Church of Scotland, 'The Second Booke of Discipline,' 79.
55. Church of Scotland, 'The Second Booke of Discipline,' 79.
56. James Kirk, introduction to *The Second Book of Discipline*, ed. James Kirk (Edinburgh: Saint Andrew Press, 1980), 65.
57. Thomas M'Crie, 'The Life of Andrew Melville,' in *The Works of Thomas M'Crie*, ed. Thomas M'Crie (Edinburgh: William Blackwood, 1856), 2: 181.
58. Steven J. Reid, 'Andrew Melville and the Law of Kingship,' in Mason and Reid, *Andrew Melville*, 47–74 (see introduction, n. 52).
59. Reid, 'Melville and the Law of Kingship,' 47.
60. Coffey, *Politics, Religion and the British Revolutions*, 208.
61. John Corbet, *The ungirding of the Scottish armour* (Dublin, 1639), 14.
62. Corbet, *Ungirding*, 31.

63. Corbet, *Ungirding*, 31.
64. Corbet, *Ungirding*, 32.
65. John Forbes, *Irenicum Amatoribus Veritatis et Pacis in Ecclesia Scoticana* (Aberdeen, 1629), 123: 'Magistratus officium praecipuum est pacem & tranquillitatem publicam procurare & conservare. Quod sanem nunquam fecerit faelicius, quam cum fuerit vere timens Dei & religiosus, qui, videlicet, ad exemplum sanctissimorum Regum Principumque, populi Domini, veritatu praedicationem, & fidem sinceram promoverit, mendacia & superstitionem omnen cum omni impietate & idololatria exciderit, Ecclesiamque Dei defenderit.' [Translations are my own].
66. Samuel Rutherford, *The divine right of church government and excommunication* (London, 1646), 416.
67. Rutherford, *Divine right*, 416.
68. Rutherford, *Divine right*, 418.
69. Rutherford, *Divine right*, 393.
70. Rutherford, *Divine right*, 395.
71. Rutherford, *Divine right*, 623.
72. George Gillespie, *Aaron's rod blossoming; or, the divine ordinance of church-government vindicated* (London, 1646), 184.
73. Gillespie, *Aaron's rod*, 189.
74. Gillespie, *Aaron's rod*, 188.
75. Gillespie, *Aaron's rod*, 191.
76. Brown, 'In Search of the Godly Magistrate,' 553–81.

CHAPTER TWO

Adiaphora and Ecclesiastical Reform

Early modern Scots broadly agreed that the civil magistrate had a responsibility to advance the true religion according to the first table of the Decalogue, yet they diverged substantially regarding the exact remit of his *cura religionis*. Was his authority only external to the church, or did he possess power over its internal affairs too? On the one hand, the king might only have power outside of the church, meaning that he could punish spiritual crimes (like blasphemy and heresy) that threatened to disrupt civil peace. On the other hand, his responsibility might extend within the church through the appointment of its authorities or the reformation of its ceremonies and liturgical practices. In the latter instance, the king had a divine right to reform the church as its temporal head, appointed to serve as God's representative on earth. As Charles asserted greater authority over the Church of Scotland – especially by instituting bishops and the prayer book through his royal prerogative in 1637 – these contrasting perspectives on the king's *cura religionis* came into blatant, explosive tension. This chapter examines the theological discussions in the years leading up to the drafting of the Covenant that specifically addressed the legitimacy of the king's reforms and the remit of his *cura religionis*. It analyses two key debates, one about the regulation of *adiaphora* (matters indifferent to God) and the other about the royal supremacy. Both concepts had a long-standing history in Scotland, reaching back to the Scottish Reformation of 1560, informing debates about the Five Articles of Perth and resurfacing at the time of the National Covenant. By exploring these two debates, this chapter illustrates initial points of intersection between ecclesiological ideas and political thought in the earliest years of the Scottish Revolution.

To do so, it first examines the evolution of the royal supremacy in Scotland from the Reformation through the National Covenant to demonstrate why this doctrine proved so contentious by 1638. It then considers how Scots supported or rejected the royal supremacy using language of *adiaphora*, a theological category which enabled them to justify or challenge the king's reforms as being in accordance with or antithetical to God's will. It concludes by analysing the political implications of this theological debate: the concept of *adiaphora* enabled Covenanters to restrict the king's legislative power and place authority over church reform in the Scottish parliament instead. By debating the ambiguous nature of *adiaphora*, Scots could either renounce or justify the royal supremacy while simultaneously restricting or increasing parliamentary power. As later chapters will show, this contrast between monarchical and parliamentary power over church reform provided a model of authority that mapped onto the state, deeply informing the political theories advanced by Scots on both sides of the conflict. Ultimately, this chapter argues that initial ecclesiological debates about *adiaphora* and the royal supremacy preceding the National Covenant provided Scots with an intellectual framework for thinking about church reform that simultaneously paved the way for parallel discussions about the king's civil and legal sovereignty over the state.

The Evolution of Royal Supremacy, 1560–1640

Following the Protestant reformations of the sixteenth century, theologians across Europe needed to determine who possessed authority over the church in the absence of the pope. But the answer to this question differed greatly among Protestant communities. In England, royal supremacy emerged as a crucial doctrine that bridged the gap between church and state, but it was not universally accepted across the British Isles. After his break with Rome over the question of his divorce, King Henry VIII (1491–1547) established his headship over the Church of England through the first Act of Supremacy, passed by the English parliament on 3 November 1534. Roman Catholic Queen Mary I (1516–1558) repealed the Act in 1554, but Parliament swiftly re-established it in 1558 when Queen Elizabeth I (1533–1603) succeeded to the throne. The second Act of Supremacy deemed Elizabeth the church's supreme governor (rather than its supreme head), a title created to placate subjects who were concerned about a woman leading the church.

The idea that the king or queen could serve as the temporal head of the church had a more complicated history in Scotland where the kingdom's Protestant reformation had not been carried out by the monarch.[1] Indeed, the Scottish Reformation occurred in direct defiance of the magistrate and was ushered in by parliamentary statute instead. As a Roman Catholic, Mary, Queen of Scots could not act as the head of the Church of Scotland in the same way that Elizabeth acted as the governor of the Church of England. As a result, the Scottish parliament did not enact royal supremacy into law as an essential component of the country's reformation. Instead, John Knox's reforms wrested control from the monarch and established the precedent that the church alone held authority over its own process of reformation. The Scots' earliest Protestant Confession of Faith (1560) provided evidence of this position. As Francis Lyall argued, this confession had been 'published by the Protestants in Scotland, and *ratified and approved* by Parliament'.[2] There was no sense in which it was 'enacted by the civil authority for the Church'.[3] The church thus became its own authority, responsible for reforming itself, while Parliament (rather than the king) enacted those reforms into law.

Yet the dynastic Union of Crowns in 1603 complicated the doctrine of the royal supremacy in Scotland. After taking up residency in England, James VI and I grew increasingly fond of his headship over the Church of England, and of its ceremonies and liturgical practices. As a strong believer in the divine right theory of kingship, James appreciated that his supremacy over the English church complimented his desire for absolute, unchallengeable power in the state. He subsequently instituted a series of reforms in the Scottish church, ones intended to bring it into closer alignment with the English one. Although scholars have debated the extent to which James desired a policy of total ecclesiastical conformity through the unification of the two national institutions as part of a larger, pan-European Protestant church, he did gradually increase his authority over the Church of Scotland's internal affairs.[4] Throughout the 1590s, he had already begun to dismantle the Presbyterian church structure instituted by the earliest reformers through the *Second Book of Discipline*. He did so by imposing episcopacy, a form of church government based upon a hierarchy of royally appointed bishops, while ensuring that the moderators of the presbyteries would be selected by the bishops that he nominated. Additionally, in 1610, the Scottish Privy Council created two courts of High Commission to judge ecclesiastical matters, effectively replacing the General Assembly as the supreme church court. The Privy Council also affirmed that bishops held the power of excommunication, enabling the king to exercise greater authority over spiritual discipline through the churchmen he appointed. According to Alan MacDonald, these changes were all intended 'to cement the royal supremacy' under James's rule as he sought a headship over the Scottish church like that which he held over the English one.[5] As a result, the kirk 'was now emphatically *part* of the state in so far as it was unambiguously integrated into the structures of civil authority as never before.'[6]

In 1616, James also introduced the unpopular Five Articles of Perth to ensure greater liturgical conformity between the kirk and the English church. These articles required the Church of Scotland to institute private communion, private baptism, episcopal confirmation, kneeling at communion and the observance of holy days. Some Scots objected to the Articles on the grounds that they threatened the purity of the Reformed faith by introducing 'popish rites and superstitious ceremonies'.[7] The most controversial Article pertained to kneeling at communion, a practice that its opponents vehemently denounced as an idolatrous and mistaken honouring of Christ's real presence in the Eucharist.[8] Given the problematic nature of the Articles, the General Assembly initially rejected them in 1617. However, another meeting of the Assembly in 1618 approved them, likely as a compromise to prevent further royal interference in the kirk. The Scottish parliament finally ratified the Articles into law in 1621, although ministers did not always institute the reforms in their parishes and the king's representatives struggled to enforce them.[9]

Scots had therefore witnessed decades of James's attempts to assert greater control of their national church after 1560. When Charles succeeded to the throne in 1625, he inherited these religious tensions in Scotland from his father, and his ecclesiastical policies alone were not to blame for escalation into armed violence. Nevertheless, he failed to stop the mobilisation of resistance to his ecclesiastical policy. Following the drafting of the National Covenant on 28 February 1638, Charles initially condemned the Covenanters who embarked on a subscription campaign, accusing subscribers of treason and threatening them with arrest. However, he later allowed the General Assembly to meet in Glasgow in November 1638, hoping that this meeting might reconcile the deep religious divisions taking root in his northern kingdom. He sent his chief advisor, James Hamilton, 1st Duke of Hamilton (1606–1649) to negotiate, but the Covenanting leadership pushed for the clear establishment of Presbyterianism and refused the bishops entry. As a result, the Covenanters' opponents deemed the Glasgow Assembly illegal and created a rival 'King's Covenant'. Rather than reconcile divisions, the Glasgow Assembly increased them, prompting both Charles and the Covenanting leadership to raise military forces in January 1639.

Military skirmishes occurred between March and June 1639 during the First Bishops' War, coming to an end with the inconclusive Treaty of Berwick. The following year, the Second Bishops' War broke out when the Covenanters marched south of the border to occupy Newcastle in August 1640. They sustained their military occupation there until the Treaty of London brought the war to an end in August 1641, albeit with disastrous terms for the king. As the rest of this chapter will show, within this broader context of their own post-Reformation history, many Scots characterised Charles's innovations as yet another attempt by the Crown to assert supremacy over the kirk, intervening in its internal affairs and corrupting true worship (contrary to the first table of the Decalogue). As a result, they returned to arguments and ideas about monarchical authority over the church that Scots had developed under James's reign, applying them anew to contest the legitimacy of Charles's reforms.

Adiaphora and Matters Indifferent to God

One of the main debates that Scots resurrected in response to Charles's reforms pertained to *adiaphora*. The category of *adiaphora* initially appeared in Scotland during disputes about the Five Articles of Perth, but it also provided Scots with a crucial intellectual framework for debating the legitimacy of Charles's reforms and royal supremacy roughly twenty years later. The Greek term *adiaphora* translates literally to 'indifferent things', and it had multiple meanings within and beyond a theological context. According to its roots in Stoic philosophy, *adiaphora* comprised all morally ambiguous or neutral actions, meaning those that were neither inherently good nor evil. As a theological term, it referred to all matters indifferent to God, or those characterised by their moral neutrality given 'the silence of natural or divine law'.[10] For example, 'the time, place, ceremonies, rites, gestures, and vestments of worship' might all be considered *adiaphora* as matters that the Bible neither prohibited nor commanded.[11] Since these matters did not affect salvation, they could be determined by human discretion rather than by biblical mandates alone. Yet *adiaphora* proved to be an ambiguous and highly contentious category for Scottish Protestants who vehemently disagreed about which elements of worship were truly 'indifferent' to God, which elements affected salvation, and which individuals possessed authority to regulate these matters when faced with the silence of scripture.

The concept of *adiaphora* emerged as a central point of dispute in the aftermath of the Protestant reformations throughout Europe. In one of the most famous cases, Holy Roman Emperor Charles V issued the Augsburg Interim in 1548, which received strong opposition from Lutheran ministers. In response, Philip Melanchthon introduced a modification affirming that some points of Lutheran doctrine, such as justification by faith alone, were essential for salvation and could not be negotiated. By contrast, other points of doctrine were not essential for salvation (given scripture's silence) and were therefore matters for compromise. These so-called *adiaphora* debates resulted in Melanchthon's drafting of the Leipzig Interim (1548), a temporary settlement between Charles V and German Lutherans following the Schmalkaldic War (1546–1547). The category of *adiaphora* therefore proved an essential, yet controversial, negotiating point in religious conflicts as Protestants began to forge their own orthodoxy and determine permissible forms of worship in the face of religious hostility.[12]

Yet debates about *adiaphora* were not exclusively theological. Within the context of the British Isles, scholars have observed multiple intrinsic connections between *adiaphora* and ideas about political power or toleration. For example, Jacqueline Rose, Charles W. A. Prior and Robert von Friedeburg have all examined how seventeenth-century English intellectuals used the concept to reassess parliamentary sovereignty over the Church of England and bring about political change.[13] More specifically, Rose argued that English authors strategically reinvigorated debates about *adiaphora* after the Restoration in 1660 to promote greater religious toleration between Puritans and anti-Puritans.[14] Simultaneously, by categorising the most controversial and divisive church ceremonies as *adiaphora*, English intellectuals also reassessed the roles of civil magistrates, Parliament and law in regulating the church. As Rose concluded, debates about *adiaphora* therefore 'had a legal dimension' because they raised 'the question of who had the right to impose such matters, and under what authority they so did.'[15]

In the Scottish context, debates about the nature of *adiaphora* and their implications for political authority surfaced much earlier than the Restoration. Prior to the 1603 union, James already recognised that *adiaphora* had the capacity to significantly threaten absolute monarchy. In 1599, he wrote *Basilikon doron* in the form of a letter to his eldest son, Henry, Duke of Rothesay (1594–1612). Across three books, James provided advice for ruling justly and efficiently. He specifically advised his son

> to discerne betwixt poyntes of salvation and indifferent thinges, betwixt substance and ceremonies; & betwixt the expresse commandemente and will of God in his word, & the invention or ordinance of man; since al that is necessarie for salvation is contained in the Scripture.[16]

James argued that kings had authority over all indifferent matters that scripture did not explicitly address. For any matters not regulated in scripture, he urged his son to 'spare not to use or alter them, as the necessitie of the time shall require.'[17] He also resisted the notion that any authorities apart from the king could regulate them, cautioning his son to think carefully about scripture and keep his conscience sound so that he would not fall into the trap of believing '(with the Papistes) The Churches authoritie, better nor your owne knowledge'.[18] James thus recognised that a fundamental tension existed between church and crown on matters of indifferency, but he concluded that kings held the ultimate authority over their determination (lest kings subordinate their power to churchmen).

While James raised the issue of *adiaphora* theoretically in 1599, he confronted it in practice during the controversies surrounding the Five Articles of Perth. The language of *adiaphora* and indifferency permeated how Scots approached the Articles' legitimacy. As John Ford observed, Scots on both sides of the debate used the 'scholastic vocabulary of law and liberty, necessity and indifferency' to criticise or support James's proposed ceremonies.[19] They primarily contested whether these practices were necessary for salvation (meaning directly mandated in the Bible), whether they were indifferent matters that did not affect salvation, or whether they posed an idolatrous threat to salvation through their implementation. Although this framework of *adiaphora* appeared in the context of the Five Articles, it resurfaced two decades later when Scots responded to Charles's new attempts to impose the Book of Common Prayer. The centrality of this theological concept to debates immediately preceding the National Covenant has received little sustained analysis, but it proved critical both for the purity of the kirk and for the limits on Charles's civil authority. As the rest of this chapter demonstrates, Scots who opposed Charles's reforms (generally Presbyterians) advocated for a restricted category of *adiaphora*, one that limited royal authority over the church to external matters alone, such as the civil punishment of spiritual crimes. They tended to argue that any elements of worship that the Bible did not explicitly mandate must be omitted from the church entirely, not left to human discretion. Practices derived from the human will would only result in idolatry, for original sin had so greatly corrupted the relationship between humans and God that the former could not discern how to worship properly without explicit biblical guidance.

Opposition to Charles's ecclesiastical reforms using language of *adiaphora* appeared in a range of printed and manuscript materials between 1637 and 1639. The manuscripts, though often of unknown authorship, provide crucial insights into popular reactions to Charles's reforms beyond printed works authored by the Covenanting leadership. They also reflect how ordinary ministers in Scotland thought about and responded to both the Five Articles of Perth and Charles's attempts to assert supremacy over the church through his royal prerogative. For example, one sixteen-page manuscript outlined twelve general arguments for why the ceremonies imposed by Charles were unlawful. Although anonymous and undated, the manuscript is held in the papers of Thomas Wylie (minister of Fenwick), and its persistent rejection of the prayer book suggests that it was authored at some point in 1637.[20] The manuscript advanced a twofold argument. First, Scottish ministers must reject Charles's reforms because they threatened to reintroduce Roman Catholicism in Scotland. Second, any ceremonies instituted by human will, rather than by divine command, constituted idolatry. The manuscript began by claiming that any individuals who accepted and instituted Charles's ceremonies committed a grave sin and gave 'special honor to Antichrist and his members' (by which the manuscript meant Roman Catholic priests).[21] By acquiescing to ceremonies derived from the will and pleasure of the Stuart kings alone, Scottish subjects would sacrifice their conformity with the practices of Reformed churches in France, Germany and the Low Countries, choosing to honour English bishops instead.[22] Lest the Scots aid the Antichrist, they must resist any elements of worship not expressly mandated in the Bible.

Along with describing Charles's reforms as idolatrous threats to the true religion, the manuscript also rejected the king's authority to regulate matters of indifferency. It claimed that Charles's reforms were 'nether lawfull in themselves to be used, nor therefor lawfull because the Magistrat commandes them to be used, tho they war matteres in ther awne nature indifferent. Ergo they ar unlawful to be used in divine service.'[23] Crucially, this implied that even indifferent matters did not become lawful or necessary in worship simply because the magistrate imposed them. Instead, the king possessed no exceptional authority to regulate *adiaphora*, for 'these thinges that God leaves as indifferent to the will, and discretione of man to doe ... ar imposed only by the will and pleasour of man.'[24] In other words, if scripture was silent on a particular point of worship, it could only be imposed upon the church by the flawed will of human beings. The king's attempts to regulate ecclesiastical reform were therefore unnecessary, unbiblical and idolatrous.

Another manuscript from 9 December 1638 likewise maintained that Charles's reforms reintroduced idolatry to the Church of Scotland, drawing upon the same framework of *adiaphora* and indifferency.[25] It claimed that all innovations introduced by the Stuart monarchs (especially the Five Articles of Perth and episcopacy) contravened previous provisions for the Reformed faith in Scotland. According to the manuscript, when they subscribed to their 1581 Confession of Faith, Scots had 'sworne to forbear the practice of all Innovationes, already introduced in the maters of the worship of God or approbation of the corruptions of the publick Governament of the kirk', especially as a means of upholding the purity of the true religion.[26] It was now necessary for Scots to renew the terms of this covenant and reject any 'maters of Religion and worshippeing of God' that derived only from 'the Invention and opinion of man'.[27] The 1581 Confession of Faith ultimately obliged them to 'detast all signes and traditions brought into the kirk without or against the word of God', leading the manuscripts' authors to emphasise the necessity of renewing the previous Confession against 'all kynd of papistrie'.[28] This manuscript therefore rejected Charles's reforms by prioritising scripture as the sole authority on worship, even on supposedly 'indifferent' matters. It again reflected the core position taken by the king's opponents: if scripture did not expressly require a ceremony, it must be omitted rather than imposed by sinful human will, lest it introduce idolatry and lead worshippers astray.

While these two manuscripts emphasised the idolatrous nature of the king's innovations, the language of *adiaphora* also appeared in printed works from the period. In 1637, George Gillespie criticised Charles's reforms in his *Dispute against the English-popish ceremonies*, a text that he claimed to write for all Reformed churches in England, Scotland and Ireland. This book fuelled hostilities about the crown's ecclesiastical policy to such an extent that, on 17 October 1637, the Privy Council ordered all copies to be confiscated and burned. The Privy Council alleged that this work had been printed in Leiden and sent to Scotland 'purposely to stirre the hearts and affections of the subjects from their due obedience and allegeance.'[29] There was perhaps some merit to this fear, for Gillespie vehemently portrayed Charles's reforms as idolatrous and 'popish' while maintaining that the king had no authority whatsoever to impose them upon the kirk.

Gillespie framed his objections to Charles's reforms in terms of *adiaphora*, questioning whether they were indifferent by nature. Ceremonies characteristic of the English church that the Stuart kings attempted to impose in Scotland (such as kneeling at communion and the observance of holy days), were not necessary, expedient or lawful. As Gillespie argued, 'The Church is forbidden to adde any thing to the commandments of God, which he hath given unto us, concerning his worship and service.'[30] Even if these ceremonies were indifferent by nature, they could never be indifferent in practice. An indifferent ceremony that scripture did not overtly ban might have idolatrous implications when enacted in practice, leading Christian subjects into idolatry.[31] Additionally, any attempt to impose reforms at the king's will or pleasure constituted blasphemy, implying 'that the commandments of God are imperfect, and that by addition they are made perfect.'[32] Much like other opponents of Charles's reforms, Gillespie therefore rejected these innovations on the grounds that scripture did not command them, nor did the king possess authority to implement them. As a result, they should be wholly omitted. Ultimately, Gillespie confirmed that the king's *cura religionis* did not extend to the church's internal governance, especially through the regulation of its ceremonies and liturgical practices.

Although the language of *adiaphora* and indifferency permeated the initial responses to the king's reforms in 1637, the same perspective appeared within the National Covenant itself. The Covenant described how the 1581 Confession of Faith presented a form of religion to which 'we willingly agree in our conscience in all points, as unto God's undoubted truth and verity, grounded only upon His written word.'[33] Given that Charles imposed reforms contrary to this confession, subscribers now swore to reject all ceremonies that reflected the Roman Antichrist's 'tyrannous laws made upon indifferent things against our Christian liberty'.[34] They also confirmed their belief that the king's reforms constituted 'erroneous doctrine against the sufficiency of the written word'.[35] However, likely in an attempt to downplay their resistance to the king himself, the Covenant framed the recent innovations against the 1581 Confession as the work of the Antichrist, not as Charles's direct fault. Nevertheless, drawing upon the same language of indifferency and *adiaphora* as debates surrounding the implementation of the Five Articles of Perth and the prayer book, the National Covenant stipulated that subjects must not contravene their conscience by accepting royal reforms that added unwarranted human interpretation to the perfection of scripture.

By contrast, Scots who supported the king's ecclesiastical reforms employed the same concept of *adiaphora* to advance the opposite interpretation. They tended to believe in limited requirements for salvation, meaning that most ceremonies, doctrines and liturgical practices could be considered *adiaphora*. Crucially, these individuals were just as concerned about the reintroduction of Roman Catholicism and idolatry into Scotland as their Covenanter contemporaries. They were not interested in modern notions of toleration, nor were they supporters of religious plurality. Instead, they believed that the intra-confessional conflicts brewing across Scotland over small points of doctrine posed a much greater threat to civil stability, opening the door fully for the return of papal influence. Additionally, they believed that the king did possess legitimate authority to impose and regulate any ceremonies that did not affect salvation; God had ultimately left indifferent matters open to human interpretation by his appointed representative on earth.

John Forbes of Corse was a leading advocate of this approach to *adiaphora*, likely as a result of his involvement with a group of religious irenicists in continental Europe. He believed that the king had legitimate authority to regulate *adiaphora*, and that God commanded subjects to obey their magistrates in all matters related to the church. Forbes is most well-known as the leader of the royalist 'Aberdeen Doctors', a group of ministers and professors in the region who engaged in a pamphlet war with Covenanter commissioners as they travelled throughout the kingdom gathering subscriptions. Traditionally, the Doctors have included the six individuals who signed the pamphlets: Forbes, Robert Baron (ca. 1596–1639), William Leslie (d. 1654), James Sibbald (1595–1647), Alexander Scroggie and Alexander Ross.[36] Forbes, Leslie and Baron were all professors at King's College or Marischal College in Aberdeen, while Scroggie, Sibbald and Ross served locally as ministers. Russell Newton has also convincingly argued that William Guild (1586–1657), minister of the East Kirk in Aberdeen, should be considered the Doctors' seventh member.[37] Most scholars have omitted Guild from the group because he eventually subscribed the Covenant when the leadership redressed his concerns about their subversion of royal authority. Yet his inclusion highlights the diverse range of concerns, rather than strict unity, within the Doctors' collective opposition. Despite their intellectual diversity, the Doctors did provide sustained dissent to the Covenant in the months following its drafting. Forbes was especially instrumental in the movement, engaging in written debates with the Covenanters and coordinating support from local noblemen, such as George Gordon, 2nd Marquis of Huntly (ca. 1590–1649), to sustain their opposition.[38] Along with writing two pamphlets against subscription, the Doctors signed the King's Covenant, reaffirmed the Five Articles of Perth and refused to abjure episcopacy.[39] The 1640 General Assembly summoned the four Doctors still alive at the time (Forbes, Sibbald, Leslie and Scroggie) to answer before a special committee, one that eventually deposed them from their ministerial and academic positions.[40]

Scholars have long been fascinated by the Doctors' campaign against the Covenant, their philosophical innovativeness and their interest in ideas about religious irenicism.[41] As a group, they engaged with an ecumenical project that emerged in continental Europe to promote confessional concord between Lutherans and Calvinists. The Doctors specifically joined forces with John Dury (1596–1680) and the Hartlib circle, a group of theologians and academics who aimed to unify the Protestant states of Europe against the greater threat of Roman Catholicism.[42] Dury was born in Edinburgh in 1596 to a Presbyterian family. He entered the ministry and studied in Sedan, France under Andrew Melville, after which time he became part of the mercantile community in Prussia in 1624. It was here that he linked up with Samuel Hartlib (1600–1662), a merchant and educational reformer of German-Polish descent who relocated to England in 1628.[43] Dury subsequently dedicated himself to an irenicist project that came to include Forbes and the rest of the Doctors. Although Dury eventually returned to England, he continued to pursue 'chronically underfunded, peripatetic endeavours in Germany, Poland-Lithuania and Sweden' where he advocated for confessional union between Calvinists and Lutherans.[44] He also wrote treatises urging ecclesiastical concord among Protestants amidst the outbreak of the civil wars and became increasingly involved in politics, eventually encouraging readmission of the Jews into England under Oliver Cromwell's Protectorate as part of his desire for unity and reconciliation among victims of Catholicism.[45]

In 1635, Dury specifically sought support for his ecumenical project from John Spottiswoode (1565–1639), archbishop of St Andrews. Spottiswoode asked the Doctors to appraise the validity of Dury's request. They drew up a treatise in favour of Protestant unity entitled *Judgment . . . regarding the peace and concord of the evangelical churches*, a work that was also published in Bremen under a different name.[46] In this work, the Doctors defended Dury's attempts to secure Protestant unity across Europe by distinguishing between fundamental and secondary doctrines (a distinction that mirrored the category of *adiaphora*). Fundamental doctrines pertained to the foundations of the faith and affected salvation, while secondary doctrines comprised those which did not affect salvation.[47] Unity could only be achieved by overlooking disagreements about secondary doctrines (i.e., indifferent ones) that had no bearing upon spiritual status.

The Doctors' affinity for Lutheran and Calvinist concord has led scholars to debate the extent to which they were early advocates of toleration.[48] Yet as Aaron Clay Denlinger has convincingly argued, they were not tolerationists in a modern sense; their arguments in favour of Protestant unity were uniquely attuned for peace-making in Scotland, not for international unity. They also refused to accommodate the Anabaptists or promote reconciliation with Roman Catholics.[49] Instead, '[t]heir entire argument for ecclesiastical concord presupposed robust theological convictions on the part of all parties involved', rather than an acceptance of religious plurality.[50] Furthermore, unlike Dury (who supported and defended the English parliamentarians, the regicide and the Cromwellian republic), Forbes and the rest of the Doctors used their belief in religious irenicism to promote temporal peace and loyalty to the king in Scotland. The Doctors' religious ecumenicism enabled them to intellectually justify prioritising civil stability over religious division through adherence to Charles's authority, especially since his reforms did not threaten salvation. As the next chapter will demonstrate, their religious irenicism therefore significantly informed the theories of political obedience that they advanced.

Of all the Doctors, Forbes especially engaged with the ecumenical project in Scotland. He had studied at the University of Heidelberg under David Pareus (1548–1622), a German Reformed minister who sought to unite Lutherans and Calvinists into a general synod.[51] Pareus defended his plans in *Irenicum sive de unione et synodo evangelicorum liber votivus* (1615).[52] He argued that a synod consisting of 'good men of both ecclesiastical and civil orders' must be convened to discuss and compile opinions regarding 'what the word of God proclaims regarding controversial articles'.[53] He concluded that this 'universal synod of the evangelicals' must unite in 'earnestly seeking to promote divine glory, truth, and peace' while simultaneously mending the wounds of schism that 'came out of Roman

Babylon'.⁵⁴ Pareus thus prioritised the meeting of an ecumenical synod – one that civil rulers of Protestant lands would also sanction and attend – to find common ground on the most controversial points of doctrine and overcome intra-confessional division. Yet Pareus was also a well-known proponent of resistance theory. For example, in his 1608 commentary on Paul's Epistle to the Romans, he maintained that inferior magistrates had a duty to resist superiors who 'persecute[d] the true religion with weapons or force[d] subjects into idolatry', marking one key point of divergence between Pareus's thought and that of Forbes, his student but later royalist.⁵⁵

In 1629, Forbes wrote *Irenicum amatoribus veritatis et pacis in Ecclesia Scoticana* – a title which closely resembled that of Pareus's work. Although Forbes wrote this book to defend the Five Articles of Perth and the restoration of bishops, it was reprinted in 1639 amid new debates about the National Covenant. Forbes argued that the most controversial requirements of the Five Articles of Perth, kneeling at communion and the institution of bishops, fell within the remit of *adiaphora*, drawing upon the distinction between elements and circumstances of worship to substantiate this argument.⁵⁶ As he claimed, Christians must partake in the Lord's Supper as an element of worship (meaning one required for salvation), but the specific posture was a circumstance that could be regulated at human discretion. Additionally, he stated that the ceremonies required by the Five Articles were 'necessary for us, not because of the necessity of the things themselves, but from the necessity of obedience, order, and peace' that would result from obeying the magistrate who prescribed them.⁵⁷ Divine law may have been silent on kneeling at communion (a circumstance), but the divisions that arose between Protestants in Scotland produced a far greater threat: civil unrest and the return of Catholicism. Obedience to the magistrate in indifferent matters must be the highest priority, rather than uncompromising theological purity. Forbes therefore took a largely pragmatic approach to the Stuart kings' reforms, most likely inspired by his religious irenicism and involvement in central European ecumenical projects. As a result, he expanded the category of *adiaphora* to secure temporal peace among Scots and justify royal intervention within the church.

Forbes also supported this argument by referencing John Calvin's ideas about obedience and the conscience. According to Calvin, God required humans to submit to civil magistrates and the laws they created, provided they were good and just. He argued that individual laws 'do not reach the conscience, yet we are bound by the general command of God, which enjoins us to submit to magistrates.'⁵⁸ This meant that humans had a duty to obey all laws – whether those produced by kings or by ecclesiastical authorities – according to God's commandments in Romans 13. Obedience to these laws would leave their consciences, souls and salvation unaffected. He therefore concluded that 'the whole necessity of observing them [human laws] respects the general end, and consists not in the things commanded.'⁵⁹ Forbes adapted Calvin's argument to the Scottish context, arguing that subjects must obey any indifferent ceremony enacted into law because God required obedience to magistrates, not because of the necessity of the ceremony itself.⁶⁰ Ultimately, the problems raised by subjects' disobedience of the Five Articles of Perth (and by extension their disobedience to Charles's reforms with the reprinted version) significantly outweighed any issues about the ceremonies' expediency or necessity. By developing a broad category of *adiaphora* and by emphasising temporal obedience over religious schism, Forbes could ultimately justify the king's supreme authority over the internal affairs of the church.

As a group, the Doctors' interest in religious irenicism informed their collective response to the National Covenant. They wrote their first pamphlet against subscription, entitled *General Demands* (1638), to challenge the Covenanters' authority to interpret previous confessions of faith and impose a new one upon the Scottish population. They followed this initial pamphlet with a second, extended response: the *Duplyes* (1638). They argued that, at this time, there was no need to create a new religious confession or challenge the king. Using examples of Reformed churches across continental Europe, ones that embraced a wide range of liturgical practices, the Doctors argued that multiple ceremonies proved acceptable under the umbrella of the 'true religion'. On these grounds, the Doctors defended the legitimacy of the Five Articles of Perth and Charles's innovations.⁶¹ Equally, they sought theological doctrines common to all Protestants, not ones that emerged and divided them after the Reformation. Like Forbes himself, the Doctors collectively maintained that if 'a doctrinall errour (not being fundamentall) prevaileth by publicke authoritie in any church', pastors had a 'more necessarie and weyghtier duetie' to preserve peace and order rather than stir up religious schism.⁶² Using a wide category of *adiaphora*, the Doctors thus argued that Charles's reforms would not fundamentally corrupt the church, and that subjects must obey all liturgical changes enacted by proper civil authority.

The Doctors additionally legitimised the king's reforms when they maintained that they, like the Covenanters, were equally committed to rooting out idolatry from the church. Yet they maintained that the diseases described by the Covenanters did not exist. Part of their argument was predicated upon the fact that Charles had already abandoned the imposition of his reforms by the time they wrote, making the Covenanters' resistance unnecessary. However, they also believed that Charles's reforms would not corrupt the true religion precisely because they constituted *adiaphora*. As they claimed, 'our church is not infected with anie such erroures, nor is in such dangers, as may give just occasion, of so fearfull a division: which in itselfe is a sore disease.'⁶³ Even if the church did experience errors in its doctrines or ceremonies, the rooting out of any disease in the church must 'bee done without a rupture, and such a dangerous division.'[64] In doing so, they ultimately prioritised the necessity of accepting Charles's reforms as the best way to respect God's commandment of obedience and to prevent schism between Protestants that might truly pave the way for Roman Catholicism.

It is therefore clear that competing strands of thought emerged in Scotland regarding the regulation of *adiaphora*, ones that first appeared during the reign of James VI and I but that resurfaced again under Charles. For those who opposed Charles's interventions, his imposition of idolatrous and 'popish' reforms by royal prerogative corrupted the purity of Reformed Protestantism and threatened the return of Roman Catholicism. Even if the Bible did not expressly prohibit certain ceremonies or practices, such as kneeling at communion or confirmation by bishops, they must be omitted. The king's *cura religionis* therefore pertained solely to the external punishment of spiritual crimes. He should not interfere within the church by deciding manners of indifferency, lest he usurp Christ's headship over the church. By restricting the category of *adiaphora*, some Scots demonstrated that the king had no special or divinely given authority to impose his own will on indifferent matters without approval of the General Assembly.

By contrast, for those who favoured (or at the very least tolerated) Charles's reforms, the practices instituted through his royal prerogative did not fundamentally affect salvation. Since scripture neither required nor prohibited them, they could lawfully be commanded by human authority. Their much larger category of *adiaphora*, and far more limited requirements for salvation, thus allowed Charles to act as the church's head and determine its liturgical practices according to his own will. These two positions reflected the broader tension between divine revelation and human will in regulating the ceremonies and practices of the Church of Scotland, highlighting the importance of *adiaphora* as a shared intellectual framework for Scottish ecclesiological debates preceding the National Covenant. But as Scots thought about the necessity, expediency, lawfulness and indifferency of church ceremonies, they also reconsidered the respective roles of king and Parliament in legislating church reform. As a result, the rest of this chapter turns to the political implications of this theological debate for models of kingship in the state.

Authority over Church Reform: Parliament or Monarch?

At stake in these debates about *adiaphora* and church reform was not just the nature of ceremonies and liturgical practices themselves, but also where authority to impose them resided. To answer this question, royalists and Covenanters advanced competing truth claims about Scotland's post-Reformation history, including how legal provisions for the church had been developed after 1560. Whereas royalists tended to emphasise the king's role in reforming the church as the author of law, Covenanters prioritised parliamentary sovereignty, even allowing Parliament to act contrary to the will of the monarch. For example, a series of manuscripts written against Charles's reforms in 1637 and 1638 defended the Scottish parliament's role in securing legal provisions for the true religion. A manuscript copy of a supplication against bishops and the Book of Common Prayer from 18 October 1637 denounced Charles's interventions in the church on the grounds that they subverted pre-existing ecclesiastical laws, ones that Parliament had enacted to protect Reformed Protestantism. According to the manuscript, Charles's reforms, especially the Book of Common Prayer, sowed 'the seeds of Diverse superstitions, Idolatry, and false Doctrines, contrare to the true religion established in this Realme by Diverse acts of Parliament'.[65] Reforms instituted via the royal prerogative not only threatened the true religion and worship of God, but they demonstrated Charles's attempts to secure royal supremacy contrary to established laws of the land. His ecclesiastical policy was therefore not just a theological concern but a legal one, subverting the power that Parliament traditionally exercised over legalising church reform after 1560.

Printed works from the period also argued for the supremacy of Parliament over reformation of the church. For example, Gillespie argued that the Scottish church had been 'blessed with a more glorious and perfect reformation, then any of our nighbour churches.' As he claimed, 'The doctrine, discipline, regiment, and policie established here by ecclesiasticall and civill lawes, and sworne and subscribed unto by the Kings Majesty' had received applause from foreign nations and agreed entirely with scripture.[66] He placed the origin of these ecclesiastical laws in the church first; these then became civil laws that bound the population following parliamentary sanction. The king only swore and subscribed laws that the General Assembly and Parliament had already enacted. Both institutions (parliament and church) therefore acted independently of the crown to enforce reformation, much as they had in 1560. Robert Baillie likewise clarified this relationship between the General Assembly and Parliament, claiming that, 'All matters spirituall and ecclesiastick, are first determined by the generall assembly, if the nature of the things require a civill Sanction, the votes of the assembly are transmitted to the Parliament.'[67] According to this order, Parliament acted independently on behalf of the church with no confirmation by the king. Crucially, the king could only swear and enforce ecclesiastical laws already determined, not author or alter them.

The National Covenant also advanced this perspective with its abundant references to Scottish legal history and Acts of Parliament. Sir Archibald Johnston of Wariston (1611–1663), one of the leading architects of the Covenant, was a well-known lawyer. The plethora of references to Scots law within the Covenant reflect his intellectual influence. For example, the Covenant claimed that Reformed Protestantism had been recognised by 'a former large confession established by sundry acts of lawful General Assemblies and of Parliaments, unto which it hath relation, set down in public catechisms.'⁶⁸ While the Covenant did not expressly prohibit episcopacy, it included a lengthy list of parliamentary Acts and Acts of the General Assembly which eliminated idolatry, superstition and 'popish influences' (which might be said to include royally appointed bishops). As the Covenant charged, 'many Acts of Parliament are conceived for the maintenance of God's true and Christian religion . . . in her national synodal assemblies, presbyteries, sessions, policy, discipline, and jurisdiction thereof.'⁶⁹ This implied that Presbyterianism had been established through parliamentary sanction and had been protected through the laws of the land. Through their emphasis on legal history and parliamentary provisions for the true religion, the Covenanting leadership thus portrayed their agenda as a dutiful restoration of the church to its former purity as established by law, while the king pursued a radical plan of innovation.

Wariston also appealed to Scottish legal history in his own writings to demonstrate how the Covenanters carried out God's vision for Scotland. He argued that all past covenants and confessions of faith, such as the Negative Confession (1581), were immutable and unchangeable despite royal interventions. Previous confessions of faith confirmed the lawfulness of the Covenanters' agenda, including the maintenance of Presbyterianism and the purification of the church from Episcopalian innovations. As he affirmed, the National Covenant 'containeth nothing in substance but that what is contained in the Confession of Faith, and general band formerly made for maintenance of Religion, & acts of Parliament made at sundie times.'⁷⁰ The Covenant did not represent an innovation but served as a renewal of the very legal precedents for the church that Parliament had already established. By emphasising the supremacy of past parliamentary legislation over the king's arbitrary royal prerogative, Wariston thus advanced one interpretation of Scottish church history that justified the Covenanters' hostility to Charles's unlawful reforms.

The idea that the church served as the source of its own reformation also permeated the manuscript from 9 December 1638 mentioned previously, which argued for the necessity of renewing the 1581 Confession of Faith. According to the manuscript, 'the question must be stated, by all parties whithir Episcopacie was professed or condemned 1580 and 1590 Be the confession of faith.'⁷¹ Previous confessions of faith and Acts of the General Assembly had clearly established Presbyterianism and outlawed episcopacy, for the office of the bishop 'is brought in by the foly and corruptions of mens inventions.'⁷² These confessions firmly established Presbyterianism, while the 1592 Act of Parliament confirmed that 'any ecclesiasticall office, should not flow from the king bot from the king of kings.'⁷³ The manuscript again prioritised parliamentary sovereignty above the royal prerogative, especially on matters of church polity. However, the manuscript equally noted that power over church government did not belong to Parliament either. As it continued, 'neither can a parliament more institute originally any ecclesiasticall offices in the church, nor the church can Institute officers of state in the com[m]onwealths.'[74] This manuscript therefore advanced one interpretation of Scotland's post-Reformation history, in which Presbyterianism had been the only legally sanctioned form of church government. It additionally assigned the power to determine polity to the church itself, rather than to Parliament or the crown, preserving a critical distinction between the two kingdoms.

By contrast, royalists also referred to Scotland's post-Reformation past, but they generally emphasised the authority of the king (rather than the General Assembly or Parliament) in providing for church government and authoring ecclesiastical laws. The king did not simply ratify confessions of faith as the Covenanters suggested. Instead, he played an integral role in their formulation and codification. By emphasising the king's authorship of confessions of faith and ecclesiastical laws, royalists could defend his episcopal innovations as wholly lawful and legitimate. For example, the royalist John Maxwell (ca. 1586–1647) adhered to such a view of the king's authority over church reform. Arguably the main political theorist of Scottish royalism, Maxwell graduated with an MA from St Andrews in 1611 and served as a pastor in four different churches around Edinburgh from 1622, until he eventually became the bishop of Ross in 1633. He also played an essential role in assisting William Laud with developing the Book of Common Prayer for Scotland.[75] When the Covenanters held their meeting of the General Assembly in Glasgow in 1638, they excommunicated Maxwell because of his affinity for Laudianism and his involvement with Charles's unpopular liturgical reforms. As a personal favour, Charles appointed Maxwell as the bishop of the Irish see of Killala and Achonry in 1640, where he remained in exile until his death.

In 1646, Maxwell denounced the Covenanters' Presbyterian agenda and claimed that they subverted the king's lawful power over reforming the church. He accused the Covenanters of arguing that 'if the King, or Queene, will not reforme Religion, they may take upon them by violence ane power to reform it', a doctrine they adapted from Knox's *History*.[76] According to Maxwell, the Covenanters believed that the people (or the entire commonwealth) might reform the church without the approval of royal authority. On these grounds, he criticised the earliest reformers who, 'without the authoritie of Soveraigntie, nay, without the knowledge of it . . . at the direction of their Ministerie, prescribe[d] Orders for Reformation of Religion.'[77] The Covenanters now engaged in a similar process by imposing reformation of the church without royal consent. Maxwell ultimately believed that 'Popular tumultuarie Reformations' were illegitimate, and that the power over reformation was 'intrinsecally inherent in the Crowne, or wheresoever Soveraigntie is fixed', not in the hands of ministers who had no authority to impose a confession upon the wider population.[78] The next chapter will demonstrate how this belief reflected Maxwell's broader interest in the concept of absolute sovereignty, a theory which stipulated that the king authored and reigned supreme over all laws in the kingdom, including those that pertained to the church. Maxwell's support for Charles's ecclesiastical reforms therefore mirrored his support for Charles's absolutism in the state.

Ultimately, those who supported and those who opposed the king's ecclesiastical policies did not simply discuss the legitimacy of his reforms in themselves. They also debated who held the authority to regulate and reform the church by law within the kingdom. To do so, they advanced competing truth claims about Scotland's own post-Reformation history, choosing to strategically prioritise either parliamentary or royal sovereignty over key ecclesiastical developments after 1560.

Conclusion

This chapter has examined the initial theological debates that emerged between the king's opponents and supporters around the time of the National Covenant. It has demonstrated that the theological category of *adiaphora* played a significant role in how Scots thought about the legitimacy of the king's reforms. But by expanding or restricting the ceremonies, doctrines and liturgical practices that counted as *adiaphora*, Scots also reconsidered the extent of the king's authority over civil laws regulating the church. Two opposing perspectives emerged. On one hand, any ceremonies not required in scripture must be omitted from worship lest they lead subjects into idolatry. The General Assembly had the ultimate authority in determining these matters, while Parliament enacted their decisions into laws that bound the consciences of the Scottish population when necessary. Those who opposed the king's reforms thus championed parliamentary sovereignty, allowing the Estates to act independently of, or even contrary to, royal authority. On the other hand, a larger category of *adiaphora*, one that comprised a broad range of liturgical practices, enabled the king's supporters to defend his authority over church reform and his authorship of ecclesiastical laws, urging subjects to obedience for the sake of temporal peace. These theological debates about *adiaphora* and royal supremacy ultimately presented an important model for how Scots articulated political ideas about absolute and limited monarchy, the subject of the next chapter.

Notes

1. MacDonald, 'Church and State,' 607–12 (see chap. 1, n. 44).
2. Lyall, *Church and State in Scotland*, 7 (see chap. 1, n. 48).
3. Lyall, *Church and State in Scotland*, 7.
4. MacDonald, 'James VI and I,' 885–903 (see introduction, n. 1); John Morrill, 'The National Covenant in its British Context,' in Morrill, *Scottish National Covenant in its British Context*, 7–9 (see introduction, n. 24); Morrill, 'A British Patriarchy?', 209–37 (see introduction, n. 1).
5. MacDonald, 'Church and State,' 622.

6. MacDonald, 'Church and State,' 623.
7. David Calderwood, *Perth Assembly* (Leiden, 1619), sig. A2r.
8. Calderwood, *Perth Assembly*, 33–62.
9. *RPS*, 1621/6/13 (accessed 2 August 2023).
10. Rose, 'Debate over Authority,' 32 (see introduction, n. 74).
11. Rose, 'Debate over Authority,' 32.
12. Markus Friedrich, 'Orthodoxy and Variation: The Role of Adiaphorism in Early Modern Protestantism,' in *Orthodoxies and Heterodoxies in Early Modern German Culture*, eds Randolph C. Head and Daniel Christensen (Leiden: Brill, 2007), 45–68.
13. Robert von Friedeburg, 'Ecclesiology and the English State: Luther and Melanchthon on the Independence of the Church in English Translations of the 1570s,' *Archiv für Reformationsgeschichte* 101, no. 1 (2013): 138–63; Charles W. A. Prior, 'Ecclesiology and Political Thought in England, 1580–c.1630,' *Historical Journal* 48, no. 4 (2005): 855–84; Jacqueline Rose, 'John Locke, "Matters Indifferent", and the Restoration of the Church of England,' *Historical Journal* 48, no. 3 (2005): 601–21.
14. Rose, 'Debate over Authority,' 31.
15. Rose, 'John Locke,' 603.
16. James VI, *Basilikon doron. Devided into three books* (Edinburgh, 1599), 23–4.
17. James VI, *Basilikon doron*, 23–4.
18. James VI, *Basilikon doron*, 23.
19. John D. Ford, 'Conformity in Conscience: The Structure of the Perth Articles Debate in Scotland, 1618–1638,' *Journal of Ecclesiastical History* 46, no. 2 (1995): 267.
20. NLS, Wodrow Octavo XXVII, no. 3, fols. 24r–31v.
21. Wodrow Octavo XXVII, no. 3, fol. 25r.
22. Wodrow Octavo XXVII, no. 3, fol. 25r.
23. Wodrow Octavo XXVII, no. 3, fol. 28r.
24. Wodrow Octavo XXVII, no. 3, fol. 24r.
25. NLS, Wodrow Folio XLII, no. 112, fols. 289r–297v.
26. Wodrow Folio XLII, no. 112, fol. 289r.
27. Wodrow Folio XLII, no. 112, fol. 290r.
28. Wodrow Folio XLII, no. 112, fol. 290r.
29. Walter Balcanquhall, *A large declaration concerning the late tumults in Scotland, from their first originals* (London, 1639), 34.
30. Gillespie, *A dispute against the English-popish ceremonies, obtruded upon the Church of Scotland* (Leiden, 1637), 117.
31. For an overview of Gillespie's argument, see Ford, 'Conformity in Conscience,' 272–3.
32. Gillespie, *A dispute*, 118.
33. 'The National Covenant: or, the Confession of Faith,' in Kerr, *Covenants and the Covenanters*, 40 (see introduction, n. 32).
34. 'The National Covenant,' 40.
35. 'The National Covenant,' 40.
36. For biographies of each of the Doctors, see Donald Macmillan, *The Aberdeen Doctors: A Notable Group of Scottish Theologians of the First Episcopal Period, 1610–1638* (London: Hodder and Stoughton, 1909), 227–64.
37. Russell Newton, 'United Opposition? The Aberdeen Doctors and the National

Covenant,' in Langley, *National Covenant in Scotland*, 55–8 (see introduction, n. 4).
38. Forbes's correspondence with Huntly can be found in: NRS, Correspondence of the Dukes of Hamilton, 1563–1712, GD406/1/432; GD406/1/446; GD406/1/457; GD406/1/664; GD406/1/667.
39. Alexander Peterkin, ed. *Records of the Kirk of Scotland* (Edinburgh: John Sutherland, 1838), 1: 92–3.
40. Aaron Clay Denlinger, 'The Aberdeen Doctors and Henry Scougal,' in *The History of Scottish Theology, Vol. 1: Celtic Origins to Reformed Orthodoxy*, ed. David Fergusson and Mark W. Elliott (Oxford: OUP, 2019), 281–2; John Spalding, *History of the troubles and memorable transactions in Scotland, from 1624–1645* (Aberdeen: John Rettie, 1792), 243–4.
41. Aaron Clay Denlinger, 'The Aberdeen Doctors (c. 1620–1641) on Tolerable and Intolerable Tolerance,' *Global Intellectual History* 5, no. 2 (2020): 137–51; Reid, 'Reformed Scholasticism,' 149–78 (see introduction, n. 50).
42. Allan I. Macinnes, introduction to *Scottish Liturgical Traditions and Religious Politics: From Reformers to Jacobites, 1540–1764* (Edinburgh: EUP, 2021), 7; Macinnes, *British Confederate*, 10–11 (see introduction, n. 54); Steve Murdoch, *Network North: Scottish Kin, Commercial and Covert Associations in Northern Europe, 1603–1746* (Leiden: Brill, 2006), ch. 8; Anthony Milton, '"The Universal Peacemaker"? John Dury and the Politics of Irenicism in England,' in *Samuel Hartlib and Universal Reformation*, ed. Mark Greengrass, Michael Leslie, and Timothy Raylor (Cambridge: CUP, 1994), 1–25.
43. Murdoch, *Network North*, 281.
44. Macinnes, *British Revolution*, 6 (see introduction, n. 3).
45. John Dury, *A memoriall concerning peace ecclesiasticall amongst Protestants* (London, 1641); John Dury, *A petition to the honourable House of Commons in England now assembled whereunto are added certaine considerations showing the necessity of a correspondencie in spiritual matters betwixt all Protestant churches* (London, 1642). See also: Haig Z. Smith, 'John Durie [Dury] (1596–1680)' in *Lives in Transit in Early Modern England: Identity and Belonging*, ed. Nandini Das (Amsterdam: Amsterdam University Press, 2022), 94–9; Jeremy Fradkin, 'Protestant Unity and Anti-Catholicism: The Irenicism and Philo-Semitism of John Dury in Context,' *Journal of British Studies* 56 (2007): 273–94.
46. This work was published under the title, *De pace inter Evangelicos procuranda, eminentiorum in Ecclesia Scoticana theologorum sententiae*, in 1639 in Bremen, and later in 1643 in Frankfurt. See Aaron Clay Denlinger, '"Men of Gallio's Naughty Faith?": The Aberdeen Doctors on Reformed and Lutheran Concord,' *Church History and Religious Culture* 92, no.1 (2012): 58–9.
47. Denlinger, '"Men of Gallio's Naughty Faith",' 64–6.
48. Denlinger, 'Aberdeen Doctors on tolerable and intolerable tolerance,' 137–51.
49. Denlinger, 'Aberdeen Doctors and Henry Scougal,' 285.
50. Denlinger, 'The Aberdeen Doctors on tolerable and intolerance tolerance,' 147.
51. Howard Hotson, 'Irenicism and Dogmatics in the Confessional Age: Pareus and Comenius in Heidelberg, 1614,' *Journal of Ecclesiastical History* 46, no. 3 (1995): 432–56.
52. David Pareus, *Irenicum sive de unione et synodo evangelicorum concilianda liber votivus* (Heidelberg, 1614).

53. Pareus, *Irenicum sive*, 23: 'Synodus legitima, libera Christiana doctrina et bonorum virorum utriusque; ordinis, Ecclesiastici et civilis, convocanda erit ... quid verbum Dei de articulis controversis pronunciet.' [All translations mine].
54. Pareus, *Irenicum sive*, 32: 'Synodi universalis Evanglicorum ... serioque divinae gloriae, veritatis, ac pacis promovendae studio ... tam necessario vulnerum publicorum remedio, orbi Christiano, ex Babylone Romana egresso.'
55. David Pareus, 'Commentary on the Divine Epistle to the Romans of St Paul the Apostle (1608)' in Campbell and Verhaart, *Protestant Politics*, 159 (see chap. 1, n. 15).
56. For an overview of Forbes's thought on elements and circumstances of worship, see Denlinger, 'The Aberdeen Doctors and Henry Scougal,' 284.
57. Forbes, *Irenicum*, 75: 'Consequenter tamen & mediante legitima Ecclesiae authoritate sit jam nobis necessaria, non quidem necessitate rei, sed necessitate obedientiae, & ordinis, & pacis, &c.' [All translations mine].
58. John Calvin, *Institutes of the Christian Religion*, trans. Henry Beveridge, vol. 2 (Edinburgh: T. & T. Clark, 1863), 417.
59. Calvin, *Institutes of the Christian Religion*, 2: 417.
60. Forbes, *Irenicum*, 75.
61. *Duplyes of the Ministers and Professors of Aberdene to second Answers of some Reverend Brethren, Concerning the Late Covenant* (Aberdeen: Edward Raban, 1638), 75–97.
62. *Duplyes of the Ministers*, 125.
63. *Duplyes of the Ministers*, 11.
64. *Duplyes of the Ministers*, 11.
65. NLS, Wodrow Octavo X, no. 1, fol. 18. This manuscript is part of a collection of documents relating to the period between August 1637 and March 1648 under the title, 'A True Relation of the Prelats carriage for introducing the Service Book, Book of Canons and other novations'. These were probably copies of papers kept by the Tables. The index for the Wodrow Collection, held at the NLS, contains further information about these manuscripts.
66. Gillespie, *A dispute*, sig. A3r.
67. Robert Baillie, *An historicall vindication of the government of the Church of Scotland* (London: Samuel Gellibrand, 1646), 61.
68. 'The National Covenant,' 48.
69. 'The National Covenant,' 44.
70. Archibald Johnston of Wariston, *Reasons against the rendering of our sworne and subscribed confession of faith* (Edinburgh, 1638), n.p.
71. NLS, Wodrow Folio XLII, no. 112, fol. 290r.
72. Wodrow Folio XLII, no. 112, fol. 291r.
73. Wodrow Folio XLII, no. 112, fol. 296r.
74. Wodrow Folio XLII, no. 112, fol. 296r.
75. James, *'This Great Firebrand'*, ch. 2 (see introduction, n. 1).
76. John Maxwell, *The burthen of Issachar: or, the tyrannicall power and practises of the presbyteriall government in Scotland* (London, 1646), 23. He specifically cited John Knox, *The History of the Reformation of Religion within the Realm of Scotland* (London, 1587), 213.
77. Maxwell, *Burthen of Issachar*, 25.
78. Maxwell, *Burthen of Issachar*, 26.

CHAPTER THREE

Royalist Political Thought

Scottish royalism has long been viewed as a minority movement restricted to 'conservative' areas of the country, such as the northeast, and to ardent Episcopalians who supported strong monarchical power over the church.[1] But as the previous chapter demonstrated, Scots who supported the king's reforms expressed theological justifications that extended far beyond an unwavering commitment to bishops. Some believed that the king possessed legal authority to reform the church according to his will, or that his ecclesiastical policy would not introduce idolatry since his proposed changes constituted *adiaphora*. We are also increasingly recognising that Scottish royalism was a widespread movement that comprised a diverse group of individuals from an array of geographic, social and professional backgrounds. Professors at universities across Scotland orchestrated resistance to the Covenant, while Glasgow's civic leaders and members of the city's merchant elite diverged regarding their loyalty to the crown.[2] Even parish clergy who refused to subscribe defended their opposition through a complex appeal to personal loyalties, their belief that the Covenant lacked legitimacy and their fear that the Covenanting movement would undermine civic order.[3]

Scottish royalism was therefore just as intellectually diverse and complex a movement as the Covenanting one. This is especially apparent in the range of political ideas that Scottish royalists advanced to defend their support for the king. Some claimed that the Covenanters did not possess the necessary authority to impose a new confession of faith without royal approval. Others asserted that the Covenanters committed treason against the king by banding together in defence of the ambiguous 'true religion'. Yet others criticised the Covenanters for failing to keep the ends of the two kingdoms distinct, thereby seeking church dominance over the state. As Andrew Lind has argued, royalists' 'most pressing concern was the defence of royal authority', suggesting that they prioritised political stability over any uncompromising commitment to one ecclesiological position.[4] As a result, Scottish royalism constituted far more than a 'diehard episcopalianism nurtured in the conservative northeast'.[5]

This chapter contributes to the growing field of scholarship on Scottish royalism by examining the range of political ideas underlying the movement. It shows that royalists drew upon nature, scripture and legal theory to emphasise the need for temporal peace above all else, achieved through a fundamental respect for the king's authority and the natural hierarchy of political society. It first examines how some Scots refused subscription of the Covenant by appealing to civil stability and the duty of obedience, incorporating arguments from nature and Scots law. It then considers how royalists defended Charles's unchallengeable authority as a monarch by appealing to innovative cross-confessional debates about the definition of sovereignty taking place in continental Europe. It concludes with an examination of constitutional royalism to demonstrate the breadth and diversity of how Scottish royalists engaged with abstract political theories.

By focusing on royalist political ideas, this chapter challenges a long-standing polity-led approach to Scottish church history, according to which Scots' beliefs about church government predicted their political allegiances and their willingness to subscribe the Covenant.[6] This perspective derives from seventeenth-century church histories – such as those by John Spottiswoode and David Calderwood (1575–1650) – that emphasised a strict Presbyterian versus Episcopalian rift within Scottish society after the Reformation parliament of 1560.[7] However, as Alexander Campbell observed, this dichotomy reflected 'a characteristically sectarian historiography of Scottish Church parties from the early seventeenth century onwards', and it did not accurately portray how most Scots thought about church government or their political allegiances.[8] Indeed, Lind has shown that many Scottish ministers expressed far more flexibility on church polity (and far more willingness to compromise) than has previously been acknowledged.[9]

Through an examination of political thought, this chapter contributes to our increasing knowledge of the range of motivations underlying Scottish royalism, ones that extended beyond a steadfast commitment to episcopacy. Equally, it counters long-standing stereotypes of royalists as conservative or antiquated in their commitment to preserving absolute monarchical power through the divine right of kingship, a characterisation retained from the Whig historiographical tradition. While much has been done to reverse this perception of English royalism, the political thought of its Scottish counterpart has not received the same level of sustained analysis or reassessment.[10] Nevertheless, these individuals engaged with cutting-edge continental European debates as they developed an organic theory of the state and defended absolute political power.

It is important to note, however, that Scottish royalists did not wholly dismiss theological concerns in favour of civil stability or the preservation of royal authority. Their ideas about the hierarchy of nature and the necessity of absolute monarchy intrinsically reflected their concerns about the nature of the church, and these two forms of argument could not be easily separated. As the previous chapter showed, royalists tended to support a broader category of *adiaphora* that extended the king's authority over the church, a model of authority that also mapped onto the civil state and directly complemented absolute monarchy. Additionally, their political ideas reflected one strand of Protestant thought about the end of politics and the godly commonwealth that emphasised civil government's coercive and absolute nature to counteract human sinfulness (discussed in Chapter 1). The temporal kingdom existed more for the preservation of peace than for the militant advancement of the true religion. As a result, God commanded magistrates to use the sword to restrain human sinfulness, while subjects had a duty to obey all the authorities that God established. God alone deposed tyrants because He ruled commonwealths directly without any mediation of His power by Christian subjects. Ultimately, while the Covenanters have been regarded as theocrats who claimed to know and enact God's will when they resisted the king for religious purposes, Scottish royalists argued more overtly for God's direct sovereignty over political life. They were no less authentically Protestant for failing to support armed defence of the true religion, nor were they wholly uninterested in theological arguments against subscription and resistance. Instead, they embraced an alternative strand of Protestant thought about political life, one that emphasised coercive government, natural hierarchies and obedience as being God's will for the temporal kingdom.

Temporal Peace and Obedience, 1638–1640

The emphasis on temporal peace and obedience in royalist writings became immediately apparent surrounding the Covenanters' subscription campaign and the Bishops' Wars. Individuals from all parts of society – such as ministers, university professors and civic leaders – advanced political arguments in opposition to the Covenant and military engagement with the king. For example, in their two pamphlet exchanges with Covenanter commissioners, the Aberdeen Doctors focused on the Covenanters' lack of authority and their rebellion against the king. The Doctors first claimed that the Covenanters had not received warrant from the king, Parliament or a national synod to impose a new version of the 1581 Confession of Faith upon an unwilling population. Instead, they 'seeme to pretend an extraordinarie calling from God, alleadging an extraordinarie necessitie at this tyme' for producing a new confession contrary to the crown.[11] As a result, all who subscribed would engage in a seditious act. For the Doctors, the Covenant was especially dangerous because it permitted the creation of a band of defence among believers, one that might require subscribers to resist their king rather than obey. Although the Covenanters claimed no 'diminution of the King's greatness and authority', they simultaneously swore to 'the mutual defence and assistance every one of us of another, in the same cause of maintaining the true religion, and his Majesty's authority, with our counsel, our bodies, means, and whole power.'[12] This contradictory stipulation within the Covenant suggested that subscribers owed obedience to the king only when he maintained the true religion according to their will.

As the Doctors argued, the very act of swearing to defend the true religion contravened a 1585 parliamentary Act in which James VI forbade his subjects from forming military alliances, known as leagues or bands.[13] Noblemen and burgh magistrates had often formed such alliances (or bands) as a 'traditional means of indicating commitment to a cause'.[14] These bands reflected friendships, kinship networks and a shared commitment to religious goals, such as protecting Protestantism in Roman Catholic areas following the Scottish Reformation. But in August 1582, several Presbyterian nobles abducted James when he was sixteen years old, holding him hostage and attempting to use his captivity to banish Catholicism and foreign influence from the kingdom. This plot, known as the Raid of Ruthven, laid precedents that bands of subjects might prioritise 'loyalty to religion above obedience to the crown'.[15] Consequently, James's parliamentary Act stipulated that no 'leagues and bonds be made amongst his subjects of any degree upon whatsoever colour or pretence without his highness's or his successors' privity and consent', thereby preventing future sedition among his subjects.[16]

Within this context, the Doctors accused the Covenanters of now creating their own band of defence to promote Presbyterianism and their own subjective interpretation of the true religion, an action that clearly broke established law. As they claimed, subscribers formed 'a band of mutuall defence, by force of armes, made without the king's privitie and consent.'[17] The Covenant represented a new instalment in the historically problematic tradition of banding, one that usurped the power of the sword from the king, transferred it to the people and permitted an unlawful rebellion among a community of believers. This band of defence was especially subversive because it depended upon a vague, subjective interpretation of the 'true religion'. Unlike earlier bands, which had been created to defend Protestantism against the Roman Catholic threat, the Covenanters formed one to defend their own definition of the Reformed faith and the customs of the Scottish church, both of which remained highly contested. The Covenant's statement that subscribers would stand to the 'defence and preservation of the foresaid true religion, liberties and laws of the kingdom' therefore threatened treason, suggesting that Christian subjects owed obedience to the king only when he followed the will of ministers.[18]

To support their criticisms of the banding tradition, the Doctors stressed that all Christian subjects had a divinely mandated duty to obey their authorities, even ungodly or tyrannical ones. They drew upon examples from scripture, Augustinian just war theory and multiple Reformed authors to prove that God never commanded Christians to carry out the armed defence of religion. For example, they referenced 1 Peter 2:13–14 and Ecclesiastes 8:2, both of which urged Christians to submit themselves to every human authority and obey all the king's commandments for the Lord's sake. Using these verses, the Doctors argued that 'the sword belongeth onlie to the king, and to them who are sent by him.'[19] As a result, 'it is vnlawfull for subjects in a monarchicall estate, (such as is this kingdome of Scotland) to take armes for religion, or for anie other pretence, without warrand and power from the prince, and supreame magistrate.'[20]

Just war theory equally proved that only superior magistrates could wield the sword, while a civil war between a superior magistrate and their inferiors would always be unjust. The Doctors' emphasis on just war demonstrated their belief in a hierarchy or order inherent within nature. They claimed that St Augustine, 'wryting of a lawfull warre, acknowledgeth that onlie to bee lawfull, which hath authoritie from the prince.'[21] War waged by the prince reflected that natural order 'which is accommodated to the peace of mortal men'.[22] His power to commence war – a power that the Covenanters now claimed for themselves – therefore never devolved to others, whether to inferior magistrates or to subjects. Additionally, a just war could only be undertaken between two legitimate kings, while a civil war contradicted natural order. Inferior magistrates (who might unjustly begin a civil war) were always merely private individuals with respect to their superiors. As the Doctors argued, 'Although Magistrates, who are vnder the king, bee publicke persons, in respect of their inferioures; yet being considered, with relation to him that is supreame, 1. Pet. 2:13. They are but private.'[23] Resistance by inferiors was illegitimate since 'what-so-ever is done agaynst the will of the supreame ruler, is destitute of that power; and consequentlie, is to bee esteemed for a private act.'[24] For this reason, it could be labelled treason. Ultimately, even if Charles had contravened the laws, liberties and religion of the kingdom (which was still debatable), no one could reclaim or challenge his political authority, which derived exclusively from God. The Covenanters therefore had no legitimate warrant for rising against their king in a just war. They could only form an illegal band of defence among private individuals, a treasonous act that contravened Scots law and subverted the hierarchy of nature.

The Doctors also directly challenged key Reformed resistance theorists – such as George Buchanan, John Knox and the Marian exile Christopher Goodman (1520–1603) – all of whom argued that God permitted (or even commanded) inferior magistrates to resist ungodly or tyrannical magistrates. The Doctors claimed that such resistance theories did not apply to Charles's reign or to the National Covenant context. They drew their critiques specifically from *Jesuita vapulans* (1635), a treatise authored by the French Huguenot theologian André Rivet (1572–1651).[25] In this work, Rivet engaged with and disproved a series of Jesuit theological and political positions, one of which included the argument that the people elected their civil rulers and could legitimately resist them with arms. Rivet argued that Protestants who permitted resistance had only done so in extraordinary circumstances or in moments of exceptional danger. Protestants generally did not approve of resistance, meaning that this doctrine could only have originated with the politically subversive Jesuits.[26] The Doctors directly adopted Rivet's argument for Scotland, claiming that Protestant resistance theorists rashly and erroneously defended resistance because of 'the hard and perilous tymes of persecution, where-in they lived'.[27] Their resistance was entirely reactive and did not represent a broader Reformed consensus.

Equally, the Covenanters did not face the same levels of religious persecution as their predecessors. They simply disagreed with the king's ecclesiastical reforms – all of which constituted *adiaphora* and could be legitimately determined by royal authority – while they continually disregarded Charles's attempts to resolve disputes. Taking Rivet's argument a step further, the Doctors maintained that Scottish reformers who supported resistance (such as Knox and Buchanan) only defended these positions because of their 'mistaking of the Governement of the *Scotish Kingdome*, as if it were not truelie and properlie *Monarchicall*', meaning absolute rather than limited.[28] Rivet had likewise criticised Buchanan for thinking 'that the Kingdom of Scotland was not complete and absolute' in *De Jure regni apud Scotos*.[29] As a result, they built their resistance theories upon a fundamental misinterpretation of monarchical power, making their ideas inapplicable to the National Covenant context. By rejecting canonical resistance theorists as outliers within a Reformed consensus on obedience, the Doctors positioned themselves as the true adherents to this intellectual tradition. Although they acknowledged that John Calvin advanced a non-committal position on whether inferior magistrates (such as the Spartan ephors) might lawfully resist their superiors, they argued that Calvin 'sayeth no more, but that *peradventure* the three Estates assembled in Parliament, have that same power, which the fore-mentioned Ephori, &c. had', meaning that only *perhaps* the Estates had that power.[30] The Doctors capitalised upon this ambiguity within Calvin's thought to claim that they (rather than the Covenanters) upheld Calvin's true position and represented the Reformed tradition.

Lastly, the Doctors compared the political commonwealth to the physical body as a strategy for encouraging unity among Scottish subjects. Referring to the 1585 Act of Parliament that made banding illegal, they affirmed that 'the whole bodie of the Common-wealth should stirre at once: not anie more as divided members, but as one consolidate lumpe.'[31] Nature confirmed that the human body could not survive if its individual components refused to obey the head. As members of the commonwealth, the Covenanters betrayed their own head (the king) and prevented the political body from moving in a unified manner. The Doctors therefore drew upon a diverse range of arguments to support the need for temporal peace above all else. But their desire for civic stability did not reflect wholly secular concerns. Rather, as the previous chapter demonstrated, they also believed strongly in the need to establish ecclesiastical concord between Protestants, viewing intra-confessional division as paving the way for the re-establishment of Roman Catholicism. Their religious irenicism, in addition to their fear of the greater Catholic threat, thus directly complemented their emphasis on temporal peace secured through obedience and the preservation of a natural hierarchy within the state.

Although the Doctors waged one of the most sustained intellectual campaigns against the Covenant, the same concern for temporal peace and upholding the duty of obedience appeared in other royalist works. On 20 March 1638, the masters of the University of St Andrews drew up a list of reasons for refusing to subscribe the Covenant. Like the Doctors, they claimed that the Covenanters lacked any authority to impose a new confession of faith without 'authoritie and commission frome the prince.'[32] As a result, the authors refused to subscribe because they believed that subjects must not take an oath 'frome any except his most sacred ma[jes]tie.'[33] It would therefore be unlawful to subscribe a confession of faith presented by 'these p[rete]ndit commissionares' who had 'no aut[hor]itie and com[m]issione ordinar or extraordinar frome our sacrad soveraine'.[34] Much like the Doctors, they also cited the illegality of banding, declaring 'all bandes and leagues amongst subiectes without the privitie and consent of the prince' treasonous and seditious.[35] As a result, all who subscribed were guilty of the 'trubleing of the publick peace of the kingdome.'[36] The St Andrews masters were therefore equally concerned with the Covenanters' lack of legal authority to make subjects subscribe the Covenant, coupled with their blatant disregard for laws against banding and the formation of leagues without the king's consent.

The Covenanting leadership took criticisms that they formed an illegal military band – one that prioritised religion over obedience to the king – seriously. They overtly disagreed with the accusation that they participated in an illegal banding tradition within Scotland, arguing that 'if no convocation, leagues, or bandes were lawfull, then if the puritie of the countrie degenerat in a tyrannie', subjects would not be allowed to 'band together to resist him [the king], which is against common sense and reason.'[37] On 6 June 1640, the Scottish parliament decreed that preceding parliamentary Acts against bonds and leagues did not prohibit those formed for the 'maintenance and preservation of the king's majesty, the religion, laws and liberties of the kingdom, or for the public good, either of kirk or state.'[38] The parliament of June 1640 thus affirmed that subjects could form bands of defence for these reasons without committing treason. The Covenanting leadership equally contended that they had no intention of fomenting resistance to the king or forcibly imposing the Covenant upon unwilling subjects. They responded specifically to the objections of the St Andrews masters, arguing that 'ther meeting was not a meeting of few, but of a great number of persons of all ranks, and not in secret but in public . . . for the generall and common good of the whole bodie.'[39] They met not to stir up sedition among the people but 'to save themselves and others from trouble for standing to the established religion.'[40] In doing so, the Covenanters had not forcibly required any subjects to subscribe the Covenant, for this was only 'to be taken voluntarlie by such as please to tak it.'[41] The Covenanting leadership therefore attempted to defend themselves against these accusations, but royalists continued to renew their emphasis on the need for civil stability that would be undermined by subscribers.

In 1638, John Strang (1584–1654), the principal of Glasgow University, similarly argued that Scots must refuse to subscribe, lest they sacrifice temporal peace. Appointed principal of the university in February 1626, Strang lectured on divinity and taught Hebrew. He initially opposed the Covenant, arguing that subscribers must compromise since Charles had agreed to withdraw his controversial liturgical innovations. However, Strang eventually subscribed the Covenant himself after he became convinced that it threatened neither royal authority nor episcopacy. Much like the Doctors, he used language of the physical body to justify his own opposition to the Covenant. As he stated,

> If the memberis of our natural bodie be out of there proper joynt or place ... the whole bodie must of necessitie com to ruine. Even so it fareth with the politick body, which is conteined and preserved, by the same proportion and harmonie of all the partes. Now the present truble of one estate seimeth to proceid from a certane disjunction betines the head and the members.[42]

One of Strang's key reasons for refusing subscription was therefore the necessity of all members of the commonwealth working together in unity to preserve the commonwealth, much as parts of the physical body must coexist harmoniously.

Other royalists looked beyond language of the body, appealing instead to the organisation of the natural world as a model for absolute monarchy. William Drummond of Hawthornden (1585–1649), for example, claimed that the structure of the universe justified monarchy alone and provided clear evidence that subjects must obey their superiors in all matters. Although Drummond's contemporaries knew him primarily for his poetry and his involvement in literary circles, he also became a political pamphleteer and satirist following the drafting of the Covenant. Drummond had graduated from the University of Edinburgh in 1605, followed by two years studying law at Bourges and Paris. During Charles I's coronation at Scone in 1633, Drummond authored both congratulatory speeches and poetry that reflected his support of Laudianism, Episcopalianism and royal authority. Yet he was not an advocate of unchallengeable, absolute royal authority and instead 'looked to outline the position of the loyal critic in some of his writings in the 1630s'.[43] Between 1638 and 1640, he wrote multiple short tracts denouncing the divisive nature of the Covenanting movement, although he circulated many of these as private manuscripts rather than widely in print. He also signed the Covenant himself in 1639 as an act of self-protection, but he nevertheless remained committed to defending and upholding monarchy. Throughout 1638 and 1639, he urged his fellow Scots to submit to the king using imagery of the strife and dissolution that would result from following the Covenanting leadership.[44] On 22 September 1638, he specifically appealed to the structure of nature to confirm human beings' duty to obey their superiors. As he argued:

> Every part of this Universe obeyeth the Supreme Maker God; the inferiour Celestial Bodies obey the Superiour; the Earth and Seas obey them; Kingdoms, Estates, Cities, yea the meanest Families, the Strong with the Weak, the Poor with the Rich, the Evil with the Good, are preserved and maintained by that Obedience, which is given to Magistrates and Superiours.[45]

He concluded that, in conformity with God's creation, subjects ought to honour kings above all else as 'the Princes of our Princes, the Sovereigns of our Governours, and the Superiours of all Magistrates.'[46] Drummond's appeal to natural hierarchy thus cemented his belief that only obedience to the monarch could protect subjects from societal disorder and the dangers of political division.

Following the outbreak of the First Bishops' War in January 1639, William Guild, the former Aberdeen Doctor who eventually subscribed the Covenant, authored a short treatise in which he too urged his fellow Scots to obedience. He called upon his contemporaries to remember the duties that they owed to their 'native and most gracious Prince, the anointed of the Lord', and to cease threatening 'that Crowne, which God hath set vpon his Head'.[47] He also accused the Covenanters of only pretending to profess their defence of the king's sacred authority when they claimed to abhor 'that Iesuiticall and damnable doctrine ... that Christian people may ryse in open hostilitie agaynst their sacred Soveraygnes.'[48] As a result, Guild urged reconciliation between the crown and Scottish subjects. He argued that good kings must be aware of their subjects' grievances and be willing to compromise as a sign of respect. According to Guild, Charles had demonstrated this compromising attitude when he reneged on his imposition of the Book of Canons and the prayer book. The king had even promised 'a patent Eare to all his Subjectes farther just complaynts.'[49] The Covenanters needed to reciprocate through their obedience. Only if Scots focused on peace rather than division, and on respecting the king's authority, would Satan be disappointed and '*Romish* Adversaries their hopes may bee frustrate'.[50] Guild's objection to the Covenanters' resistance to the king thus depended upon an appeal to Charles's sacred and divine status, as well as to a fear that the evils wrought by civil unrest would far outweigh any positive reformation of religion.

In 1639, John Corbet likewise incorporated language of the natural body to argue that the Covenanters only pretended to urge unity across society, when 'to recommend unitie, and not with the head, is in effect, to urge separation and division.'[51] He also claimed that the Covenanters sought to refashion the entire form of civil government. They replaced the king with the nobility as the head of the commonwealth, made the burgesses of the burghs the thighs, and installed ministers as the feet. The Covenanters' dangerous attempt to craft a 'new sort of Government' that consisted of nobles, barons and burgesses constituted 'neither a *Monarchie*, nor *Aristocracie*, nor *Democracie*, nor *Oligarchie*, & c. And you will offend, if we call it, *Anarchie*.'[52] Using such physical imagery, Corbet therefore maintained that union must be sought 'between the head and the rest of the body, the King and his subjects, which you have so much withstood, seeking only union of the members without the head, which is to make one monster of many heads.'[53] This example of the body also justified the need for absolute, rather than limited, monarchy in the state. As Corbet continued, monarchs must hold absolute power only, for 'if their power were not absolute, there would be some other power above them, which is absurd.'[54] As a result, he declared that 'the people wanting a King cannot have the *supreme power* over itself ... none can give that to another which they have not themselves.'[55] Crucially, this meant that the king did not derive authority from his inferiors, nor could he be held accountable to them. By portraying the nobility, ministers and burgesses of the burghs as different limbs of the body, Corbet defended absolute monarchy as critical for securing political unity and peace.

As these examples have demonstrated, the earliest royalist responses to the National Covenant and the Bishops' Wars demonstrated a shared, overarching concern with civil stability and obedience to the king. Yet such arguments from nature, scripture and law also reflected a view of the temporal kingdom as a place for coercive government and the preservation of peace above all else. Royalists saw unity as essential for countering greater threats posed by Roman Catholics or by political anarchy. They thus actively opposed a competing strand of Protestant political thought that emphasised the militant defence of the true religion (the very nature of which remained highly contested), as this would only foment disorder and contravene natural order. While some of these royalists supported episcopacy (such as Strang or Drummond) or advocated for Protestant unity over theological division (the Doctors), their theological concerns paralleled their desire for obedience, civil stability and absolute monarchy.

Political Thought after the Solemn League and Covenant (1643)

Royalist political thought developed further after the Covenanters allied with the English parliamentarians in the Solemn League and Covenant (1643). By this time, some of the earliest royalists, such as Corbet and two of the Aberdeen Doctors, had died. Others had been sent into exile in continental Europe or elsewhere in the British Isles, while the Covenanting leadership deposed yet others from their offices or coerced them into subscription. As a result, fewer royalist works exist from the mid and late 1640s that document clear opposition to the Covenanting agenda based upon political principles. Yet a few examples do remain that demonstrate how royalists responded to the Covenanting agenda after 1643. These are the focus of the rest of this chapter.

Following the Solemn League and Covenant, Drummond renewed his opposition to the Covenanting agenda on the grounds that the Scots should not enter a war with unclear religious objectives. He maintained that, 'No subjects under a Monarchy and ancient Sovereignty, without their Sovereign's Consent, may enter into a League or Covenant with a stranger Nation', especially one that would require them to 'defend the Religion of England, in catechism and discipline, and yet know not what they are'.[56] He further argued that, 'It is a great folly to make a people swear to maintain the liberties of stranger-nations, of which they are ignorant', especially at the behest of 'this oligarchy, now assembled at London'.[57] Drummond believed that the Covenanters' intention to export Presbyterianism throughout the British Isles reflected their misconception about the purpose of war. He claimed that 'leagues contracted for the propagation of the doctrine of heaven, were seldom or never prosperous, or had a happy event.'[58] As a result, the Solemn League and Covenant was an illegitimate alliance on both the English and the Scottish side. It incorrectly assumed that 'the Parliament and General Assembly, have an omnipotency and arbitrary power, the one to establish what religion they think fittest, over men's consciences . . . the other, to dispose of their bodies, lands and moveables, after their Pleasure.'[59] For Drummond, the Solemn League and Covenant therefore reflected the Covenanters' final usurpation of the king's power over the sword to enter into an unjust war, one that was equally unwise in its unclear religious ends.

In 1644, John Maxwell authored *Sacro-sancta regum majestas* (1644), one of the most comprehensive articulations of royalist political theory to emerge in Scotland. He wrote this treatise during his time in exile in Ireland, and it prompted Samuel Rutherford to respond with *Lex, Rex* that same year, a treatise which laid out a competing theory of limited monarchy in defence of the Covenanters' actions. Unlike earlier royalists who responded directly to the threat posed by the National Covenant and the Bishops' Wars, Maxwell offered a much more comprehensive, abstract political theory in defence of both absolute monarchy and obedience. His primary aim was to show that monarchy must be absolute, not limited, and that kings held their authority solely from God, not from their subjects. He drew upon a range of arguments from nature and scripture to prove these points.

First, he capitalised upon the idea that civil government existed to mitigate the negative effects of sin within the temporal kingdom. As a result, divine law mandated absolute monarchy as the only form of government (*jure divino*) that could protect humans from their wickedness. Maxwell argued that all human beings possessed an inclination to submit to government for their own protection, while God ordained the sovereign to combat 'mans corruption and untowardnesse by reason of sinne'.[60] Individual families grouped together for protection under civil laws that enforced morality, because '[n]ecessity forceth them to a government, (without it they can have neither society, nor safety, nor peace, nor happinesse).'[61] However, like the earliest Protestant reformers, Maxwell agreed that civil government had positive benefits for all Christians, challenging the 'mad haeresie of the Anabaptists who condemne all government whatsoever as sinfull and unlawfull'. He maintained that the Anabaptists' belief that all government among Christians was sinful constituted an '[i]mpious blasphemous error, destructive not onely of humane society but mankind itselfe.'[62] For Maxwell, all humans, even godly 'saints', required government to counteract their sinful natures, making the institution a gift from God rather than a wholly natural one (as Roman Catholics maintained).

Maxwell's emphasis on human depravity also reflected the Augustinian interpretation of the temporal kingdom outlined in Chapter 1. He resisted a Thomistic or civic humanist interpretation of political life, according to which humans formed political associations to fulfil their sociable natures, attain rational flourishing and strive after civic virtue. His theory provided little space for the sense that people became most fully human when they participated rationally in political life, or that they formed societies to advance God's glory. Instead, he embraced an Augustinian perspective on coercive government, one that characterised the primary end of politics as the restraint of human sinfulness through obedience.

Maxwell's belief that humans entered political society for protection laid a foundation for his larger theory about natural subjection and equality. He maintained that humans had a natural disposition to live in structures of inferiority and superiority. They did not possess some inherent sense of equality that prompted them to consent to government by magistrates through a process of election. Rather, 'all the people have is a capacity to be governed, with a vehement desire to be stated in a condition of peace and safetie', a desire which could not be realised unless all members of the community submitted to structures of government.[63] If humans were inherently equal, government would be elective and subjects would have to voluntarily give up their freedom to be ruled by governors. But God would not permit flawed human beings to make such a weighty decision about the election of magistrates. As Maxwell questioned,

> How can it then be conceived, that God hath left it to the simple consent and composition of man, to make and establish a herauldry of sub and supra, of one above another, which neither Nature nor the Gospel doth warrant?[64]

Human beings' natural desire for political subjection therefore provided God with greater direct or immediate agency over the selection of rulers, and human beings with far less.

Scripture also confirmed this natural human instinct for subjection, evidenced by the hierarchy that God imposed upon the family unit between Adam and Eve in the Garden of Eden. Maxwell departed from an Augustinian perspective on government when he maintained that subordination existed prior to the Fall. Political subjection therefore did not result from human sinfulness but became a positive gift from God. For example, in the Book of Genesis, God made Adam superior to all of creation and fashioned Eve from his rib to be his subordinate, demonstrating the inherent goodness of hierarchy and subjection. God did not create two fully independent human beings, knowing that they would be incapable of living peacefully together if they were not formed within a hierarchical relationship.[65] Likewise, God prevented political equality after the Fall, for equality would only produce tensions between individuals vying for power. Domestic society equally confirmed God's hierarchical structure for the world. From birth, humans knew that they must be subject to higher authorities since God commanded children to obey their parents.[66] To counter the problems that would arise from the human desire for power, God saw fit for 'the man to have power over his wife, a father to have power over the sonne, a King to rule, and subjects to obey.'[67] Only absolute monarchy allowed the king to fulfil this patriarchal role in the commonwealth, while 'of Aristocracie or Democracie you have not one word in Holy Writ to commend them.'[68] Maxwell thus weaved together a complex set of arguments drawn from both natural and divine law, ones that affirmed inherent structures of hierarchy and subjection, to justify absolute monarchy in the state.

After confirming that absolute monarchy was the best form of civil government and one explicitly mandated by scripture, Maxwell described how kings practically attained their power. He appealed to the divine right theory of kingship, rejecting the idea of any contractual obligation between king and subjects. As Chapter 5 will show, the theory of a covenant or contract was a central tenet of Catholic scholastic thought that equally permeated Covenanting political theory. It maintained that God ordained the 'office' of a magistrate, while the people themselves elected specific rulers.[69] Humans mediated God's power on earth and could recall magistrates who did not uphold the conditions upon which they agreed to rule. Maxwell directly challenged Francisco Suárez (1548–1617) and Robert Bellarmine (1542–1621) – a Spanish Jesuit and an Italian Jesuit respectively – on this point, condemning this component of Jesuit political thought as exceptionally subversive of monarchical authority. Instead, Maxwell maintained that God directly ordained magistrates with no human mediation or interference.[70]

However, Maxwell anticipated that his enemies would accuse him of claiming that God still spoke directly and prophetically in New Testament times to appoint rulers. As a result, he acknowledged that God used means other than revelation to designate officials in modern times, claiming that all should know 'that some thing may immediately proceed from God, and be his proper worke, without a revelation or manifestation extraordinary from Heaven.'[71] Although God no longer revealed His will through dreams or prophets, He did not relinquish agency over political life. Instead, as with baptism, human actions had no divine significance until God infused them with power. In the same way, political power derived directly from God even though the people bestowed it through election, succession or conquest. As Maxwell concluded, 'the designation of the person is from men and an humane act; but the endowment with supernaturall power to act, doe, and exercise supernaturall acts, is immediately from God and Christ.'[72] These elements of Maxwell's political theory therefore prioritised God's direct agency over government and political life, at the expense of human involvement. Sinful humans had no role beyond obedience to the magistrates whom God established over them, a necessary requirement for government to fulfil its end of preserving peace and order.

The Defence of Absolute Sovereignty

Maxwell next turned away from nature and scripture to engage with a prominent debate taking place in continental Europe about the definition of absolute sovereignty. He drew upon legal theories developed by sixteenth-century Catholic jurists to defend Charles's supremacy above all laws governing the commonwealth, both civil and ecclesiastical. Debates about absolute sovereignty pertained to a long-standing concept in political theory, the *societas perfecta* (perfect political community), used to explain the origins and purposes of commonwealths. Aristotle employed the term to describe the most sovereign political association (the *polis*) as that which could best attain the common good of all subjects. The *polis* consisted of many smaller units, such as families and villages, but it achieved its aim through its own resources, making it the highest and most self-sufficient level of association.[73] This concept also permeated Catholic political theory. Thomas Aquinas adopted an Aristotelian approach, arguing that the perfect political community was that which tended toward the common good of all its members.

Later Jesuit authors, including Bellarmine and Luis de Molina (1535–1600), used the concept to defend absolute monarchy. They maintained that humans chose to enter different levels of associations loosely arranged according to Aristotle's order, culminating in the *societas perfecta* which could best be protected by an absolute monarch.[74] Francisco de Vitoria (1483–1546), a Spanish theologian and the founder of the School of Salamanca, also connected the commonwealth's self-sufficiency to political power, stating that

> the temporal commonwealth is self-sufficient (*perfecta*), and therefore cannot be subject to anyone outside itself, otherwise it would not be self-sufficient. Therefore it can set up a prince for itself who is in no way subject to another in temporal matters.[75]

The self-sufficient political community thus necessitated absolute monarchy to fulfil its own end (the common good of its subjects), while it represented the natural culmination of multiple levels of voluntary political association.

The concept of the *societas perfecta* resulted in two distinct intellectual traditions regarding the type of political power that would best ensure the commonwealth's self-sufficiency. The French jurist and nominal Catholic Jean Bodin (1530–1596) developed one strand when he created a new definition of absolute sovereignty based upon the monarch's absolute power over the law. His definition of sovereignty depended on its undivided nature, challenging the Aristotelian interpretation of the self-sufficient commonwealth as one which was democratic in nature. The German Reformed jurist Johannes Althusius (1563–1638) provided an alternative federalist approach to government in which sovereignty lay in the groups that constituted the commonwealth (popular sovereignty). Both strands of thought permeated Scottish discourse, with Bodin providing a basis for Maxwell's political theory and Althusius providing the basis for Rutherford's (as discussed in Chapter 5). Bodin's concept of absolute sovereignty, in addition to later developments made by Scottish Catholic jurists Adam Blackwood (1539–1613) and William Barclay (1546–1608), offered an essential legal framework for Maxwell's defence of Charles's unchallengeable sovereignty.

Bodin was born around 1530 near Angers in France. He studied at the University of Paris after moving to the city in 1549, followed by his study of Roman law at the University of Toulouse in the late 1550s. He then taught law at the same institution until 1560. The next year, Bodin was licensed as an attorney of the French *parlement*, during which time he took an oath affirming his Catholic faith following the outbreak of the French Wars of Religion. Amidst these religious wars, he advanced a theory of sovereignty in which he affirmed the need for a strong centralised monarchy to overcome internal divisions within the country. In 1576, he authored *De republica libri sex* (*Six Books of the Commonwealth*) to advance this theory. He challenged Protestant reformers who believed that subjects were more important in power than the prince, and that they could therefore hold him accountable by revolting against tyranny. Bodin accordingly developed a new legal defence of absolute sovereignty that was especially innovative for sixteenth-century political thought. As David Stevenson remarked, Bodin made a 'radical break with the past' when he 'separated politics from religion and sought to justify submission to the "sovereign power" in the state', taking a distinctly legal rather than theological approach to the nature of political power.[76] Quentin Skinner also argued that Bodin's career as a legal theorist led him to the innovative conclusion that sovereignty was 'fundamentally legislative in character'.[77]

While Bodin defined sovereignty as a power absolute and undivided in nature, his definition was fundamentally grounded in the ruler's relationship to law. He contended that 'persons who are sovereign must not be subject in any way to the commands of someone else and must be able to give the law to subjects.'[78] This meant that all legislative bodies in a commonwealth, such as parliaments, held no coercive authority over their sovereign. As he stated:

> It is thus that the grandeur and majesty of a truly sovereign prince is manifested – when the Estates of all the people are assembled and present requests and supplications to their prince in all humility . . . what the king pleases by way of consent or dissent, command or prohibition, is taken for law, for edict, or for ordinance.[79]

However, Bodin did not suggest that sovereigns may rule entirely according to their own will. Instead, divine and natural law (but not human law) limited their power. As he argued, 'Every prince on earth is subject to them [natural and divine law], and it is not in their power to contravene them unless they wish to be guilty of treason against God.'[80] Although these two types of law checked a prince's power, he could never be held accountable by inferiors. Bodin challenged authors who suggested that princes must keep the laws and customs of their land, claiming that 'by doing this they weaken and degrade sovereign majesty, which should be sacred, and produce an aristocracy, or even a democracy.'[81] Absolute monarchy could therefore never be compatible with a prince's accountability to his subjects, other magistrates or parliaments. The idea that the parliamentary Estates held any power over the prince would lead subjects 'to revolt from the obedience they owe'.[82] Referring specifically to the parliaments of England, France and Spain, all of which could only assemble in the king's name, Bodin argued that these very institutions derived their power from the king and could not turn that power against him.[83] For Bodin, the distinctive mark of the sovereign was therefore their ability to make, repeal and impose all laws without the consent of any other.[84]

Barclay and Blackwood, two Scottish Catholic jurists, articulated similar ideas about the king's authorship of the law to justify absolute monarchy. Both authors built upon Bodin's theory in direct response to Buchanan's *De Jure Regni apud Scotos* (1579), printed three years after *De Republica*, which defended elective kingship. Buchanan advanced a theory of contractual government, according to which the king and his subjects formed a binding agreement, one that stipulated that the king would rule for his subjects' good. This contract also subordinated the king to law since the people possessed the legislative power. Buchanan argued that the people were 'the parent, or at any rate the author, of the law, since they can make or repeal it as seems appropriate'.[85] This position created a hierarchy in which 'the law is more powerful than the king . . . and the people more powerful than the law.'[86] As a result, the king could be held accountable to the law like any private individual. To refute Buchanan and other 'monarchomachs' who defended a contractual relationship between the king and subjects – one that subordinated the monarch to the rule of law – Barclay and Blackwood expanded upon Bodin's definition of sovereignty. To his legal perspective, they added the divine right theory of kingship, or 'the originally Protestant belief that all powers are ordained of God, so that to offer any resistance to the king is strictly equivalent to resisting the will of God.'[87] It was through the union of these two strands of thought that 'the distinctive concept of the "divine right" of kings is articulated'.[88]

Blackwood produced two texts in which he discussed the monarch's authority above human laws: *De coniunctione religionis et imperii libri duo* (1575) and *Adversus Georgii Buchanani* (1581).[89] He argued that the king was not necessarily the author of the law, but that he was its primary interpreter. The king's duty included carrying out the law in such a way that his power became synonymous with the law itself. Blackwood distinguished between human laws (those which are changeable) and divine laws (those which are eternal and unalterable). The magistrate needed to interpret and administer human laws so that they mirrored divine ones, ultimately ordering the state towards perfection.[90] However, the law also depended upon the magistrate's will. According to Blackwood,

> I call a law what is pleasing to the prince by his right, not at the request of the ruled, for not only the laws and customs of every city and township, but also the public laws are subject to his will.[91]

Contrary to what Buchanan had argued, civil law did not derive from the people but depended exclusively on the king. Ultimately, since the king might change or create laws at his own pleasure, he could not be held accountable to them.

Barclay presented a similar theory of absolute sovereignty in *De regno et regali potestate* (1600), a treatise in which he also refuted Buchanan's views on the king's subjection to the laws of the land.[92] He primarily advanced his theory of absolute sovereignty to restrict papal authority over temporal affairs, deeming civil power absolute and unchallengeable. He argued that political power originated from the need for protection, and that laws provided safety within the commonwealth.[93] The king's duty included implementing justice and protecting his people. To fulfil this duty, he instituted laws to act in his place, since he could not ensure personal protection to his people at all times and in all places.[94] As David Baird Smith summarised, 'Laws were established by kings, not for the purpose of limiting themselves, but with the object of regulating the people.'[95] Ultimately, because the king held absolute authority above the law, he could not be held accountable to it by any earthly standards. Although he should follow divine and natural law to serve his own best interest, neither the pope nor inferior magistrates could coerce him to do so.

Referencing these authors, Maxwell provided an in-depth examination of Charles's legal sovereignty, one that supplemented his appeal to *jure divino* monarchy and divine-right kingship. As Stevenson acknowledged, scholars of Scottish political thought have widely accepted that Maxwell 'was the first in Britain's mid-seventeenth century revolutions to place Bodin's concept of sovereignty at the centre of royalist theory in a published work', although Ian Campbell has demonstrated an earlier reception of his theory in the writing of Sir John Davies, attorney general for Ireland, in 1612.[96] Drawing explicitly upon the work of Bodin, Barclay and Blackwood, Maxwell argued that the king acted as the sole author of the law, not just as its enforcer. As a result, inferior authorities in Parliament, subjects and church leaders could not hold him accountable. Maxwell began with high praise for the discipline of law, accounting 'the knowledge of that science next to Divinity, and farre more excellent and usefull than all others besides.'[97] More specifically, he maintained that, 'None have written more divinely almost, nor rationally, in maintenance of the sacred right and person of Kings, than some excellent and eminent in the knowledge of the Law; as Bodin, Barcklay, Blackwood, and others.'[98] Maxwell used these jurists to demonstrate the prerogatives that were inherent in the crown, and how these prerogatives meant that the king could never be opposed. For Maxwell, the king held the 'prerogative of the *Suprema potestas*' or that 'Sovereignty which giveth the Law'.[99] The superiority of the king as the highest sovereign who authored the law meant that he was free from 'Coercion humane, or any humane coactive power, to punish, censure, or dethrone'.[100] Maxwell therefore adapted the legal arguments that Bodin, Barclay and Blackwood advanced about sovereignty to Scotland, concluding that the commonwealth could only be sustained by an absolute monarch unified and unchallengeable in power. A limited or representative government would simply never be able 'to preserve itself, and to right what is amisse'.[101]

By engaging with these cutting-edge legal arguments advanced by sixteenth-century Catholic jurists, Maxwell effectively challenged the power of ecclesiastical authorities to hold civil rulers accountable. While Barclay and Blackwood specifically denounced papal intervention in temporal affairs, Maxwell applied their logic to Presbyterian ministers who overextended their power and intervened in politics. As the previous chapter demonstrated, Maxwell also believed that the king, not Parliament, held supreme authority over authoring and altering ecclesiastical laws. In this sense, Maxwell's belief in the theological legitimacy of Charles's reforms equally complemented his view of absolute sovereignty in the state. Rather than simply reiterate that civil magistrates held authority from God and could not be resisted, Maxwell thus situated his own political theory in the context of wider sixteenth-century Catholic debates about papal power and the king's relationship to the law. This cross-confessional debate ultimately allowed him to reject the Scottish constitutional settlement, arguing that Parliament did not possess supreme legislative power and therefore could not challenge the king according to the law, traditions and customs of the land. Nor could Parliament assume independent authority over authoring the ecclesiastical laws that reformed the church.

Together, these various facets of Maxwell's political theory justified his belief that God called subjects to obedience alone. He relied predominantly on biblical precedents to assert that God held direct, unmediated power over magistrates that included deposing or sustaining them. Scripture revealed first and foremost that God would punish and remove magistrates from positions of authority. He never required Christians to take this action themselves; instead, humans contravened God's authority if they sought to control tyrants according to their will. The Old Testament provided clear evidence that God would deliver His people by His own hand. The Israelites did not free themselves from Egypt by drawing on a power vested in the community, nor did God require Moses to deliver the people through his own wisdom and strength. Instead, God 'did with an high hand by his own immediate might and power' work through Moses.[102] In this sense, Moses did not act as an inferior magistrate invested with the community's original power. If God chose not to rescue his people, this was to be taken as a sign of punishment on a sinful community. According to Maxwell, 'God maketh and sendeth kings, as in his wise providence hee thinketh for the punishment of our sinnes, or in his mercy and bounty to blesse us when we walke in his wayes.'[103] As a result, the people must 'submit in patience, and wait till God send a remedy, either rectifying or removing the bad governour.'[104] To give subjects the authority to remove tyrants themselves would ultimately undermine both the supremacy and sovereignty of God over human affairs. Instead, Christians must 'reserve the rectifying of the soveraigne, and his errours in government, to God himselfe', lest they attempt to serve God against His will without express warrant.[105] Maxwell therefore struck a balance between human activity and divine agency over political life that gave the people a passive role in the construction of civil magistrates.

For many Scottish royalists, the case for obedience did not derive from the divine right theory of kingship alone, or the argument that God ordained the king directly so he could never be resisted. Instead, they drew upon a diverse range of examples from nature, scripture, law, historical precedent and just war theory to emphasise that God required humans to obey the natural hierarchy of the world rather than take up arms. Common to these various theories, however, was the belief that the temporal kingdom existed to maintain peace and order among Christians and non-Christians above all else. Resistance on behalf of the true religion would undermine this end of political life and therefore could not be warranted or commanded by God. Obedience constituted the only divinely mandated duty in the temporal kingdom because it followed God's structure of the world and maintained His right over government.

Constitutional Royalism

Not all royalists drew theories of absolute sovereignty to the conclusion that kings must never be limited in their power, nor was Maxwell the only royalist to apply Bodin's legal theory to Scotland. Bodin's definition of sovereignty played an equally important role in constitutional royalism. An anonymous, undated manuscript, entitled the 'Letter on Sovereign Power', also incorporated Bodin's theory of sovereignty to strike a constitutional equilibrium between king and subjects. The letter's authorship and content has been the source of significant scholarly debate. It was vaguely addressed to a 'Noble Sir' and signed 'Montrois', leading scholars to originally assume that its author was James Graham, 1st Marquis of Montrose (1612–1650).[106] Montrose initially joined the Covenanters but changed his support to the king in 1644 following his wavering commitment to Presbyterianism. However, Stevenson has made a more convincing case that Archibald Napier, 1st Lord Napier (ca. 1576–1645) wrote the letter instead.[107] Napier, who was Montrose's brother-in-law and former tutor, had supported the king from 1640. Questions about the letter's authorship have also affected interpretations of its content. Assuming that Montrose (who initially supported the Covenant) authored it, some scholars have argued that it defended the Covenant, rejected royal absolutism, and maintained that magistrates could be held accountable to divine and natural law for the protection of their subjects' liberties.[108] As a result, many scholars have placed the letter firmly within a Scottish constitutionalist tradition that affirmed parliamentary sovereignty.[109] By contrast, under the assumption that the royalist Napier wrote the letter, Stevenson highlighted its contrary absolutist implications, ones derived directly from Bodin.

While the authorship and political implications of the letter remain ambiguous – although Stevenson makes the most convincing case for Napier's authorship – the letter incorporated Bodin's ideas about sovereignty to argue for a constitutional balance between king and subjects. It drew upon the same legal debates that Maxwell had used, but it brought Bodin's theory to a different conclusion. The letter used Bodin's ideas to defend strong monarchical power unchallengeable by inferiors, but it also placed limits upon the king's authority by urging his obedience to the laws of the land.

It began with the assertion that civil society could not exist without government, nor could government exist without some sovereign power that forces subjects to obey the laws, an argument drawn directly from Bodin.[110] This sovereign power had to be supreme, meaning one 'whose acts cannot be Rescinded by any other, Instituted by god for his Glory, and the Temporall and eternall happiness of men.'[111] Notably, the letter also emphasised that civil magistrates existed to preserve peace and order while carrying out duties related to the external body. This position was apparent in the specific duties that the letter assigned to civil magistrates, ones also derived from Bodin: creating laws, making peace and war, and serving as a figure to whom appellations for justice could be made.[112] The letter incorporated Bodin's definition of sovereignty to argue that the 'soveraigne being strong and in full possession of his la[wf]ull power and prerogative, is able to protect his subjects, from oppression and mentain their libertys.'[113]

Nevertheless, the letter differed from Bodin when it argued that sovereign power was 'limited by the Lawes of god and nature, and some lawes of nations, and by the foundamentall lawes of the country', all different types of law upon which sovereign power rested.[114] Whereas Bodin had maintained that a prince could never be limited by laws of the land (as their only author), this letter suggested the opposite. Like many other royalist works from this period, the letter capitalised on the temporal kingdom as a place for the preservation of peace and order, part of which required the king to conform to laws of the land.

Although this position seemed to champion limited monarchy, according to which the king had to obey all civil laws, the letter crucially did not permit resistance. As it stated, 'Its not the peoples part towards that end, to take upon them to limite and circumscribe royall power.'[115] Instead, to argue that the people might recall power from the king was 'the language of the spirits of division' between the king and his people.[116] Furthermore, limiting the prince's sovereignty was 'the oppression and Tyrranny of subjects'.[117] Even if a king ruled contrary to civil laws and devolved into tyranny, subjects must obey and wait for God to rescue them. Rebellion would only result in greater oppression and pain. This highly pragmatic argument about obedience thus established a theoretical constitutional equilibrium between subjects and magistrates. On the one hand, kings should be limited in their power by natural, divine and civil law. On the other hand, subjects could not resist the king, even if he failed to conform to these laws. Within Scottish royalism, Bodin's theory of sovereignty could therefore be adapted to support absolute monarchy (as Maxwell did), but it could also be used to develop a more pragmatic, constitutionalist position. Significant diversity thus existed within royalist political thought, even among the small group of authors who advanced theories about absolute monarchy in this period.

Conclusion

The political thought of Scottish royalists was far from monolithic, nor were they unanimously committed to episcopacy in their denunciation of the Covenanting agenda. Even though many royalists prioritised civil stability and respect for monarchy above religious division, great variety existed in how they thought about the aims and nature of the temporal kingdom. They defended absolute monarchy using a variety of arguments pertaining to the need for civil stability, the natural hierarchical order of the universe, scriptural warrants and legal theories about absolute sovereignty. Although these arguments have sometimes been interpreted as 'secular' political ones, they must also be interpreted within wider Protestant intellectual traditions about the end of politics and the magistrate's *cura religionis*. Royalists feared that the Covenanters wanted to limit the king's civil authority by resisting (and potentially deposing) him if he ruled contrary to their subjective interpretation of the true religion. This meant that subjects would pledge their primary allegiance to ministers rather than to their civil magistrates, the ones whom God ordained to preserve peace and order in the temporal kingdom. As a result, royalist approaches to the Covenanting agenda frequently reflected a strand of two-kingdoms thinking that prioritised God's immediate sovereignty over politics, and minimised human agency over furthering religion through civic institutions. Since God ordained civil government to preserve peace and order among sinful human beings, he also required subjects to submit to their magistrates in all circumstances. Scottish royalists – rather than the supposedly theocratic Covenanters – therefore maintained a high view of direct divine sovereignty over political life, one that left little room for human agency at any level. As a result, Covenanters would need to produce a markedly different theory about politics to counteract this vision of an organic, hierarchical commonwealth that necessitated absolute monarchy.

Notes

1. Donaldson, 'Scotland's Conservative North,' 65–79 (see introduction, n. 55).
2. Paul R. Goatman and Andrew Lind, 'Glasgow and the National Covenant in 1638: Revolution, Royalism and Civic Reform,' in Langley, *National Covenant in Scotland, 1638–1689*, 39–52 (see introduction, n. 4); Cipriano, 'Scottish Universities and Opposition,' 12–37 (see introduction, n. 56).
3. Andrew Lind, 'Royalism, Resistance and the Scottish Clergy, c. 1638–41,' in *The National Covenant*, 125–44.
4. Lind, 'Royalism, Resistance,' 144.
5. Lind, 'Royalism, Resistance,' 144.
6. David George Mullan, *Scottish Puritanism, 1590–1638* (Oxford: OUP, 2000); David George Mullan, '"Uniformity in Religion": The Solemn League and Covenant (1643) and the Presbyterian Vision,' in *Later Calvinism: International Perspectives*, ed. W. Fred Graham (Kirksville, MO: Sixteenth Century Journal Publishers, 1994), 249–266; James Kirk, *Patterns of Reform: Continuity and Change in the Reformation Kirk*, 154–231 and 334–367; David George Mullan, *Episcopacy in Scotland: The History of an Idea* (Edinburgh: John Donald, 1986); Donaldson, *Scottish Church History*, 60–70 (see chap. 1, n. 47).
7. David Calderwood, *The True History of the Church of Scotland* (Edinburgh, 1678); John Spottiswoode, *History of the Church and State of Scotland* (London, 1677).
8. Campbell, *Life and Works of Robert Baillie*, 85 (see introduction, n. 54). For an analysis of the emergence of these trends, see Mullan, *Episcopacy in Scotland*, 136–150. See also: Julian Goodare, 'The Rise of the Covenanters' in *The Oxford Handbook of the English Revolution*, ed. Michael J. Braddick (Oxford: OUP, 2015), 43–59; Alasdair Raffe, *The Culture of Controversy: Religious Arguments in Scotland, 1660–1714* (Woodbridge: Boydell, 2012); John R. Young, *The Scottish Parliament, 1639–1661: A Political and Constitutional Analysis* (Edinburgh: John Donald, 1996).

9. Steven J. Reid, 'Cultures of Calvinism in Early Modern Scotland,' in *The Oxford Handbook of Calvin and Calvinism*, eds Bruce Gordon and Carl R. Trueman (Oxford: OUP, 2021), 220–236; Lind, 'Royalism, Resistance,' 144; Alan R. MacDonald, *The Jacobean Kirk, 1567–1625: Sovereignty, Polity and Liturgy* (Aldershot: Ashgate, 1998).
10. Jason McElligott and David L. Smith, eds, *Royalists and Royalism during the English Civil Wars* (Cambridge: CUP, 2007); Jerome de Groot, *Royalist Identities* (Basingstoke: Palgrave, 2004); John Sanderson, *'But the People's Creatures': The Philosophical Basis of the English Civil War* (Manchester: MUP, 1989), ch. 2.
11. *Duplyes of the Ministers*, 10 (see chap. 2, n. 62).
12. 'The National Covenant,' 49–50 (see chap. 2, n. 33).
13. *RPS*, 1585/12/15 (accessed 14 June 2023).
14. Keith M. Brown, *Noble Power in Scotland from the Reformation to the Revolution* (Edinburgh: EUP, 2011), 86.
15. Brown, *Noble Power*, 6.
16. *RPS*, 1585/12/15.
17. *Duplyes of the Ministers*, 14.
18. 'The National Covenant,' 49–50.
19. *Duplyes of the Ministers*, 26.
20. *Duplyes of the Ministers*, 26.
21. *Duplyes of the Ministers*, 29; Augustine, 'Contra faustum Manichaeum libri XXII,' in *Corpus scriptorum ecclesiasticorum latinorum*, ed. Joseph Zycha (Leipzig: Tempsky, 1972), 25: 249–797. For an English translation, see also: St Augustine, *Contra Faustum (Answer to Faustus, a Manichean)*, trans. R. J. Teske (Hyde Park, NY: New City Press, 2007).
22. *Duplyes of the Ministers*, 29.
23. *Duplyes of the Ministers*, 30.
24. *Duplyes of the Ministers*, 30.
25. André Rivet, *Jesuita vapulans* (Lyon, 1635), ch. Xiii, 274–5.
26. Ibid., 275: 'Et tamen nemini nostrum probantur, quae vel ex *Goodmanno*, vel ex *Knoxo*, vel ex *Buchanano*, in eam sententiam describuntur, quamvis eò usque non procedant, quo Iesuitae processerunt.'
27. *Generall demands, concerning the late covenant propounded by the ministers and professsors of divinitie in Aberdene* (Aberdeen: Edward Raban, 1638), 11.
28. *Generall demands*, 11.
29. Rivet, *Jesuita vapulans*, 275: 'Putavit Buchanus, fortè etiam ea fuit mens Knoxi, Regnum Scotiae plenum non fuisse, & absolutum.'
30. *Duplyes*, 31.
31. *Generall demands*, 10.
32. NLS, Wodrow Folio XLIII, no. 140, fol. 273r.
33. Wodrow Folio XLIII, no. 140, fol. 273r.
34. Wodrow Folio XLIII, no. 140, fol. 273r.
35. Wodrow Folio XLIII, no. 140, fol. 273r.
36. Wodrow Folio XLIII, no. 140, fol. 273r.
37. NLS, Wodrow Quarto LXXVI, no. 4, fol. 57r.
38. *RPS*, 1640/6/29 (accessed 14 June 2023).
39. Wodrow Quarto LXXVI, fol. 57r.
40. Wodrow Quarto LXXVI, fol. 57r.
41. Wodrow Quarto LXXVI, fol. 56r.

42. NLS, Wodrow Folio XXXI, no. 2, fol. 7r.
43. Barry Robertson, *Royalists at War in Scotland and Ireland, 1638–1650* (London: Routledge, 2016), 38.
44. William Drummond of Hawthornden, 'A speech (Which may be called A Prophecy) to the noblemen, barons, gentlemen, &c. who have leagu'd themselves for the defence of the Religion and Liberties of Scotland, 2 May 1639,' in *Works of William Drummond of Hawthornden*, eds John Sage and Thomas Ruddiman (Edinburgh: James Watson, 1711), 179–82.
45. William Drummond of Hawthornden, 'Irene: a remonstrance for concord, amity and love, amongst his majesty's subjects; written after his declaration publish'd at Edinburgh, 22nd of September, 1638' in *Works of William Drummond*, 165.
46. Deummond, 'Irene,' 165.
47. William Guild, *To the Nobilitie, Gentrie, Burrowes, Ministers, and others of this late combination in Covenant, a friendly and faythfull advice* (Aberdeen: Edward Raban, 1639), 4. The copy referenced here is from: NLS, Rb.S.3013.
48. Guild, *To the Nobilitie*, 5.
49. Guild, *To the Nobilitie*, 6.
50. Guild, *To the Nobilitie*, 7.
51. Corbet, *Ungirding*, 4 (see chap. 1, n. 61).
52. Corbet, *Ungirding*, 47.
53. Corbet, *Ungirding*, 5.
54. Corbet, *Ungirding*, 19.
55. Corbet, *Ungirding*, 30.
56. William Drummond of Hawthornden, 'Remora's for the National League between Scotland and England, 1642,' in *Works of William Drummond*, 188.
57. Drummond, 'Remora's for the National League,' 188.
58. Drummond, 'Remora's for the National League,' 188.
59. Drummond, 'Remora's for the National League,' 189.
60. John Maxwell, *Sacro-sancta regum majestas; or, the sacred and royal prerogative of Christian kings* (Oxford, 1644), 85.
61. Maxwell, *Sacro-sancta*, 86.
62. Maxwell, *Sacro-sancta*, 1.
63. Maxwell, *Sacro-sancta*, 92.
64. Maxwell, *Sacro-sancta*, 83.
65. Maxwell, *Sacro-sancta*, 84.
66. Maxwell, *Sacro-sancta*, 86.
67. Maxwell, *Sacro-sancta*, 86.
68. Maxwell, *Sacro-sancta*, 179.
69. For an overview of this position, see Harro Höpfl, *Jesuit Political Thought: The Society of Jesus and the State, c.1540–1630* (Cambridge: CUP, 2004), chs 9–10.
70. Francisco Suárez, *Tractatus de legibus ac deo legislatore: in decem libros distributes* (Antwerp, 1613), bk III, ch. II. For an English translation, see; Francisco Suárez, *Selections from Three Works of Francisco Suarez, S. J.*, ed. and trans. Thomas Pink (Indianapolis: Liberty Fund, 2015); Robert Bellarmine, *De laicis, or the treatise on civil government*, ed. and trans. Kathleen E. Murphy (New York: Fordham Press, 1928), 25.
71. Maxwell, *Sacro-sancta*, 19.
72. Maxwell, *Sacro-sancta*, 22.

73. Aristotle, *Politics*, ed. and trans. Ernest Barker and R. F. Stalley (Oxford: OUP, 1995), bk 1, ch. 1.
74. Robert Bellarmine, 'On Laymen or Secular People,' in *On Temporal and Spiritual Authority: On Laymen or Secular People. On the Temporal Power of the Pope: Against William Barclay. On the Primary duty of the Supreme Pontiff*, ed. and trans. Stefania Tutino (Indianapolis: Liberty Fund, 2012), 18–20; Luis de Molina, *De iustitia et iure tractatus* (Venice, 1611), bk II, disp. XXII.
75. Francisco de Vitoria, 'De potestate ecclesiae prior: on the power of the Church,' in *Vitoria: Political Writings*, ed. Anthony Pagden and trans. Jeremy Lawrance (Cambridge: CUP, 1991), quest. 5, art. 3, 87.
76. Stevenson, '"Letter on Sovereign Power",' 31 (see introduction, n. 64).
77. Skinner, *Foundations of Modern Political Thought*, 2: 289 (see introduction, n. 13).
78. Jean Bodin, 'Book I, Chapter 8: On Sovereignty,' in *Bodin: On Sovereignty*, ed. Julian H. Franklin (Cambridge: CUP, 2012), 11.
79. Bodin, 'On Sovereignty,' 18–19.
80. Bodin, 'On Sovereignty,' 13.
81. Bodin, 'On Sovereignty,' 27.
82. Bodin, 'On Sovereignty,' 19.
83. Bodin, 'On Sovereignty,' 19–23.
84. Jean Bodin, 'Book I, Chapter 10: On the True Marks of Sovereignty,' in *Bodin: On Sovereignty*, 56.
85. George Buchanan, *A Dialogue on the Law of Kingship among the Scots: A Critical Edition and Translation of George Buchanan's De Iure Regni apud Scotos Dialogus*, eds Roger A. Mason and Martin S. Smith (London: Routledge, 2004), 135.
86. Buchanan, *Dialogue on the Law*, 135.
87. Skinner, *Foundations of Modern Political Thought*, 2: 301.
88. Skinner, *Foundations of Modern Political Thought*, 2: 301.
89. Adam Blackwood, *Adversus Georgii Buchanani dialogum, de iure regni apud scotos, pro regibus apologia* (Poitiers, 1581); Adam Blackwood, *De coniunctione religionis et imperii libri duo* (Paris, 1575).
90. Howell A. Lloyd, 'The Political Thought of Adam Blackwood,' *Historical Journal* 43, no. 4 (2000): 922.
91. Adam Blackwood, *Adversus Georgii Buchanani*, 110: 'Legem voco principis placitum iure suo, non precario regnantis, cuius imperio non modo singularum ciuitatum ac municipiorum iura consuetudinesque, verumetiam publicae leges sunt obnoxiae.' English translation taken from Lloyd, 'Political Thought of Adam Blackwood,' 926.
92. David Baird Smith, 'William Barclay,' *SHR* 11, no. 42 (1914): 145–54.
93. Smith, 'William Barclay,' 146.
94. William Barclay, *De regno et regali potestate aduersus Buchananum, Brutum, Boucherium, & reliquos monarchomacos, libri sex* (Paris, 1600), 83.
95. Smith, 'William Barclay,' 148.
96. Ian W. S. Campbell, 'Aristotelian Ancient Constitution and Anti-Aristotelian Sovereignty in Stuart Ireland,' *Historical Journal* 53, no. 3 (2010): 586–8; Stevenson, '"Letter on Sovereign Power",' 43.
97. Maxwell, *Sacro-sancta*, 144.
98. Maxwell, *Sacro-sancta*, 144.
99. Maxwell, *Sacro-sancta*, 175.

100. Maxwell, *Sacro-sancta*, 140.
101. Maxwell, *Sacro-sancta*, 156.
102. Maxwell, *Sacro-sancta*, 152.
103. Maxwell, *Sacro-sancta*, 75.
104. Maxwell, *Sacro-sancta*, 148.
105. Maxwell, *Sacro-sancta*, 157.
106. For an overview of the contested claims about its authorship, see Stevenson, '"Letter on Sovereign Power",' 25–6 and 28–31.
107. Stevenson, '"Letter on Sovereign Power",' 28.
108. John Buchan, *Montrose* (London: Thomas Nelson, 1928); William Law Mathieson, *Politics and Religion: A Study in Scottish History from the Reformation to the Revolution* (Glasgow: Maclehose, 1902); Mark Napier, *Memorials of Montrose and His Times*, vol. 2 (Edinburgh: Maitland Club, 1850), 35–6; Mark Napier, *Montrose and the Covenanters, their Characters and Conduct* (London: James Duncan, 1838).
109. Stevenson, '"Letter on Sovereign Power",' 26–31; Cowan, *Montrose* (see introduction, n. 54); Ronald Williams, *Montrose: Cavalier in Mourning* (London: Barrie and Jenkins, 1975); William Cunningham, 'The Political Philosophy of the Marquis of Montrose,' *SHR* 14, no. 56 (1917): 354–69; John Buchan, *The Marquis of Montrose* (London: Nelson, 1913).
110. For a comprehensive comparison of the letter to Bodin's *De republica*, see Stevenson, '"Letter on Sovereign Power",' 36–41.
111. NLS, Wodrow Quarto XL, no. 2, fol. 3r.
112. Wodrow Quarto XL, no. 2, fol. 3r.
113. Wodrow Quarto XL, no. 2, fol. 5r.
114. Wodrow Quarto XL, no. 2, fol. 3r.
115. Wodrow Quarto XL, no. 2, fol. 4r.
116. Wodrow Quarto XL, no. 2, fol. 4v.
117. Wodrow Quarto XL, no. 2, fol. 4r.

CHAPTER FOUR

Church Government and the Commonwealth

Scottish royalists opposed the National Covenant and military conflict with the king for a variety of theological and political reasons which extended far beyond a simple, unwavering commitment to episcopacy. While we are increasingly recognising that a staunch Presbyterian versus Episcopalian divide did not characterise early modern Scottish society, it would still be erroneous to downplay the importance of debates about church government within its intellectual culture. Church polity was not just a theological concern but a deeply political one that had drastic implications for Scotland's civic institutions. On the one hand, as the previous chapter demonstrated, royalists sought civil stability that could only be attained through the rule of a strong, absolute monarch. They feared that the Covenanters' desire for Presbyterianism – a form of church government that placed authority in elders, presbyteries, synods and the General Assembly rather than in royally appointed bishops – threatened absolute monarchy by subordinating the king to the church and making him subject to spiritual discipline. Only episcopacy and absolute monarchy were compatible, whereas Presbyterianism would produce the very civic disorder that royalists so ardently sought to avoid. On the other hand, many members of the Covenanting leadership – especially those who served as commissioners to the Westminster Assembly (1643–1653) – believed that scripture explicitly mandated Presbyterianism (making it *jure divino*), and that no alternative could be legitimate. Scots therefore had an obligation to mould a form of civil government that complemented and protected the Presbyterian church, such as limited monarchy.

This chapter examines these strands of thought about church government as another key point of intersection between political and ecclesiological ideas during the Scottish Revolution. It first analyses how royalists criticised Presbyterianism as politically subversive by directly comparing it to two debates within the Roman Catholic intellectual tradition: the papal deposing power and conciliarism. It then considers how Covenanter commissioners to the Westminster Assembly responded to these accusations by defending the *jure divino* status of Presbyterianism and emphasising its necessity in the church. It concludes with an analysis of how they defended a specific element of Presbyterianism that proved so problematic for the crown: the power over excommunication. Ultimately, this chapter demonstrates the various ways that debates about church government confirmed royalists' belief in absolutism or laid foundations for Covenanting defences of limited monarchy (examined in the next chapter).

Debates about church government became increasingly important after the Scots entered the Solemn League and Covenant with England in 1643. Through this alliance, they endeavoured to 'bring the Churches of God in the three kingdoms to the nearest conjunction and uniformity in religion, confession of faith, form of church-government, directory for worship and catechising.'[1] They additionally swore to extirpate 'Prelacy, (that is, church-government by Archbishops, Bishops, their Chancellors, and Commissaries, Deans, Deans and Chapters, Archdeacons, and all other ecclesiastical Officers depending on hierarchy)'.[2] Despite the Covenanters' goal of achieving uniformity in church government and liturgical practices across England, Scotland and Ireland, recent scholarship on Scottish church history has demonstrated the complex and malleable nature of beliefs about Presbyterianism during this period. The extent to which the Covenanting leadership collectively desired a Presbyterian settlement for all of Britain and Ireland, especially through their participation in the Westminster Assembly, has been called into question. Eight Scottish commissioners were appointed, including George Gillespie and Alexander Henderson (who arrived first in September 1643), followed by Robert Baillie and Samuel Rutherford. Two non-ministerial elders joined the Assembly later: John Maitland and Sir Archibald Johnston of Wariston. David George Mullan originally argued that four of the Commissioners – Baillie, Gillespie, Henderson and Rutherford – remained rigidly committed to Presbyterianism as part of a 'self-consciously inflexible and anti-tolerationist program that embraced the whole of society'.[3] They consequently imposed their brand of Presbyterianism as 'the immutable and eternal will of God', offering little toleration for English Independents.[4]

However, John Coffey, Hunter Powell and Alexander Campbell have shown that great diversity existed within the Scottish commissioners' positions on church polity. They did not conclusively agree on all aspects of Presbyterianism, such as where God located original power in the church.[5] The commissioners also disagreed amongst themselves regarding the threat that Independency posed, blurring the boundaries between Presbyterianism and congregationalism to such an extent that multiple strains of Presbyterian thought emerged at the Assembly.[6] Interactions with English divines thus prompted Scottish commissioners to debate and defend the nature of Presbyterianism, especially in light of the criticism that they faced from royalists and Episcopalians back home. Despite these variations, some common ground existed. As Chad Van Dixhoorn has shown, 'one of the points that came to unite the majority of assembly presbyterians was a conviction that a form of church government could be deduced from Scripture.'[7] Nevertheless, the Scottish commissioners still developed a range of ideas about church government during their time in London, ones that complicated the exact Presbyterian settlement they sought to achieve through the Solemn League and Covenant.

Recent scholarship has also proved the relationship between church polity and political life during the civil wars to be an especially fruitful line of enquiry. As Elliot Vernon has argued, debates about church government during the seventeenth century were fundamentally political, for 'structures of church governance . . . had the potential to impact substantially on the lives of the vast majority of people.'[8] Although the average Scot may not have expressed a deep interest in abstract defences of Presbyterianism or Episcopalianism, these debates did matter for the everyday structures under which they lived and the forms of spiritual discipline that they experienced. Indeed, struggles over church polity in Reformation Scotland 'left a residual body of thought, together with a deep layer of resentment within Scottish political and religious culture.'[9] Given renewed scholarly interest in the connections between church polity and politics, this chapter thus examines how reflections on church government raised questions about the nature of political power and forced royalists and Covenanters to defend their preferred forms of civil government. Ideas about church polity thus bore heavily upon Scotland's civic institutions, for the two were inseparable within Scottish thought.

Catholic Political Thought and the Presbyterian Threat

After the Reformation of 1560, Scots began to diverge in their opinions about the form of government that best suited their national church. Although James Kirk and Gordon Donaldson debated the extent to which Andrew Melville and the earliest Scottish reformers explicitly provided for Presbyterianism, they pointed to the *Second Book of Discipline* (1578) as the beginning of an anti-episcopal movement in Scotland.[10] This movement included a definitive iteration of the 'Melvillian' two-kingdoms theory that thoroughly ousted royal authority from the church. However, early provisions for Presbyterianism were not turned into parliamentary statues, and '[t]he government adopted an aggressively authoritarian approach' to securing the royal supremacy to counter political instability between 1583 and 1585.[11] This aggressive policy included banning presbyteries, while a parliamentary Act of 1584 claimed that the king held authority over all civil and ecclesiastical affairs.

However, presbyteries were reinstated and given legal sanction in the 'Golden Act' of 5 June 1592.[12] Yet James began to slowly dismantle this system after 1597, proposing that the clerical Estate return to Parliament, a proposal that the General Assembly approved in 1600.[13] According to Alan MacDonald, James claimed that he restored the episcopate only to remedy the church's 'long-standing desire for parliamentary representation.'[14] Yet his alterations to church government presaged the emergence of a strong anti-episcopal tradition that gained momentum throughout his reign.[15]

Tensions escalated further when Charles attempted to align the kirk more closely with the Church of England, reaffirming his imposition of bishops (and his unpopular liturgical reforms) in the process. Ultimately, the meeting of the General Assembly held at Glasgow in 1638 abolished episcopacy, while the parliament of June 1640 abolished the clerical Estate.[16]

However, the abolition of the episcopate did not stop debate about the proper form of church government in Scotland. Many defences of government by bishops emerged. Some Scots believed in episcopacy's *jure divino* status, providing scriptural warrants for its imposition. For example, John Maxwell clearly maintained that, 'Episcopacy with all its essential power is immediately from God, and of his institution.'[17] Scripture permitted no other form of church government. Others maintained that church government was *adiaphora*, meaning that God allowed humans to determine church polity according to their own will. For example, a partial draft of a treatise written against episcopacy criticised this perspective. The manuscript is in David Calderwood's hand, although it is unclear whether he authored the work or simply transcribed it. Nevertheless, the author, a firm supporter of Presbyterianism, accused Episcopalians of maintaining 'that presbytericall government is no more warranted by the word of God then episcopal'.[18] Since scripture provided no overt guidance, the form of polity could be determined by human will. Similarly, even though he served in the Church of Scotland as a presbyter, John Forbes of Corse challenged those who condemned episcopacy and the Five Articles of Perth as 'Abominable, and Antichristian' by asking: 'These doctrines how can wee receave, without condemning the doctrine and practise of sound antiquitie, and of manie famous Reformed kirks, in Britane, France, Germanie, and else-where?'[19] Many Scots who opposed the Covenant therefore held that God either mandated episcopacy in scripture, or that He allowed humans to choose this form of church government through their own will (as seen in the practice of other Protestant churches).

More frequently, however, royalists directly criticised Presbyterianism for its politically subversive implications, including the threat that it posed to absolute monarchy and the duty of obedience. They believed that the king must remain insulated from any who attempted to challenge his power, whether inferior magistrates in the temporal realm or ecclesiastical authorities in the spiritual one. Their desire to maintain civic peace and order through a strong, unchallengeable monarch significantly informed how they responded to Covenanting ideals on church government. Presbyterianism was so dangerous because it gave divine warrant to potential tyranny of the church over the state while blurring boundaries between the two kingdoms. As a result, Scottish royalists sought to prove that Presbyterianism had not been divinely mandated, and that it threatened absolute monarchy in the state contrary to God's will. To do so, some royalists compared Presbyterianism to two debates within Catholic intellectual circles: conciliarism and the papal deposing power. This section examines how Scottish royalists used both debates to portray Presbyterianism as politically subversive and accuse their Covenanter contemporaries of drawing their ideas from the corrupted thought of the Catholics (rather than from any Reformed consensus).

In 1638, John Corbet clearly described the threat that Presbyterianism posed to the civil state: the independence of individual parishes and presbyteries from royal oversight might give ecclesiastical authorities power over the king. As Corbet argued, 'But now in Scotland, not only the whole church takes the supreme power to itselfe, but also every parish takes upon it to be an absolute independent society.'[20] This structure of the Church of Scotland, one inherently liberated from royal oversight, enabled it to maintain its own authority and act independently with no external control. As a result, ecclesiastical authorities of these independent churches might encourage subjects to depose their king. Corbet argued that the Covenanters drew their ideas from Thomas Cartwright (1534/5–1603), an English minister who preached a series of controversial lectures at the University of Cambridge in 1570 in which he advocated for a Presbyterian polity in the Church of England.[21] According to Corbet, Cartwright 'layeth down a ground for this overthrow of Kings ... for he holdeth that the *Common-wealth* is in the Church, and not the Church in the *Common-wealth*.'[22] According to Presbyterianism, ministers could treat the king as any other subject, not as the church's temporal head. As a result, ecclesiastical authorities held supreme power over his spiritual discipline. Corbet charged the Covenanters with similarly using Presbyterianism to limit the king's control over the church while giving ministers absolute authority.

Furthermore, Presbyterianism threatened to collapse the boundaries and jurisdictions between the temporal and spiritual kingdoms by giving ministers authority over the king. Corbet criticised the Covenanters for their intellectual similarity to Catholics who defended the papal deposing power. According to this highly controversial power, the pope could deem a civil ruler heretical and illegitimate based upon their spiritual status. The power originated from Pope Gregory VII's *Dictatus Papae*, which stipulated '[t]hat it may be permitted to him [the pope] to depose emperors' and '[t]hat he may absolve subjects from their fealty to wicked men'.[23] A ruler's civil legitimacy therefore depended directly upon their spiritual standing, not upon the quality of their own rule. But not all Catholics agreed with this power of the pope. William Barclay, the Scottish Catholic jurist who Maxwell used to defend absolute sovereignty, rejected any coercive power of the church over temporal rulers. In 1609, he wrote a treatise entitled *De potestate papae* in which he argued that spiritual and temporal powers must remain entirely distinct.[24] The pope could never use the excuse of excommunication to deem a magistrate politically illegitimate, for his end was not to engage in politics. Robert Bellarmine responded directly to Barclay, defending the papal deposing power with a treatise in which he cited the consensus of Italian, French, Spanish, German, English and Scottish Roman

Catholics on the matter.[25] He also systematically challenged Barclay's arguments to reach the conclusion that

> the Pope has authority to dispose of temporal matters, to the point of deposing kings and emperors themselves; indeed, through this spiritual authority the Supreme Pontiff can bind secular princes with the bond of excommunication, he can absolve peoples from their oath of allegiance and obedience, he can oblige those peoples under pain of excommunication not to obey an excommunicated king and to choose for themselves another king.[26]

Although Catholics themselves did not agree on the legitimacy of the papal deposing power, especially the extent to which it blurred the purposes and authorities of the two kingdoms, these debates provided Scottish royalists with an intellectual framework for challenging Presbyterianism.

Writing from the perspective of the fictional Lysimachus Nicanor, a Jesuit congratulating the Covenanters for the political upheaval they created in Scotland, Corbet claimed that absolute monarchy hindered the pope from exercising supremacy over civil rulers. As he told the Covenanters, enduring absolute monarchy would be 'a great impediment to the *ends* you aime at', meaning the subordination of the king to the presbytery, just as temporal rulers had been subordinated to the pope.[27] Having rejected the pope's authority, the Covenanters transferred the papal deposing power to the General Assembly. As Corbet claimed, the Assembly exercised a power 'not only *Directive*, but also *Coactive*' over the king, meaning that the Assembly could forcibly compel the king to obey its commands rather than simply offer spiritual guidance and direction.[28] The inherent way that a Presbyterian church structure isolated and protected individual churches from royal oversight was so subversive because the General Assembly (like the pope) could deem the king heretical, excommunicate him and absolve subjects of their due obedience.

For Corbet, absolute monarchy was the only way to circumvent this Presbyterian threat. If church leaders functioned independently from the king, then they had no impetus to submit to any political authorities. Corbet argued that the Covenanters did not see their rebellion as treason 'because they are not subject to the king in church matters'.[29] However, this logic paved the way for church rule over the state. As Corbet continued, the Covenanters might begin by holding the king accountable to church censure alone, but they would soon 'rob him of his *Supremacy* in matters civill'.[30] If the king could be limited by ministers, he might also be held accountable by his subjects at their command. Corbet ultimately told the Covenanters that they had to borrow their intellectual weapons from the Roman Catholics, for 'they maintain the *Supremacy of the Pope over Kings*; and you now use them to maintain the *Power of the People* over *Kings*.'[31] For Corbet, the Covenanters therefore promoted Presbyterianism not to protect the church from royal oversight. Instead, they carried out a nefarious political agenda to overextend their own authority into temporal matters. This included holding the king accountable to the General Assembly's coactive power, thereby giving the church dominance over the state. By using the papal deposing power as a precedent, and replacing the pope with the presbytery, the Covenanters could therefore undermine absolute monarchy in addition to the separate jurisdictions of the two kingdoms.

A similar emphasis on the Covenanters' intellectual similarity to Roman Catholic debates appeared in other royalist literature. For example, Maxwell engaged with the same idea of the papal deposing power to defend Charles from church censure in 1644. He argued that, even in a Protestant community which did not recognise the pope, ministers could never possess a coercive power over temporal rulers. The General Assembly could not declare the king illegitimate simply because he ruled heretically by failing to conform to their subjective interpretation of the 'true religion'. In his opening letter to James Butler, Marquis of Ormond (1610–1688) in *Sacro-sancta regum majestas*, Maxwell affirmed that, 'Sound Reformed Catholique Protestants denie justly such a subordination of the Prince to the Priest ... and that Kings by any Church-man or men whatsoever, Pope or Presbyterie, is censurable, dethronable, deposable.'[32] According to Maxwell, Presbyterians inappropriately tried to subordinate the king to the General Assembly when he held absolute power. Like Corbet, Maxwell claimed that the Covenanters sought not only to spiritually discipline the king, but to attain total control over the state. He argued that the Covenanters had already attempted to take hold of civic institutions through their presbyteries and assemblies, for the ecclesiastical sovereignty inherent within Presbyterianism 'may restraine and constraine the king at pleasure. It may repeale his Lawes; correct his Statutes; reverse judgments. It may establish its owne, urge disobedience, cite, convent, and censure in case of disobedience.'[33] Indeed, Scotland had already become a 'despoticall Soveraignty' in which ecclesiastical leaders tyrannised over both the king and subjects, requiring them to give up their money, arms, and life for their religion.[34]

Maxwell also framed his criticisms of Presbyterianism in the context of Catholic intellectual traditions. First, he specifically challenged Jacques Almain (ca. 1480–1515), Jean Gerson (1363–1429), and William of Ockham (ca. 1287–1347), three Catholic authors who granted 'that the Pope for Heresie may depose a king, and the people for transgressing against the Commonwealth.'[35] As Maxwell argued,

> To make pope or presbyterie, as the immediate vicegerents of Christ, and to authorize them with a coactive, a coercive power, to confirme their orders, to force him [the king] to repeale his own lawes, and ... to stirre up people against the Lords anointed, to sedition, to rebellion ... is truely the disgrace of religion, the highest of treasons against God and man.[36]

Maxwell claimed that, since these authors wrote before the Reformation, any belief that the church held a coercive power above the king – one that might even warrant deposition – could not have emerged from a Protestant consensus.[37] Corbet and Maxwell both demonstrated royalists' overarching fear that Presbyterianism inevitably collapsed the boundaries of the two kingdoms, an argument that they articulated using Catholic debates about the legitimacy of the papal deposing power.

Maxwell also introduced a second Roman Catholic debate as a parallel for the Covenanting context: conciliarism. He argued that the Covenanters erroneously drew parallels between conciliarism – a debate about the authority of general councils to oppose the pope – and the authority of inferior civil magistrates to depose their superiors. Conciliarism arose during the Western Schism (1378–1417) when two rival popes emerged in Rome and Avignon. When the Council of Constance (1414–1418) met to end the schism, it determined that ecumenical councils held supreme authority in the church, challenging the doctrine of papal infallibility.[38] Building upon this precedent, fifteenth-century Catholic conciliarists such as John Mair (1467–1550), a Scottish philosopher at the Sorbonne, granted general ecumenical councils authority to depose or challenge the pope in instances where papal power had been abused.[39] Francis Oakley has argued that this conciliarist thought laid foundations for seventeenth-century constitutionalism, according to which inferior magistrates might challenge the king in the same way that ecumenical councils might challenge the pope.[40] Maxwell's criticisms of the Covenanters corroborate Oakley's assessment; he accused the Covenanters of adapting this Catholic theological concept into a constitutional one that they applied to Scotland. But Maxwell maintained that the conciliarism debate should never map onto the state to absolve subjects of their civil obedience. Those who supported limits on the king's authority drew their argument from Catholic conciliarists who believed that the power of the papal office was given by Christ, but the specific pope derived his authority from the community of the faithful. If papal power was abused, the pope was deposable by a general council.

According to Maxwell, the Council of Constance still

> made the communitie of the People, the prime, first, proper, and immediate subject of all Civill Power, intending at this time onely to vindicate Princes from the sacrilegious and violent invasion of the Pope of Rome, who most impiously and tyrannically usurped upon them.[41]

Even though ecumenical councils might challenge a pope, conciliarism never placed princes under the authority of their inferiors. Nor did it absolve the people from their duty to obey civil authorities. This paradigm for the internal governance of the church therefore could not be transferred as a proper model of power for the state, as the Covenanters attempted to do. Maxwell thus concluded that the Covenanters developed their ideas about the church and civil power from the 'polluted cisterns' of Catholic conciliarist thought.[42]

The Defence of Presbyterianism

Some Covenanters responded to these accusations by claiming that they too respected a strong boundary between the ends, authorities and jurisdictions of the temporal and spiritual kingdoms. For example, Baillie argued that Scottish Presbyterians were not interested in radically altering the form of civil government to impose church rule over the state. As he maintained, those who opposed Presbyterianism were 'mistaken in fastning upon presbiteriall government any furtherance of democracy'.[43] Although Presbyterians arranged church government according to elders, synods and presbyteries, this structure did not pose a threat to the state or reflect a desire to subvert pre-existing civic structures. Instead, Baillie reaffirmed the traditional distinction between the two kingdoms, claiming that the church 'medles not to the prejudice of any civill government which it finds established by law, but what ever that be, it supports it to its power.'[44] Baillie's interpretation of the two kingdoms therefore allowed different forms of church and civil government to be complementary, rather than diametrically opposed. Other Presbyterians responded to these criticisms by claiming that they were only recovering the original church settlement instituted at the time of the Scottish Reformation. As Coffey has noted, the Covenanting leadership 'never lost their vision of its restoration' despite decades of royal interference.[45] Simultaneously, others defended Presbyterianism as a *jure divino* form of church government expressly required by divine law. It constituted the only form of polity ordained by scripture, and any alternative (especially Episcopalianism or congregationalism) would prove unbiblical, threaten the Reformed faith and corrupt the church. For example, Gillespie and Rutherford wrote extensively in defence of *jure divino* Presbyterianism, both when they responded to royalist criticism and when they participated in the Westminster Assembly.[46]

Gillespie had already begun to defend the *jure divino* basis of Presbyterianism as early as 1637 in his *Dispute against the English-popish ceremonies*, the same work in which he developed a limited category of *adiaphora* to denounce the lawfulness of Charles's liturgical reforms. He argued that, in the New Testament, Christ specifically ordained elders and deacons, not bishops.[47] God established elders to carry out discipline and teaching, although they might also assist pastors by overseeing the people and censuring their faults.[48] Deacons were responsible for the 'collecting, receiving, keeping, and distributing of ecclesiasticall goods' that were necessary for the maintenance of the church and schools, for aid to the poor and for the administration of the sacraments.[49] Apart from these two offices, God did not provide for any other forms of ecclesiastical authority.

As Gillespie maintained, 'As for the order and degree of bishops, superior to that of elders, there is no divine ordinance nor institution for it.'[50]

A few years later, Gillespie more fully explained the scriptural and historical warrants for Presbyterianism in *An assertion of the government of the Church of Scotland* (1641). He authored this treatise primarily to defend against English theologians who championed *jure divino* episcopacy, such as Bishop Joseph Hall (1574–1656).[51] Gillespie cited multiple verses of scripture – Matthew 18:17, Romans 12:8, 1 Corinthians 12:28 and 1 Timothy 5:17 – along with patristic works to provide the scriptural warrants for Presbyterianism. He also maintained that other Reformed churches throughout Europe had embraced Presbyterian church government, as was apparent from the French, Belgic and Helvetic confessions.[52] Presbyterianism therefore constituted the only good and divinely warranted form of church government, one that other Reformed churches throughout Europe already upheld. But more importantly, scripture expressly required Presbyterianism, making that form of church government an essential component of worship for which there could be no compromise.

However, Gillespie's views on church government also tended toward congregationalism, whereby the entire church body acted as the source of original power and played an active role in electing its elders.[53] This position distinguished him from his Covenanter contemporaries, including Rutherford and Baillie. According to Gillespie, the example of the ancient church and scripture demonstrated that 'the right of election pertaineth to the whole church'.[54] Relying on 2 Corinthians 8:19–23, Gillespie argued that Paul and Barnabas ordained men as elders only after the entire church approved them through the raising of their hands.[55] On these grounds, he concluded that 'the election of ministers, according to the apostolicke institution, pertaineth to the whole body of that church, where they are to serve'.[56] Regardless of where Gillespie placed the original power over the election of elders, he did firmly believe that scripture mandated Presbyterianism alone, rather than episcopacy or congregationalism.

Gillespie's belief in the *jure divino* status of Presbyterianism was not just important for the governance of the church. It also informed how he conceived of civil authority and the remit of the magistrate's *cura religionis*. For example, Gillespie directly connected church and civil government when he described Presbyterianism as partially monarchical, partially aristocratic and partially democratic. Unlike the papacy, which generally mirrored absolute monarchy, Presbyterianism best combated tyranny from within because it provided checks on its own ecclesiastical power, like limited monarchy. Gillespie also defended Presbyterianism as the only way to keep the temporal and spiritual kingdoms separate and distinct, contrary to the accusations levelled by his royalist contemporaries. He specifically addressed John Whitgift, archbishop of Canterbury (ca. 1530–1604) who argued that scriptural precedents for ruling elders only pertained to communities that did not have a Christian magistrate. According to Whitgift, the very existence of

Christian magistrates meant that the church already had a temporal head who could appoint bishops and exercise supreme ecclesiastical authority in a godly manner.[57] As a result, a kingdom governed by a Christian prince had no need for the Presbyterian form of government based upon elders. Gillespie responded by arguing that even Christian magistrates did not hold power to institute governors in the church, because the temporal and spiritual kingdoms were separate. As he maintained, 'Ecclesiasticall power is distinct from the civil, both in the subject, object, and end: so that the one doth not hinder the other.'[58] The magistrate could never intervene within the church, even by instituting bishops, because he 'seeketh not the repentance and salvation of the delinquent by his punishment (as the Presbytery doth).'[59] Ultimately, Christian magistrates could not perform the duties that God required of ecclesiastical authorities, meaning that they must not take authority over the appointment of the church's governors upon themselves.

However, Gillespie did give the civil magistrate some role in providing for church government, even if not by directly appointing bishops. He argued that the magistrate should ensure a steady supply of elders by providing for schools and colleges that could train godly men for the office. Christian princes must also guarantee that only qualified and godly men became elders by ensuring that 'a whole presbytery or company of Elders ... take triall of him who is to be taken into the number of preaching Elders', examining his piety, doctrine and fitness for teaching.[60] Furthermore, the magistrate had indirect power to convene councils, meaning that 'they ought to give help and aide, to the convocation of the same, especially when church men either will not, or can not assemble themselves together.'[61] Even though magistrates could not intervene directly in church government by appointing bishops, they could provide the proper external conditions for Presbyterianism to thrive.

Like Gillespie, Rutherford defended the *jure divino* status of Presbyterianism in two key treatises: *The due right of presbyteries* (1644) and *The divine right of church-government and excommunication* (1646). He wrote both during his time at the Westminster Assembly, where he sought to influence his fellow divines to provide for Presbyterianism in the Confession of Faith. In both works, Rutherford demonstrated that forms of church government were neither artificial nor based upon human will. As he claimed,

> neither hath the wisdome of Christ appointed a governor in generall, and left it to the churches discretion to specifie what this governour shall be, whether a prelate, a pastor, a ruling elder ... hee [must] have determined such and such governors, ruling elders, rather than a certain creature named a diocesan prelate.[62]

For Rutherford, God did not leave matters of church polity to human discretion, much like God did not leave humans to regulate *adiaphora* when faced with the silence of scripture. As the next chapter will demonstrate,

Rutherford believed that God gave human beings agency to create their own civil governments and appoint their own magistrates using their reason. But Rutherford reversed this position when discussing church polity. While civil governments were malleable by nature, church governments were not. As Coffey has observed, Rutherford had a strong conviction 'that true religion was not simply a matter of passionate subjectivity. For him, it also involved biblically prescribed forms of church government.'[63]

On these grounds, Rutherford challenged divines in the Westminster Assembly who 'acknowledge[d] the word of God perfect in general, but left particulars to the church'.[64] Their argument that 'God may instit[ut] the genus & the church may specificate' regarding church polity was 'the forme of argumentation that the papists used', particularly John Duns Scotus, Francisco Suárez, and Bellarmine.[65] God did not give humans agency to determine church government according to their own will, nor was polity an 'indifferent' matter. Instead, humans needed to seek guidance about church polity from revelation alone, much like they did for liturgical practices and ceremonies. Rutherford's rejection of episcopacy was therefore not from a negative perspective, according to which scripture did not mandate bishops so they were unnecessary. Instead, church government comprised a fundamental part of worship. As a result, God expressly ordained Presbyterianism as a means of restricting excessive royal oversight of the kirk, leaving no room for human interpretation.

Unlike Gillespie and Rutherford, Baillie demonstrated less unequivocal commitment to *jure divino* Presbyterianism, especially as he became wearied with prolonged warfare towards the end of the 1640s. Campbell documented how Baillie's views on Presbyterian government changed over the course of his lifetime, both for pragmatic reasons (such as avoiding further conflict) and for intellectual ones.[66] According to Campbell, 'Baillie was torn between his belief in the scriptural warrant of episcopacy and his hatred of the "Canterburian" bishops holding office in Scotland.'[67] Furthermore, he detested the congregational views of the English Independents and was far less amenable to allying with them at the Westminster Assembly than either Gillespie or Rutherford. Baillie's approach to church government, and especially to the threat posed by congregationalism, appeared in a pamphlet he wrote to condemn the congregationalist approach to conscience. In *A dissuasive from the errours of the time* (1645), Baillie outlined the theological errors committed by the Brownists (separatist congregationalists) and Independents in New England and the Netherlands.[68] His criticisms pertained to the primacy they gave to individual conscience as the determination for obedience to civil laws. Independents removed all civil authority over the church, for any matter of worship and doctrine could be determined 'by every mans owne conscience, his owne light and reason'.[69] Problematically, Independents also esteemed 'all matters of religion free and exempt' from the regulatory authority of Parliament.[70] As a result, they established congregations within the king's dominion without his approval, and controlled membership of their churches according to their own consciences. Without some checks upon ecclesiastical authorities by civil ones, all members would simply follow their own conscience, resulting in the proliferation of heresies and spiritual crimes.

In light of the threats posed by Independency, Baillie expanded upon and reconsidered the magistrate's *cura religionis*. He believed that the church did require some form of external regulation, either by civil magistrates or by Parliament. To combat the idea that the 'placing of a legislative power in kings or parliaments is to usurp the property and prerogative of God', Baillie gave the king and Parliament important roles in ratifying and enforcing the doctrines of the church.[71] The king should restrain 'Idolaters, Apostats, Blasphemers, Seducers or the greatest enemies of Religion' as the protector of both tables of the Decalogue.[72] He should also use his power of ratification to produce laws that would prevent Christian subjects from falling into blasphemy or heresy by following their own consciences. The church must not operate wholly independently of civil power (as the congregationalists argued), for this would allow heresy and civil instability to run rampant. Baillie therefore serves as a useful counter-example to Gillespie and Rutherford, both of whom ardently supported *jure divino* Presbyterianism. He demonstrated less sustained commitment to Presbyterianism, but he also recognised the important political implications of church government, using these debates to defend the magistrate's *cura religionis* and legislative authority. Although all three men participated in the Westminster Assembly, they reveal diverse approaches to Presbyterianism and the king's *cura religionis* among the Covenanting leadership.

As these examples have shown, conversations about church government had important political implications and were not simply theological in nature. Scottish Presbyterians sought to preserve the purity of their church from royal interference by advocating independent governance through elders and synods. The king had little role apart from punishing heretics and blasphemers externally in the commonwealth. Since God expressly required Presbyterianism, this church polity must be prioritised above all else. By contrast, many royalists prioritised absolute monarchy in the civil sphere, giving the king supreme power that likewise applied to the church. Since God mandated absolute monarchy (evident from both nature and scripture), church government should be altered to reflect this form of civil government. As a result, only Episcopalianism and absolute monarchy could coexist as the best way to ensure peace and order within the commonwealth. While not all Scots concretely adhered to these positions, their various strands of thought demonstrate key areas of intellectual overlap between ideas about church polity, civil government and political stability. Scots could not discuss the legitimacy of church polity without also considering its implications for the state.

The Power of Excommunication and Erastianism

Another problem raised by church government pertained to the question of who held authority over excommunication and who could be subject to spiritual discipline, two prominent debates at the Westminster Assembly. Excommunication, or the power to exclude an unrepentant church member from participation in the sacraments and services of the church, became an important yet controversial theological debate for multiple reasons. Excommunication was inherently intertwined with church government, for it considered how each church might exercise the power of the keys (established in Matthew 16:19), meaning the authority to bind and loose sin by disciplining recalcitrant church members. This was especially important for the Scots. As Scott Spurlock has argued, 'presbyterian government in the Scottish context was understood to be primarily about discipline', and discipline could only be carried out if the church held the power to excommunicate recalcitrant members.[73] Excommunication was equally essential for maintaining the purity of their godly commonwealth. As John Young has demonstrated, the Covenanters enforced spiritual discipline by seeking 'civil sanctions to the religious sanctions endorsed by the Church' in their drive for a godly society.[74] Additionally, W. D. J. McKay noted that, 'Faced with the task of reforming a nation, the Church had to maintain doctrinal and moral purity within her own ranks . . . It is not surprising that discipline loomed large in the thinking of leaders such as Gillespie and Rutherford.'[75]

Although the Covenanters looked to the legal apparatuses of the state to enforce spiritual discipline, they also reserved a spiritual weapon for the church itself: excommunication. The legitimacy of excommunication became an increasingly important point of debate in the 1640s because it called into question whether the church could operate independently from, and even contradictory to, the civil magistrate on matters of discipline. For Presbyterians, the power over excommunication belonged to each congregation and could even be used to discipline the king if he had been spiritually led astray. While Scots broadly agreed that the king had a duty to wield the sword to prosecute spiritual crimes with civil punishments, they strongly disagreed about whether the church reserved its own distinct power over spiritual discipline.

Conversations about excommunication in Scotland reflected broader sixteenth-century debates about the church's power over discipline. Two general approaches emerged. One model was 'disciplinarian', and maintained that the church possessed its own power to administer and enforce discipline separate from the state.[76] This position was common in Geneva where it derived primarily from the political theology of John Calvin and Theodore Beza. The second model, the 'magistratical' view, 'emphasised the prerogative of civil authorities to administer discipline within both the ecclesiastical and civil jurisdictions'.[77] Seventeenth-century intellectuals who affirmed the authority of the state over the church commonly referred to this model as 'Erastianism', derived from the writings of the Swiss Calvinist theologian Thomas Erastus (1524–1583). However, Erastus was concerned first and foremost with excommunication, not with justifying unlimited state power over the church.[78]

In 1598, Erastus authored a treatise in which he rejected the *jure divino* power of excommunication that the English Puritan George Withers (ca. 1525–1605) defended in his doctoral thesis at the University of Heidelberg.[79] According to Erastus, the state, rather than the church, should punish Christians who committed sins. He claimed that, for the people of Israel, 'the Power of punishing the Debaucheries, and restraining the looseness and licentiousness of manners, was wholly in the Magistrate.'[80] This meant that, 'in whatever Nation the Civil Magistrate is Christian, Pious, and Orthodox, there's no need of other persons, who under another name or title should set a governing us, and call us to account, or punish us for our misdeeds.'[81] Since God provided no distinction between ecclesiastical and secular discipline in Old Testament Israel, the power over discipline devolved to the civil magistrate alone in New Testament times. Authority over all discipline thus resided in the state, not in ecclesiastical bodies or individual congregations. For Erastus, the idea that the church might possess its own power over discipline ultimately threatened the authority that God assigned civil magistrates.

Erastus's views became equated with Erastianism, a theory that emerged as a key point of tension between royalists and Covenanters in Scotland who sought to clarify the king's position to the church. Most Covenanters supported the church's power over excommunication – a power intrinsically linked to Presbyterian churches as wholly independent from royal oversight – and refuted Erastus. In doing so, they equally challenged absolute monarchy by restricting the magistrate's power in the state. For example, a central premise of Gillespie's *Aaron's Rod Blossoming* (1646) was that the church retained its own power of excommunication because it needed a form of discipline distinct from civil punishment.[82] Gillespie wrote this treatise specifically to challenge the Erastian views of Thomas Coleman (1598–1647), a Westminster Assembly divine who maintained that the Christian magistrate served as the governor of the church, and that Presbyterianism robbed the magistrate of his due authority.[83] Gillespie provided a breakdown of four types of ecclesiastical authority the corresponded to the keys of the kingdom: the key of knowledge and doctrine, the key of order and decency, the key of corrective discipline and censures, and the key of ordination of church officers.[84] All four powers were distinct from the authority of the civil magistrate, who had a duty only over the outward part of man using 'the earthly scepter and temporal sword'.[85] Gillespie defended the separation of powers and the church's authority over excommunication using two-kingdoms language. As he stated,

> there is a two-fold power of external jurisdiction which is exercised . . . one by Church-Censures, Excommunication, lesser and greater, which

is not committed to the magistrate, but to church-officers: Another, which is civil and coercive, and that is the magistrates.[86]

For Gillespie, excommunication was the highest power within the church, for ecclesiastical authorities could do nothing more than excommunicate a recalcitrant member. They must then leave that person to the judgment of God – unlike civil magistrates, who might use the temporal sword to enact temporal judgments.

Gillespie used this analysis of separate civil and ecclesiastical powers to reach broader conclusions about the legitimacy of excommunication. He maintained that Christ never gave civil magistrates power over church censures because these could only be executed in the name of Christ. As a result, excommunication pertained only to those who had been specifically commissioned for the binding and loosing, or forgiving and retaining, of sins.[87] The civil sword could never enact spiritual discipline for sins related to the status of the soul. Gillespie concluded 'that no administration formally and properly ecclesiasticall (and namely the dispencing of church censures) doth belong unto the magistrate.'[88] This was especially problematic in the case of the Court of High Commission, instituted by James in 1610 to further secure his supremacy over the church. Gillespie argued that the High Commission conflated the boundaries of the two kingdoms by making temporal and ecclesiastical authority synonymous. He argued first that the king had no authority to depose ministers himself, and therefore he could not delegate this authority to others in the Court.[89] Furthermore, according to Gillespie, 'In this Commission, Ecclesiasticall and Temporall men are joined together, and both armed with the same power.' This proved especially problematic, for 'temporall men take hold of the keyes, and ecclesiasticall men take hold of the civill sword. And this monstrous confusion and mixeture, giveth sufficient demonstration that such a forme of Iudgement is not from the God of order.'[90] For Gillespie, excommunication was integral to preserving the distinction between the two kingdoms while restricting the scope of the king's temporal authority.

Rutherford agreed that the church possessed its own power of excommunication by divine right. But for Rutherford, the entire congregation did not play as active a role in the process of spiritual discipline as Gillespie had suggested. Rutherford maintained that scripture warranted excommunication because this type of censure required a type of authority different from that of the civil magistrate. He drew upon 1 Corinthians 5 – in which Paul commanded an incestuous man to be purged from the church – as a biblical precedent for the church's authority over excommunication.[91] God thus gave the church a power beyond preaching to ensure the purity of its own members. Additionally, the purpose of excommunication differed substantially from the aim of civil punishment. Rutherford argued that civil magistrates held a two-fold power: 'one to command what is good and just, another to reward and punish'.[92] But they did not have the power to execute spiritual censures that included excommunication, meaning the 'receiving into the bosome of the Church, and casting out by rebukes'.[93] God did not call civil rulers to discern their subjects' spiritual status and deem whether they ought to be excluded from the sacraments.[94] Giving the authority over church censures to the civil magistrate therefore made the magistrate a minister, conflating the aims and jurisdictions of the temporal and spiritual kingdoms.

Baillie also defended excommunication while drawing out the broader political implications of this ecclesiastical power. In his *Historicall vindication of the government of the Church of Scotland* (1646), Baillie explained that the church must retain a power over discipline separate from the civil magistrate's, in case the church needed to discipline the king himself. As a result, the king stood before God as any other individual, and he had no special authority as the head of the church. Baillie defended the Covenanters' actions toward Charles by maintaining that they did not transgress their proper spiritual authority when holding him accountable to discipline.[95] Likewise, the power of excommunication did not interfere with civil affairs. As Baillie argued, the General Assembly 'meddle with no temporal case at all', while any accusation that the 'Assembly medles with any mans life or goods' was a lie.[96] Excommunication was thus a wholly legitimate and necessary power, one which the civil magistrate could never possess because it required spiritual discernment.

By contrast, some royalist authors claimed that excommunication provided the church with dangerous oversight of the state. If ecclesiastical authorities could discipline and excommunicate the king, they might use that same process of excommunication to warrant the deposition of an apparently illegitimate ruler, much as Roman Catholics used the papal deposing power to condemn heretical ones. Maxwell specifically criticised the Covenanters for the threat that excommunication posed to civil stability. The wholly independent authority of the General Assembly meant that

> the magistrate is at their command ... If the king obey not, he is to be excommunicated; and to strengthen this, the nobilitie, gentrie, collective bodie, nay, every individual person is to concurre, to compell and censure him to the utmost of his power, to punish, to dethrone, to un-king, to kill, &c.[97]

Whereas some Covenanters viewed excommunication only as a divine instrument to maintain purity within the church, Maxwell highlighted its subversive political implications, ones that might result from disciplining the king at the behest of ministers.

The fear that the Covenanters sought church rule over the state through the power of excommunication appeared again in 1649 in a debate between John Bramhall (baptised 1594, d. 1663) and Baillie, in which Bramhall condemned the Covenanters' attempts to limit the king's sovereignty through Presbyterianism. Although Bramhall was the archbishop of Armagh and did not reside in Scotland, his writings received detailed responses from Baillie in 1649.[98] In his *Faire Warning for England* (1649), Bramhall criticised the Covenanters' perception of their authority over the church in comparison to that of the king. As he argued, in Scotland, '[t]he king hath no more legislative power in ecclesiasticall causes, than a cobler, that is a single vote in case he be chosen an elder, otherwise none at all.'[99] As a result, Scottish Presbyterians had 'trampled upon the laws, and justled the civil magistrate out of his supremacy in ecclesiastical affairs.'[100] Bramhall also levelled accusations against the Covenanters' position on excommunication, vehemently denouncing that 'Trojan horse of ecclesiasticall discipline, (A practise never justified in the world either by the Turk or by the Pope)', and asserting that their discipline was 'the very quintessence of refined popery'.[101] By allowing ecclesiastical discipline through excommunication, Scots 'will sooner endure a bishop or a superintendent to govern them, than the civil magistrate'.[102] In his corresponding *Review of Dr Bramble* (1649), Baillie denounced Bramhall for believing that all ecclesiastical power 'flowes from the magistrat, that the magistrat himself may execute all church censures . . . that the spirituall sword and keies of heaven belong to the magistrate by vertue of his supremacy.'[103] Instead, for Baillie, the power of excommunication was a rare punishment that protected the distinctions between the two kingdoms and kept the magistrate's power within its proper bounds.

Debates about excommunication in Covenanted Scotland were thus theological ones about the church's power over spiritual discipline, including the binding and loosing of sin. Yet they intrinsically reflected broader questions about the king's supremacy over the church and the meaning of his *cura religionis*. Many royalists and Erastians feared that, improperly used, excommunication had the power to become a politically subversive doctrine that subordinated princely power to the whims and oversight of church officials. They maintained that the power over discipline (both civil and ecclesiastical) comprised an integral element of the king's *cura religionis*, exercised through the civil sword. By contrast, Covenanter commissioners at the General Assembly believed that excommunication enabled the spiritual discipline of the king and ensured the purity of the kirk. The spiritual kingdom had to be insulated from obtrusive and potentially idolatrous royal interference. Ultimately, debates about excommunication provided royalists and Covenanters with another theological avenue for limiting or extending the king's sovereignty over both the temporal and spiritual kingdoms.

Conclusion

This chapter has explored multiple facets to debates about church government in Covenanted Scotland. While acknowledging that not all Scots conformed to rigid Presbyterian versus Episcopalian distinctions, it has examined how royalists and Covenanters appealed to historical, legal and scriptural precedents to defend their competing views of proper polity. Most importantly, these debates were not exclusively about the internal governance of the church: they had significant implications for civil government and theories of political power. For some Scots, scripture and historical precedent warranted episcopacy, or at least demonstrated that royally appointed bishops were lawful in the church. At the same time, God mandated absolute monarchy for the civil state, evident through nature and scripture. This meant that church government (which He left to human will and interpretation) must instead be modified to complement civic institutions and uphold temporal peace and order. By contrast, as the next chapter will show, for many Covenanters, Presbyterianism required limited monarchy in the state. Limited monarchy that prized parliamentary sovereignty allowed the church to be its own highest authority over making and interpreting confessions of faith, or regulating its own ceremonies, doctrines and government. Since God required Presbyterianism in the church, the form of civil government should therefore be adapted to uphold the true religion first and foremost. Ecclesiological concerns pertaining to the proper form of church government were thus paramount to how royalists and Covenanters thought about the respective sovereignty of Parliament and the king. To examine the political ideas that Scots advanced about absolute and limited monarchy in this period without examining the ecclesiological context to which they applied overstates their 'secular' nature. Instead, compatible forms of church and civil government could not easily be distinguished within seventeenth-century Scottish intellectual culture.

Notes

1. 'Solemn League and Covenant,' 132 (see introduction, n. 32).
2. 'Solemn League and Covenant,' 133.
3. Mullan, '"Uniformity in Religion",' 260 (see chap. 3, n. 6).
4. Mullan, '"Uniformity in Religion",' 249.
5. Campbell, *Life and Works of Robert Baillie*, 85–113 (see introduction, n. 54); Hunter Powell, *The Crisis of British Protestantism: Church Power in the Puritan Revolution, 1638–44* (Manchester: MUP, 2015); Coffey, *Politics, Religion and the British Revolutions*, 202–19 (see introduction, n. 54).
6. Powell, *Crisis of British Protestantism*, 35–57.
7. Chad Van Dixhoorn, 'Presbyterian Ecclesiologies at the Westminster Assembly,' in *Church Polity and Politics in the British Atlantic World, c. 1635–66*, eds Elliot Vernon and Hunter Powell (Manchester: MUP, 2020), 106.
8. Elliot Vernon, introduction to *Church Polity and Politics*, 1.
9. Vernon, introduction to *Church Polity and Politics*, 4.
10. James Kirk, *Patterns of Reform: Continuity and Change in the Reformation Kirk* (Edinburgh: T. & T. Clark, 1989); Gordon Donaldson, *Scotland: James V – James VIII* (Edinburgh: Mercat Press, 1987); Gordon Donaldson, *The Scottish Reformation* (Cambridge: CUP, 1960).

11. MacDonald, 'Church and State,', 615 (see chap. 1, n. 44).
12. *RSP*, 1592/4/26 (accessed 27 July 2023).
13. For a comprehensive overview of these ecclesiastical changes, see MacDonald, 'Church and State, 612–20.
14. MacDonald, 'James VI and I,' 889 (see introduction, n. 1).
15. Jenny Wormald, *Court, Kirk, and Community: Scotland, 1470–1625* (London: Edward Arnold, 1981), 145–66.
16. John R. Young, *The Scottish Parliament, 1639–1661: A Political and Constitutional Analysis* (Edinburgh: John Donald, 1996), 19–24; Church of Scotland, 'Act of the Assembly at Glasgow, Sess. 16, December 8, 1638, declaring Episcopacie to have been abjured by the Confession of Faith, 1580, and to be removed out of this Kirk,' in *Acts of the General Assembly of the Church of Scotland 1638–1842*, ed. Church Law Society (Edinburgh: Edinburgh Printing & Publishing Co., 1843), 1–35.
17. Maxwell, *Sacro-sancta*, 138 (see chap. 3, n. 60).
18. NLS, Wodrow Quarto LXXVI, no. 5, fo. 61.
19. John Forbes, *A peaceable warning, to the subjects in Scotland* (Aberdeen, 1638), 19.
20. John Corbet [Lysimachus Nicanor], *The epistle congratulatorie of Lysimachus Nicanor of the Societie of Jesu, to the Covenanters in Scotland* (London, 1640), 7.
21. Thomas Cartwright, *A replye to an ansvvere made of M. Doctor Vvhitgifte Against the admonition to the Parliament* (n.p., 1573), 173–5; Peter Lake, *Anglicans and Puritans? Presbyterianism and English Conformist Thought from Whitgift to Hooker* (London: Unwin Hyman, 1988), 55.
22. Corbet, *Ungirding*, 47 (see chap. 1, n. 61).
23. Pope Gregory VII, 'The Dictate of the Pope,' in *Select Historical Documents of the Middle Ages*, ed. and trans. Ernest F. Henderson (London: G. Bell, 1903), 366–7.
24. William Barclay, *De potestate papae; an & quaetenus in reges & principes seculars ius & imperium habeat* (Hanover, 1609).
25. For an English translation, see Robert Bellarmine, 'On the Temporal Power of the Pope. Against William Barclay,' in Robert Bellarmine, *On Temporal and Spiritual Authority*, ed. and trans. Stefania Tutino (Indianapolis: Liberty Fund, 2012).
26. Bellarmine, 'On the Temporal Power,' ch. 3.
27. Corbet, *Epistle congratulatorie*, 5.
28. Corbet, *Ungirding*, 17.
29. Corbet, *Ungirding*, 17.
30. Corbet, *Ungirding*, 17.
31. Corbet, *Ungirding*, 38.
32. Maxwell, *Sacro-sancta*, sig A2r.
33. Maxwell, *Sacro-sancta*, 62.
34. Maxwell, *Sacro-sancta*, 63.
35. Maxwell, *Sacro-sancta*, 15.
36. Maxwell, *Sacro-sancta*, 66.
37. Maxwell, *Sacro-sancta*, 16.
38. Francis Oakley, *The Conciliarist Tradition: Constitutionalism in the Catholic Church, 1300–1870* (Oxford: OUP, 2003), 15–17, 39–43.
39. John Mair's 'Disputatio de authoritate concilli supra pontificem maximum' was first printed in his *Matthaeum ad literam expositio* (Paris, 1518). It was

reprinted later as: John Mair, 'Disputatio de authoritate concilii, supra pontificem maximum,' in Jean Gerson, *Opera omnia, novo ordine digesta, & in V. Tomos distributa*, ed. Ellies Du Pin, vol. 2 (Antwerp, 1702), 1,131–45. For an overview of Mair's ideas on conciliarism, see James K. Cameron, 'The Conciliarism of John Mair: A Note on the *Disputation on the Authority of a Council*,' *Studies in Church History Subsidia* 9 (1991): 429–35; Francis Oakley, '"Anxieties of Influence": Skinner, Figgis, Conciliarism and Early Modern Constitutionalism,' *Past & Present*, no. 151 (1996): 60–110.
40. Francis Oakley, 'On the Road from Constance to 1688: The Political Thought of John Major and George Buchanan,' *Journal of British Studies* 1, no. 2 (1962): 1–31.
41. Maxwell, *Sacro-sancta*, 12.
42. Maxwell, *Sacro-sancta*, 16.
43. Baillie, *An historicall vindication*, 64 (see chap. 2, n. 68).
44. Baillie, *An historicall vindication*, 64.
45. Coffey, *Politics, Religion and the British Revolutions*, 199 (see introduction, n. 54).
46. For a helpful overview of Gillespie's writings on *jure divino* Presbyterianism, see James Kevin Culberson, '"For Reformation and Uniformity": George Gillespie (1613–1648) and the Scottish Covenanter Revolution' (PhD Diss., University of North Texas, 2003), 111–15.
47. Gillespie, *A dispute*, 160 (see chap. 2, n. 30).
48. Gillespie, *A dispute*, 161–2.
49. Gillespie, *A dispute*, 162.
50. Gillespie, *A dispute*, 161.
51. Joseph Hall, *Episcopacie by divine right asserted* (London, 1640).
52. George Gillespie, *An assertion of the government of the Church of Scotland* (Edinburgh, 1641), 73–75.
53. Van Dixhoorn, 'Presbyterian Ecclesiologies,' 112–13.
54. Gillespie, *A dispute*, 164.
55. Gillespie, *A dispute*, 166.
56. Gillespie, *A dispute*, 166.
57. John Whitgift, 'The Defence of the Answer to the Admonition, Against the Reply of Thomas Cartwright: Tractates I–VI,' in *The Works of John Whitgift, D.D.*, ed. John Ayre, vol. 1 (Cambridge: CUP, 1851), 417–25. See also: Dan Eppley, 'Defender of the Peace: John Whitgift's Proactive Defense of the Polity of the Church of England in the Admonition Controversy,' *Anglican and Episcopal History* 68, no. 3 (1999): 312–35.
58. Gillespie, *An assertion*, 88–9.
59. Gillespie, *An assertion*, 89.
60. Gillespie, *A dispute*, 163.
61. Gillespie, *A dispute*, 174.
62. Samuel Rutherford, *The due right of presbyteries; or, a peaceable plea, for the government of the Church of Scotland* (London, 1644), 155.
63. Coffey, *Politics, Religion and the British Revolutions*, 188.
64. Chad Van Dixhoorn, ed., *The Minutes and Papers of the Westminster Assembly 1643–1652*, vol. 2: *Minutes, Sessions 45–119, 155–198 (1643–1644)* (Oxford: OUP, 2012), 400.
65. Van Dixhoorn, *Minutes and Papers*, 411.
66. Campbell, *Life and Works of Robert Baillie*, 85–113; Alexander D. Campbell,

'Episcopacy in the Mind of Robert Baillie, 1637–1662,' *SHR* 93, no. 1 (2014): 29–55.
67. Campbell, 'Episcopacy,' 34.
68. The Brownists were a group of early separatists from the Church of England who followed Robert Browne (c. 1550–1633) after he seceded from the Church of England and established a congregational church in Middelburg in the Netherlands in 1581. The Pilgrims who travelled on the *Mayflower* were also part of the Brownist movement.
69. Robert Baillie, *A dissuasive from the errours of the time* (London, 1645), 127.
70. Baillie, *A dissuasive*, 127.
71. Baillie, *A dissuasive*, 127.
72. Baillie, *A dissuasive*, 129.
73. R. Scott Spurlock, 'Polity, Discipline and Theology: The Importance of the Covenant in Scottish Presbyterianism, 1560–c.1700,' in Vernon and Powell, *Church Polity and Politics*, 88.
74. John R. Young., 'The Covenanters and the Scottish Parliament, 1639–51: The Rule of the Godly and the "Second Scottish Reformation,"' in *Enforcing Reformation in Ireland and Scotland, 1550–1700*, eds Elizabethanne Boran and Crawford Gribben (Farnham: Ashgate, 2006), 131–58, at 134.
75. W. D. J. McKay, *An Ecclesiastical Republic: Church Government in the Writings of George Gillespie* (Carlisle: Paternoster Press, 1997), 17.
76. Jordan J. Ballor, 'Church Discipline and Excommunication: Peter Martyr Vermigli among the Disciplinarians and the Magistraticals,' *Reformation & Renaissance Review* 15, no. 1 (2013): 102.
77. Ballor, 'Church Discipline and Excommunication,' 101.
78. John Neville Figgis, 'Erastus and Erastianism,' *Journal of Theological Studies* 2, no. 5 (1900): 66.
79. Figgis, 'Erastus and Erastianism,' 73.
80. Thomas Erastus, *A treatise of excommunication wherein 'tis fully, learnedly, and modestly demonstrated that there is no warrant . . . for excommunicating any persons . . . whilst they make an outward profession of the true Christian faith* (London, 1682), 75.
81. Erastus, *A treatise of excommunication*, 77.
82. Gillespie, *Aaron's rod*, especially bk 1, chs 4–7 (see chap. 1, n. 72).
83. Thomas Coleman, *Hopes deferred and dashed* (London, 1645).
84. Gillespie, *Aaron's rod*, 186.
85. Gillespie, *Aaron's rod*, 185.
86. Gillespie, *Aaron's rod*, 185.
87. Gillespie, *Aaron's rod*, bk 2, ch. 8.
88. Gillespie, *Aaron's rod*, 247.
89. Gillespie, *Aaron's rod*, 195.
90. Gillespie, *Aaron's rod*, 197.
91. Rutherford, *The Divine right of church government and excommunication* (London, 1646), 238.
92. Rutherford, *Divine right of church government*, 220.
93. Rutherford, *Divine right of church government*, 220.
94. Rutherford, *Divine right of church government*, 396–7.
95. Baillie, *An historicall vindication*, 19.
96. Baillie, *An historicall vindication*, 33.

97. Maxwell, *Burthen of Issachar*, 18 (see chap. 2, n. 77).
98. Jack Cunningham, *James Ussher and John Bramhall: The Theology and Politics of Two Irish Ecclesiastics of the Seventeenth Century* (Aldershot: Ashgate, 2007), 23–40; John McCafferty, *The Reconstruction of the Church of Ireland: Bishop Bramhall and the Laudian Reforms, 1633–1641* (Cambridge: CUP, 2007).
99. John Bramhall, 'A faire warning to take heed of the Scotish discipline, as being of all others most injurious to the civil magistrate, most oppressive to the subject, most pernicious to both (1649),' in John Bramhall, *Three Treatises Concerning the Scotish Discipline* (Hagh, 1661), 6.
100. Bramhall, 'A faire warning,' 8.
101. Bramhall, 'A faire warning,' 3.
102. Bramhall, 'A faire warning,' 4.
103. Robert Baillie, *A review of Doctor Bramble, late Bishop of Londonderry, his Faire warning against the Scotes discipline* (Delft, 1649), 21.

CHAPTER FIVE

Covenanter Political Thought

Given the wide range of concerns that Scottish royalists expressed about the dangers of the Covenanting movement (especially for civil stability and absolute monarchy), the Covenanters had to work especially hard to legitimise resistance to the king. They also had to justify imposing Presbyterianism across the British Isles by making this form of church polity appear less politically subversive than their royalist contemporaries believed. The Covenanting leadership therefore undertook a propaganda campaign to garner support at home and in England, resulting in a greater number of Covenanter works that articulated distinct political theories. This chapter analyses Covenanter political ideas, especially their defences of limited monarchy. It argues that their emphasis on parliamentary sovereignty allowed them to restrict the king's power over church and state while pushing through their vision of a Reformed, godly commonwealth. It first examines how they engaged favourably with natural law and human reason to encourage political participation. It then considers their ideas about the origins of government and the election of authorities, followed by a discussion of the role that covenantal obligations and the coronation oath played in the Covenanters' theoretical defence of limited monarchy. This analysis demonstrates that, unlike many of their royalist contemporaries, the Covenanting leadership believed that God retained full sovereignty over the state but that he delegated power to subjects so that they could make and unmake their own governments. This perspective ultimately enabled Covenanter leaders to increase parliamentary sovereignty and prescribe more active duties for Christian subjects in politics, ones that even came to include resistance on behalf of the true religion.

Despite being staunchly Reformed, many Covenanters developed their political ideas in the context of cross-confessional debates about the origin and purpose of civil governments. They did not make arguments for limited monarchy and parliamentary sovereignty from within an emerging Reformed intellectual tradition alone. Instead, they engaged with Catholic scholastic ideas about liberty and the natural origins of government to increase the space for human agency in political life. They also merged traditionally Catholic ideas about the creation of civil governments with a Reformed emphasis on the threefold covenant between God, king and subjects as the ultimate standard for contractual rule.

Many scholars have situated Covenanting political ideas within broader European Reformed intellectual traditions.[1] For example, Shaun de Freitas placed Samuel Rutherford within a tradition of constitutional thought advanced by a range of Reformed authors.[2] He argued that Rutherford's *Lex, Rex* and Johannes Althusius's *Politics* represented the 'two most comprehensive political and legal works of the theologico-political federalist tradition stemming from the sixteenth and seventeenth centuries', a tradition that also laid foundations for modern constitutionalism.[3] Others have analysed distinctively Scottish elements within the political thought of the Scottish Covenanters, such as their views on elective monarchy, the nobility or the parliamentary Estates. Edward Cowan argued that Scottish noblemen 'had claimed the right to control their kings since time immemorial', making the Covenanters' resistance 'initially both aristocratic and conservative'.[4] Ian Michael Smart highlighted a different element of their resistance theory, stating that the National Covenant 'was in effect a declaration of the monarch's subordination to the rule of law'.[5] This position enabled Covenanters to implement their distinctly 'presbyterian concept of constitutional monarchy', one based upon a mutual contract between the king and the people.[6] Yet the cross-confessional elements of Covenanting political theory, especially their deep similarities to Catholic scholastic ideas, have received only limited analysis.[7]

Simultaneously, Scots experienced the revival of Hebrew texts and engagement with the idea of the Hebrew Republic.[8] This tradition informed the writings of multiple theorists within the British Isles, such as John Selden (1584–1654), James Harrington (1611–1677) and Thomas Hobbes (1588–1679).[9] Like Reformed communities elsewhere in Europe, Scottish authors turned toward Jewish writings for an example of the theological-political covenant. They also increasingly referenced the Old Testament as a model for contemporary political commonwealths. As Graeme Murdock observed, Reformed clergy throughout Europe pursued 'Hebraic patriotism with extraordinary zeal, offering thoroughgoing applications of comparisons with ancient Israel to their congregations.'[10] Scotland was no exception. For example, John Coffey has shown that '[r]eferences to the New Testament in Rutherford's political theory were overwhelmingly outnumbered by those to the Old Testament', likely as a reflection of his belief that 'Israel was still to be a model for contemporary Christian nations.'[11] Yet the influence of non-Protestant traditions remains a notable gap in our understanding of Covenanter leaders' intellectual formation.

Scottish Covenanters also drew upon an Aristotelian interpretation of human rationality commonly advanced by neo-Thomists in the School of Salamanca. That Reformed intellectuals engaged so favourably with this tradition is unsurprising given their education. Although the Scottish universities served as vehicles for inculcating Reformed orthodoxy across society after the Reformation in 1560, they were not bastions of repressive or backwards Calvinist theology.[12] They instead operated at the vanguard of philosophical and theological debates taking place across Europe, and their curricula and methodologies crossed confessional boundaries.[13]

Additionally, many Covenanters attended or taught at Scottish universities where they would have acquired an awareness of key treatises written by their Catholic scholastic contemporaries. Library catalogues and lists of book donations from the Universities of Edinburgh and St Andrews, two institutions with which Rutherford was affiliated, show holdings of multiple works by Catholic scholastic authors, including but not limited to Robert Bellarmine, Francisco Suárez and Francisco de Vitoria.[14] University education therefore gave Scots substantial opportunities to think about legal, philosophical and political ideas from beyond a Protestant tradition that they strategically adapted to their own context.

Roman Catholic authors also had different priorities in post-Reformation Europe, ones which made them particularly useful sources for the Scottish context. Whereas Reformed authors frequently authored treatises justifying resistance in terms of inferior magistrates, self-defence and protection of the true religion, Catholic scholastics strategically expanded upon legal categories. Missionary work and imperial expansion required them to develop a set of moral standards that they could apply to non-Christian peoples and nations.[15] They accordingly developed classical and medieval natural law traditions to a greater extent than many contemporary Reformed writers. As a discipline, law was also not strictly confessional. Protestants could thus draw upon these legal categories without the confessional baggage that permeated theological discourse. For these reasons, we should view Covenanters' engagement with Catholic scholastic political theory as a strategic and intentional choice, not as an accidental or coincidental one, or as a simple polemical strategy to discredit their enemies as 'Jesuitical' or 'popish'.

The favourable use of Catholic scholastic political ideas is most apparent in Rutherford's case. As Coffey observed, the revival of scholasticism in the Spanish universities deeply informed the political ideas that Rutherford advanced in *Lex, Rex* (1644).[16] His education enabled him to employ Catholic ideas about equality, the origins of government and the election of authorities strategically, ones that increased the space for human activity (rather than direct divine agency) in political life. Notably, however, he merged these ideas with a traditional Reformed emphasis on a threefold covenant between God, king and subjects as the standard for a good ruler. As a result, this chapter focuses primarily on how Covenanter authors engaged with Catholic scholastic political theory to supplement the wealth of pre-existing scholarship on their relationship to Reformed intellectual traditions in continental Europe. In doing so, it opens new lines of enquiry into Covenanting political thought by better accounting for how the movement's leaders integrated Catholic scholastic ideas into a traditionally Protestant view of the godly commonwealth.

Simultaneously, this analysis challenges the notion that the Covenanters were fundamentally theocratic in seeking church rule over the state.[17] I. B. Cowan claimed that Covenanter leaders 'preferred a presbyterian theocracy to defence of kingship', while other scholars have characterised them as exceedingly zealous for the supremacy of the church, especially when compared to their English Puritan contemporaries.[18] But this perspective is based predominantly on a misinterpretation of the term 'theocracy', which, for early modern Scots, would have implied the direct rule of the state by God himself (as in Old Testament Israel) or by an ecclesiastical representative, such as a priest. It also echoes a contemporary royalist interpretation of Presbyterianism (as demonstrated in the previous chapter) without understanding how the Covenanting leadership perceived their own agenda.

Instead, this chapter shows that their legal-constitutional and religious ideas coexisted harmoniously to produce a comprehensive view of the godly commonwealth. The supposedly theocratic Covenanters delineated and respected the boundaries between the temporal and spiritual kingdoms just as much as their royalist contemporaries. They also viewed the temporal kingdom as a place governed by reason and natural law, not by divine command alone. However, their emphasis on natural law did not mean that they were 'secular' in the political ideas that they advanced either. Although some elements of their political thought have been regarded as precursors to the modern state (such as constitutionalism, consent of the governed and elective government), they advanced these ideas within an overarching covenantal context as they tried to attain a godly commonwealth. Using the Covenanters as an example of Reformed political thought more broadly, this chapter therefore reconsiders the respective positions of Catholicism and Calvinism in shaping the political ideas commonly associated with secularisation and modernity.

Human Reason and Natural Law

First and foremost, Reformed intellectuals did not uniformly believe that the Calvinist doctrine of total depravity meant humans could not contribute positively to civil society through their reason. Indeed, many respected the ability of humans to discern natural law and govern political associations without the aid of additional revelation. This was important for political thought because it challenged the notion that government had to be exclusively coercive to restrain human wickedness. Sin and a broken relationship with God did not prevent humans from comprehending the moral injunctions of natural law, although their sinful nature prevented them from following these commands fully. For example, Richard Muller has shown that the doctrine of total depravity did not correlate to a negative perception of human rationality among the Reformed.[19] Theologians believed that humans could discern the natural law and use it to contribute positively to political life through their own agency. Claiming that they rejected this ability – as Carl Friedrich and John F. H. New have done – misapplies the doctrine of total depravity.[20] Instead, this theological doctrine applied more accurately to the ability of human beings to understand the spiritual kingdom and God's workings within it. As Coffey observed, total depravity 'implied nothing about [man's] ability to establish complex forms of human association.'[21] Instead, Christians and non-Christians alike could create political associations that functioned according to the moral injunctions and standards of justice derived from natural law.

This rather favourable impression of human reason and natural law appeared in multiple Covenanting works from this period. In his *Dispute against the English-popish ceremonies*, George Gillespie addressed the difference between natural law (that knowable by reason) and divine law (that knowable by revelation). He first described the difference between natural law before the Fall (*ius Divinum naturale*) and natural law after the Fall (*ius naturale*) as a way to describe the illegitimacy of Charles's ecclesiastical reforms. The *ius naturale*, or the law that God imprinted in human nature, showed humans how 'they may be ledde to that good, which is in the end proprotionat to nature.'[22] After the Fall, this end included the preservation of humankind through procreation and self-defence. But the law of nature could also teach creatures that 'there is a God, and that this God is to be worshiped.'[23] For this reason, a human being 'should not live as a reasonlesse creature' and must instead 'live honestly and virtuously, that he should observe order & decency in all his actions.'[24]

By contrast, the *ius Divinum* (divine law) was inspired. Drawing upon Thomas Aquinas's categorisation of law, Gillespie clarified that divine law alone guided humans '*ad finem supernaturalem*', or toward 'a supernaturall good, which is an end exceeding the proportion of nature'.[25] Although humans still exercised reason in the natural world, original sin damaged their relationship with God so that they could not discern supernatural matters. For example, natural law might teach humans to recognise the moral principles that would guide them toward their common good (peace and order) or show them that God existed. But only divine law could teach them the proper way to worship. While Gillespie thus gave original sin and human depravity an important role in damaging human knowledge of the spiritual kingdom, it did not fundamentally corrupt their ability to form and participate in political associations.

Alexander Henderson employed natural law in a similar way when he argued that nature proved the existence of God, but that scripture alone dictated how He ought to be worshipped. In a fast-day sermon preached to the House of Lords on 28 May 1645, Henderson stated that, 'Nature which teacheth that there is a Godhead, leadeth also to a providence, but the other is a grand mystery, which cannot be conceived but supernaturally.'[26] Like Gillespie, Henderson suggested that humans could not comprehend any matters related to the spiritual kingdom without special revelation, but they could discern their temporal end and follow natural law by reason. Total depravity thus applied to the spiritual kingdom alone. These treatments of natural law by Gillespie and Henderson reveal that both Covenanter leaders were interested in the ends of the two kingdoms, especially the extent to which humans could fulfil their temporal duties through their own reason and agency.

However, natural law was not a 'secular' category for Covenanter leaders. As Chapter 1 demonstrated, some scholars have argued that Lutheran two-kingdoms theology established a fully secular temporal kingdom governed by natural law alone. This position is equally erroneous when applied to Reformed Scots for whom the temporal kingdom derived from God as the creator. God authored natural law and revealed it to Christians and non-Christians through common grace. As Rutherford argued in *Lex, Rex*, 'What is warranted by the direction of natures light is warranted by the Law of Nature, and consequently by a divine Law; for who can deny the Law of nature to be a divine Law?'[27] Rutherford further explained that, '[A] great part of the Bible, of the Decalogue, is Printed in the reasonable soul of man', meaning that God's moral commandments could be discerned through reason unaided by revelation, but that God remained the source.[28] This framework for natural and divine law reflected the two-kingdoms distinction between the temporal and spiritual, and it enabled many Reformed Covenanter leaders to look favourably upon the ability of humans to participate in politics using their reason (despite their belief in the theological doctrine of total depravity) as affecting the human relationship to God.

Nevertheless, not all Reformed theologians looked as favourably upon human rationality and its capabilities as the Covenanters did. Indeed, comparing Covenanter and royalist political thought highlights a key tension in Reformed theories more broadly. As Chapter 1 demonstrated, on the one hand, an Aristotelian strand emphasised the human proclivity for rational political engagement (common among the Catholic scholastics). On the other hand, an Augustinian view of politics emphasised total depravity and coercive government. This tension played out in the Scottish context with direct political implications. Whereas many Scottish royalists drew upon the latter Augustinian perspective to defend the coercive nature of government to preserve peace and order, Covenanter leaders instead embraced Aristotelian ideas about human engagement in political life (primarily advanced by intellectuals in the School of Salamanca) to prioritise human agency. As the rest of this chapter will demonstrate, these favourable perspectives on human reason had important implications for how the Covenanters limited direct divine agency over rulers and governments while extending human agency.

Liberty and Government

The emphasis on the positive contribution of human reason to the civil state helped the Covenanters to increase human agency over the establishment of governments, ultimately leading to their defences of limited monarchy and parliamentary sovereignty. While Henderson and Gillespie made only brief observations about human reason and natural law to explain worship and church ceremonies, the most thorough exposition of these ideas in a political context appeared in Rutherford's *Lex, Rex*. Rutherford was the only Covenanter leader to produce a full and comprehensive theory of politics.[29] Henderson and Sir Archibald Johnston of Wariston primarily authored short, popular works to defend resistance or subscription of the Covenant, while Gillespie and Baillie wrote lengthy ecclesiastical treatises about worship and church ceremonies. As Henderson wrote to the Aberdeen Doctors in 1638, their arguments about civil authority could 'so hardlie bee disputed and discussed, except in a large treatise', but such a defence of the Covenanters' political position had not yet been written.[30] Rutherford answered this call six years later, and it is likely that other Covenanter leaders agreed with the political theory he advanced. Henry Guthry remarked that members of the General Assembly meeting in Edinburgh on 22 January 1645 idolised *Lex, Rex* to such an extent that Buchanan's *De Jure Regni apud Scotos* 'was slighted (as not Anti-Monarchical enough)' even though the work contained 'positions, that in the time of peace and order, would have been judged damnable treasons.'[31] Coffey has additionally speculated that Wariston had considerable input into *Lex, Rex*, assisting Rutherford with the legal sections of the treatise pertaining to Acts of the Scottish parliament.[32] The conclusions that Rutherford drew about the civil state were therefore partially informed by the expertise of other Covenanters, and they also likely represented the political views of the leadership more broadly.

In his treatise, Rutherford first drew upon Catholic scholastic political thought to defend the natural origins of government against royalists who believed in *jure divino* absolute monarchy. This enabled him to work at the crossroads between an Augustinian perspective of government as a divinely mandated and coercive institution, and an Aristotelian one that viewed government as a wholly natural institution necessary for human flourishing. Rutherford began *Lex, Rex* with two broad questions about the origins of government: 'Whether Government be warranted by a divine Law', and 'Whether or no Government be warranted by the Law of nature'.[33] As Coffey observed, Rutherford referenced ten authors in response to these questions: Aristotle and nine Catholic scholastics.[34] Most of the Catholics he cited were Thomists from the School of Salamanca who looked favourably upon the role of natural law and human rationality in the organisation of civil states. In his answer to both questions, Rutherford sought to prove that government existed equally by divine command and by nature. Drawing upon Aristotle, Rutherford argued that government was natural because 'God hath made man a sociall creature, and one who inclineth to be governed by man.'[35] Just as people were born into domestic societies, they naturally desired political associations. This was not an unusual position for Rutherford to take. For example, Gillespie advanced a similar perspective when he argued that, 'The law of nature teacheth man to hold fast friendship and amiti with his nighbors, for as much as he is *Animal sociale.*'[36] Human beings were inclined to form civil societies given their sociable natures, a perspective derived from Aristotle.

However, humans also needed society for self-preservation and protection from violence, a perspective more akin to an Augustinian view of government's coercive nature for restraining sin. As Rutherford argued, 'God and nature intendeth the policie and peace of mankinde', both of which could only be guaranteed through a power of government.[37] Wariston agreed that people 'were drawn by necessitie to enter into a mutuall Union and Conjunction.'[38] As he continued, upon entering this union, subjects were 'bound not only by the Laws of God and nature, but by Our solemne Oath and subscription' to ensure that they were not divided.[39] The idea that human beings naturally gravitated toward societies because of their sociable natures (an Aristotelian concept), but that those societies provided protection against wickedness through coercive laws (an Augustinian concept), dually informed Covenanting ideas about the end and purpose of temporal government. By arguing that government had natural origins and contributed to rational human flourishing, Rutherford challenged divine-right royalists who believed that God ordained civil authorities exclusively to restrain human sinfulness. As he argued, 'There is no cause why Royalists should deny Government to be naturall, but to be altogether from God, and that the Kingly power is immediately and only from God.'[40] Crucially, if governments were both natural and divine, humans could play a greater role in how those governments functioned through their own reason.

Rutherford's argument about the natural origins of government also resembled distinctly Catholic scholastic approaches to the temporal world. Indeed, Rutherford cited a range of Catholic authors – Luis de Molina, Fernando Vázquez de Menchaca, Domingo de Soto, Vitoria and Suárez – to prove that government had its origins in nature. Many Catholic scholastics, and especially Thomists at Salamanca, had embraced the same Aristotelian perspective that human beings formed and lived in political communities by natural inclination, not just by divine command or for their own safety and preservation. Stefania Tutino and Anthony Pagden have demonstrated that Thomist authors advanced their ideas about the natural origins of government in direct response to the emerging Protestant consensus that government depended on God's grace (although Rutherford challenges the extent to which all Protestants adhered to this view).[41] For example, Vitoria argued that cities and commonwealths were 'a device implanted by Nature in man for his own safety and survival.'[42] Humans also had a natural inclination to submit to government because 'the final and necessary cause of public powers is the same.'[43] Suárez and Molina took a similar approach, stressing the human proclivity to political association and the natural origins of civil power.[44] Eminent Catholic scholastic authors – many of whom Rutherford favourably and strategically cited in the opening pages of *Lex, Rex* – thus agreed that political society and government were natural, not simply divine, in origin.

However, Rutherford departed from a Catholic consensus regarding the extent to which humans were born free and equal before entering political communities. Instead, he turned toward the work of Fernando Vázquez de Menchaca, a Spanish jurist and dissenting voice within the School of Salamanca. Although he was well-known to his contemporaries, Vázquez has generally been overlooked in modern English-language scholarship; his treatises remain untranslated from the original Latin and are less accessible. Furthermore, according to Annabel Brett, his thought placed him on the outskirts of the School of Salamanca as a 'notoriously free-thinking' jurist, making him less representative than his contemporaries.[45] However, Vázquez advanced an important voluntarist position on individual subjective rights, one which focused primarily on natural human liberty and the artificiality of government. This perspective came to greatly shape Rutherford's own political theory. For this reason, the core tenets of Vázquez's ideas about natural liberty and equality warrant brief consideration.

Vázquez developed his ideas about the artificiality of government and human equality in a treatise he wrote during his time accompanying King Philip II to the Council of Trent: *Controversiarum illustrium, aliarumque usu frequentium, libri tres* (1564). Vázquez notably diverged from the approach taken in other Catholic schools of thought, especially among the Jesuits, regarding natural liberty and equality. As Harro Höpfl has demonstrated, Jesuits generally agreed that all human beings were born free and equal, but only in the sense of freedom from slavery, not in a political sense.[46] Obedience to civil authorities demonstrated virtue, while submission to government entirely accorded with nature. For example, Suárez maintained that subjects elect their civil authorities by voluntary choice, but not as the result of freedom from political subjection or natural equality. Instead, as he stated, 'a civil magistracy accompanied by temporal power for human government is just and in complete harmony with human nature.'[47] Other Jesuits, such as Molina, also denied that government existed from the will of free and equal individuals who voluntarily ceded power to a superior upon their election.[48] Vitoria likewise rejected the artificial origins of government, claiming that, 'If all members of society were equal and subject to no higher power, each man would pull in his own direction as opinion or whim directed, and the commonwealth would necessarily be torn apart.'[49] Many preeminent Catholic authors thus maintained that humans were not born politically equal, but that they had a natural inclination toward subjection. Civil power was ultimately an extension of the human desire to live in society.

By contrast, Vázquez developed a theory of natural liberty according to which human beings could live fully and effectively in societies without magistrates. Political power was instead an artificial construction of the people's will. Vázquez began his argument on the grounds that all humans were free and equal by birth, both in the sense of slavery and in terms of political subjection. Necessity and utility, rather than natural inclination, drove humans to voluntarily submit to political authority. Although humans desired to live in societies, they were inherently prone to strife. According to Vázquez: 'There is no doubt that society and community or close friendship tend to produce disagreements . . . Indeed, human nature is inclined toward discord.'[50] As a consequence, 'the origin and creation of kings is written to have proceeded from the law of nations for the sake of avoiding wars, calamities, injustice, pillaging, violent attacks, massacres, sedition, and strife.'[51] Necessity and utility alone caused human beings to submit to authority and avoid the negative repercussions of entering political societies.

Since people made a voluntary, not natural, choice to submit to government, they could also change its form according to their own will. Humans served as the original source of political power and could subsequently recall that power if their chosen magistrate failed to serve their utility. As Vázquez wrote, 'the kingdom is not on account of the king, but the king is on account of the kingdom, and indeed [on account of] the utility of the kingdom and citizens.'[52] If the king failed to benefit his subjects, they could depose and replace him. Vázquez thus foregrounded human equality in his political theory, distinguishing him from his Catholic contemporaries. Civil power and political submission were simply not natural for Vázquez as they were for other Catholic scholars.

Vázquez's unique paradigm proved essential for the political theory that Rutherford advanced in the 1640s. Rutherford incorporated Vázquez's distinctive view of equality when he too claimed that human beings were born free from all political subjection. He specifically referenced Vázquez to argue that, 'Man by nature is borne free, and as free as beasts.'[53] On this basis, he constructed a similar stage between political association and the institution of government. According to Rutherford, outside of the domestic family unit, 'there is no law of nature agreeing to all living creatures for superiority.'[54] No human would submit to a higher authority knowing that they could be punished for their transgressions. This meant that 'all men equally are not borne kings, as is evident; and all men are not equally borne by nature under politique subjection to kings.'[55] This position usefully disproved divine-right royalists like John Maxwell who claimed that God demanded absolute monarchy through the hierarchy He instituted in nature. As Rutherford summarised, '[I]f some be by Gods grace made Kings above others, they are not so by nature.'[56] Instead, civil government required the consent of naturally free human beings, and they could fashion their own forms of government according to their will. Like Vázquez, Rutherford maintained that, 'I conceive all jurisdiction of Man over Man, to be as it were Artificiall and Positive, and that it inferreth some servitude, whereof Nature from the womb hath freed us.'[57] This position was far removed from that advanced by Scottish royalists who maintained a natural hierarchy in the world. Instead, Rutherford claimed that the political power of a magistrate was 'in its spece and kind, warranted by a positive law, and in the generall only warranted by a law of nature.'[58] Crucially, neither nature nor scripture demanded a specific form (democracy, aristocracy or monarchy).

However, Rutherford did not ecumenically endorse all types of civil government. He maintained that monarchy was the best and most legitimate form, although he certainly believed in strengthening parliamentary sovereignty. Unlike his royalist contemporaries – many of whom argued that God ordained absolute monarchy by divine law – Rutherford feared that this form of government devolved too easily into tyranny or arbitrary rule. As a result, it could not be divinely mandated. Referencing Vázquez, he argued that, 'Absolute government in a sinfull and peccable man is a wicked government, and not a power from God, for God never gave a power to sin.'[59] Its capacity for tyranny also meant that, 'An absolute and unlimited Monarchy is not onely not the best forme of Government, but it is the worst.'[60] By contrast, Rutherford claimed that a 'limited and mixed Monarcy . . . seeme to me the best government' in which Parliament played a substantial role.[61] Drawing upon examples from the Book of Judges, Rutherford argued that parliaments had the power to convene without the king's order so that they could execute God's judgment if the king would not. Rutherford most clearly explained his ideal relationship between king and Parliament when he stated that

> The speciall ground of Royalists is to make the King the absolute supreame, giving all life and power to the Parliament and States, and of meere grace convening them . . . but this ground is false, because the Kings power is fiduciary, and put in his hand upon trust, and must be ministeriall, and borrowed from these who put him in trust, and so his power must be lesse, and derived from the Parliament.[62]

Although the king might convene Parliament, the latter possessed its own power to act independently. It functioned as a representative body responsible for holding and exercising the people's original power. In this sense, it became the fountain-power for the king himself. On the basis of natural equality, Rutherford therefore argued that the people could choose their own forms of government, increase parliamentary sovereignty over the king and exercise greater agency over political life.

Although Rutherford employed Vázquez's ideas about natural liberty and the artificiality of government to refute *jure divino* monarchy arguments, he returned to a more mainstream Catholic perspective regarding the role of the people as the mediators of God's power when electing their officials. He specifically employed a Jesuit distinction between immediate and mediate power. God either ordained magistrates directly ('immediately') or indirectly by transferring his power to the people ('mediately'). This paradigm, including the terminology of mediacy and immediacy, proved essential for Rutherford's own interpretation. He first maintained that God no longer spoke to men directly as he did in Old Testament times, nor did 'God now immediately by Prophets anoint men to be Kings.'[63] God's direct agency over temporal affairs had been obvious in the Old Testament because the temporal and spiritual worlds were one and the same for the Israelites. They truly lived under a theocracy where God acted as the head of the state and chose kings to rule through prophets. Yet in contemporary times, the people did not have access to such direct divine guidance. Thus, while God ordained political authority in general for the common good of humankind, the person holding that specific office received their power through election based on the will of the people.

Rutherford returned to traditional Catholic scholastic arguments to substantiate his claim that 'power of Government is immediately from God, and this or that definite power is mediately from God, proceeding from God by the mediation of the consent of a Communitie.'[64] Rutherford's view also represented how other Covenanters conceived of the origins of political power. Henderson, for instance, stated in his 1645 fast sermon that, 'Magistracie and Civill government in the generall, is from God, and is ordained of him: But the particular different formes of Civill government are from men, and yet all of them lawfull.'[65] For this reason, 'Civill power is not absolute, but limited: First, by the will of God, whose Minister the Magistrate is. And next, by such lawes and limitations as are agreed upon to be the foundation of that power.'[66] Like Rutherford, Henderson confronted divine-right royalists by arguing that absolute monarchy was not the only legitimate form of civil government. Instead, God delegated authority to humans to lawfully choose and limit their own magistrates.

However, just because the people had greater authority over government did not mean that they lived without divine guidance. Instead, the people had to exercise their reason alongside scriptural guidelines. Once God bestowed the gift of governing and its relevant attributes on a particular person, the people needed to determine which ruler possessed that gift by exercising their rationality and verifying their decisions against the Bible. As Rutherford argued,

> I am sure he [God] doth not immediatly designe the man, but doth onely mark him out to the people, as one who hath the most royall indowments, and the due qualifications required in a lawfull Magistrate, by the Word of God.[67]

God therefore allowed human beings to use their reason to construct governments and institute their own godly kings. Parliament also played a foundational role in this process, for political authority was constituted by the 'free suffrages of the States choosing a man whom they conceive God hath endued with these royall gifts required in the King whom God holdeth forth to them in his Word.'[68] Rutherford thus incorporated the political ideas of Catholic scholastics who had a high respect for human rationality and activity in the temporal kingdom to conclude that Christian subjects mediated divine power through Parliament. While scripture advised God's people, Rutherford still relied on a fundamental respect for human rationality in political life.

This position was so important to Rutherford because he saw clear dangers inherent within divine-right royalism. If political power originated with God alone, then 'Majors, sheriffs, Provosts, Constables, are by the Prelate [Maxwell] extolled as persons, sacred, irresistible.'[69] Subjects would have no recourse if any individual in a position of power acted tyrannically, not just the king. Furthermore, the argument that every civil authority ruled with direct divine authority overturned any semblance of order within society. If all authorities claimed to be divinely chosen, the king would be unable to reprimand any of his inferiors or act contrary to Parliament. This would even mean that 'it is unlawfull to make war against any forraign King and Prince, for in invading him, or resisting him, you resist that divine majestie of God, that is in him.'[70] Defending the power of subjects to elect magistrates themselves therefore allowed Rutherford to maintain civil stability while preventing a host of tyrants from ruling in God's name.

Crucially, this position paved the way for resistance thinking. Although the people elected their magistrates, they never surrendered their original power or transferred an individual right of self-defence to the supreme magistrate. Instead, the people could always recall their original power if the king failed to rule for their good according to the laws of the kingdom. As Rutherford declared, the 'power of the king is but fiduciary, and that is (whether the Prelate think it or think it not) a sort of power by trust, pawn'd or loane.'[71] Since the king constantly borrowed power from those who elected him, he could never claim it absolutely, even after election. Rutherford drew this position to the conclusion that, since the community makes a king, 'upon law-grounds and just demerit, they may unmake him again; for what men voluntarily doe upon condition, the condition being removed, they may undoe again.'[72] Rutherford's argument again resembled that of Vázquez, who claimed that the people never fully surrendered their rights of natural equality and liberty when they entered societies. That the king existed to serve the people and could be held accountable was also commonly accepted in other Covenanters' political theory. For example, when urging the Scots to mobilise against a potential invasion by the king in 1639, Henderson wrote that, 'Princes principally are for the people and for their defence, and not the people principally for them ... The people make the magistrate, but the magistrate maketh not the people.'[73] Henderson equally affirmed that if the king failed in his covenantal obligations, especially his duty to protect the true religion, the people might reclaim their original power by taking up arms to defend themselves.

Although Rutherford drew a substantial part of his argument about the origins of government and the election of authorities from the Catholic scholastics, these ideas also appeared within Reformed intellectual traditions. The simultaneous importance of the Reformed context should therefore not be diminished or overlooked. For example, Rutherford drew substantially upon Althusius's argument that the people voluntarily constitute their kings, a point which Althusius also adapted from Vázquez. In *Politica Methodice Digesta* (1603), Althusius had defended the Dutch Revolt by promoting a federal theory of 'symbiotics' constructed around the understanding that human beings are naturally social creatures who voluntarily form societies. Althusius also presented an alternative to Jean Bodin's theory of absolute sovereignty and the *societas perfecta* that so deeply informed Maxwell's political theory (as seen in Chapter 3). According to Althusius's paradigm, humans formed associations beginning with primordial units, such as the family, and progressed to the larger unit of the commonwealth (or the *polis*). Althusius drew this arrangement of society to the conclusion that the people retained sovereignty and chose their king as the original source of his power. As Althusius stated, 'Fernando Vasquez and Lambert Daneau rightly say, and refute those who disagree, that the people is prior in time and more worthy by nature than its magistrate, and has constituted him.'[74] As a result, 'the people can exist without a magistrate, but a magistrate cannot exist without a people.'[75] While Rutherford did not construct a systematic analysis of the progression from smaller natural associations to self-sufficient ones in his own work, he incorporated Althusius's definition of sovereignty as resting in the people (who existed prior to the king), and how they voluntarily constituted magisterial authority.

Similarly, Philippe de Mornay, the probable author of the *Vindiciae, Contra Tyrannos* (1579) presented a similar perspective on the power of the people over their magistrates. As he claimed, 'the people constitutes kings, confers kingdoms, and approves the election by its vote [*suffragio*]. Indeed, God willed that it should be done this way', so that humans might exercise His original power and hold the king to account.[76] He also argued that kings 'should remember that they are born entirely by the same lot as other men, and that they are elevated from the ground to their position by the votes.'[77] The notion that kings depended upon on their subjects for their authority, and that the people existed prior to the king, thus permeated Reformed political theories. Rutherford merged this intellectual tradition with Catholic scholastic ideas about the natural origins of government and Vázquez's unique treatment of human liberty to increase the agency of human beings over the king and within political life.

Rutherford may have strategically incorporated Catholic scholastics, rather than relying on Reformed resistance theorists like Althusius or Mornay alone, to provide a level of detachment. Catholic authors had no vested interest in the intra-Protestant conflict within Britain at this time, and they served as neutral, outside observers. By showing that Aristotle and Catholic scholastics defended the same position on the natural origins of government, Rutherford could argue that Covenanter political thought had validity in wider Christian and classical intellectual traditions beyond a Reformed one alone. By drawing upon such cross-confessional political ideas – primarily ones about the natural origins of government and the human election of authorities – Rutherford ultimately demonstrated that God provided human beings with greater agency over their own political affairs in New Testament times. This analysis challenges simplistic portrayals of the Covenanters as strict biblical voluntarists who were theocratic in their political thought. For Rutherford at least – the main political theorist of the Covenanters – civil authority was not exclusively divine in its origin, and human beings should exercise their rationality to participate in political life. While scripture gave God's people invaluable advice about who they might elect, Rutherford ultimately gave human beings significant political agency in a way that counteracted the emphasis that royalists placed on God's immediate sovereignty.

Covenant and Coronation

Although civil magistrates received their power through election and the will of the people, they also had to rule according to a set of standards to retain their power. These standards were established through both a religious compact with God and a civil compact with the people, according to which the king swore to follow the laws of the land and protect the true religion. On the one hand, the king and the people jointly entered a covenant with God to serve Him faithfully by adhering to the true religion and eradicating idolatry. This covenant mutually bound subjects and the king, while each party compelled the other to perform their duty appropriately. Rutherford described this covenant when he stated that, '[T]he King is obliged to God for the maintenance of true religion, so are the people and princes no lesse in their place obliged to maintaine true religion.'[78] He drew upon multiple examples from the Old Testament, such as when the Israelites were rebuked for burning incense, to justify this type of covenant.[79] As he claimed, even when the judges (inferior magistrates) 'decline from Gods way, and corrupt the law, we finde the people punished and rebuked for it.'[80] Rutherford engaged with Old Testament examples of the covenant between God and the Israelites as a parallel for the Scots' covenant with God. This type of engagement with the history of the Israelites and their covenant with God permeated Reformed thought more broadly, especially in the Dutch Republic and in England.[81] Murdock has also shown that this typology extended to Calvinists in lesser-studied areas of central Europe, such as Hungary and Transylvania.[82] The Old Testament therefore provided a crucial model for the covenant between God and his people in Reformed thought, a model that also permeated Rutherford's own perspective on modern political communities.

But Rutherford also established a second type of covenant, or 'the sociopolitical notion of a contract of government.'[83] This covenant was predicated upon the king's oath to rule his subjects according to the laws of the land. If he broke this covenant with the people, thereby threatening the commonwealth, he could be held accountable by inferior magistrates who had also been appointed to keep the king in check. Chapter 3 demonstrated that royalists such as Maxwell and John Corbet believed that the king authored all laws, both civil and ecclesiastical, and could not be held accountable by any inferior magistrates or ecclesiastical authorities. Even if the king ruled tyrannically, contravening the established laws of the kingdom, he must be unconditionally obeyed as God's chosen ruler on earth. By contrast, Rutherford presented a different interpretation of the king's relationship to the law, one that emphasised his contractual obligations as foundational for political legitimacy.

To challenge the royalists' argument, Rutherford drew upon a different legal principle: the distinction between the directive power of the law (*potestas directiva*) and the coactive power of the law (*potestas coactiva*). This distinction meant that the king could be under the guidance or direction of positive law but not under its compulsion. While the king should obey good laws, he was not compelled to do so. Rutherford challenged Bodin, de Soto, and Gregory of Valencia (1550–1603) on this point, criticising all three as authors who 'subject the King to the directive power of the law, and liberate him of the coactive power of the law.'[84] For Rutherford, this was no better than the royalist doctrine that the king ruled with absolute power. Indeed, Vázquez had proved 'that the Prince, by Royall dignitie, leaveth not off to be a Citizen, a member of the Politique body; and not a King, but a keeper of Lawes.'[85] According to Vázquez, the king must keep and enforce the laws for the good and happiness of his people, not break them or rule above them. Since the people formed civil societies for protection and the king had a duty to carry out justice, he could not be above the very law he enforced.

These two types of covenant – one that depended upon upholding the true religion and one that depended upon the king's defence of the laws of the land and agreement not to rule tyrannically – symbolically came into being through the coronation oath. During the coronation ceremony, the king entered a contract with the people to rule for their good. For royalists, the king never formed this contract with his people, for it suggested that his authority might be limited. Indeed, Maxwell used William Barclay and Adam Blackwood to refute George Buchanan's very theory of the contract between ruler and ruled. By contrast, Rutherford drew upon Vázquez's language of the king as a 'keeper of the laws' to argue that

> Now the king, at his Coronation-covenant with the people, giveth a most intense consent, an Oath, to be a keeper and preserver of all good Laws: and so hardly he can be freed from the strictest obligation that Law can impose.[86]

In his 'Instructions for defensive arms', Henderson had similarly referenced this oath as the standard for the king's behaviour as a ruler.

Magistrates were meant to reign for the good of the people, evidenced by 'the mutual contract between the king and the people; as may be seen in the acts of parliament, and order of the coronation.'[87] Henderson also emphasised that inferior magistrates in Parliament could legitimately check the power of the king if he failed in these covenantal obligations. Covenanter political theory thus reflected multiple perspectives on greater human agency over politics, the rule of law over the king, and the election of authorities alongside a standard Reformed emphasis on the covenant that prioritised the king's *cura religionis*. Determining whether the king had devolved into tyranny depended on the very terms of the covenant established at the king's coronation, ultimately leaving the door open for justifications of armed resistance, as will be discussed in the next chapter.

Conclusion

To counteract royalist emphases on *jure divino* absolute monarchy, Covenanter leaders presented a theory of the civil state centred around greater human agency. The people could establish governments, elect kings, and hold authorities accountable to covenantal obligations by exercising their own reason in accordance with scripture. Rutherford expressed these ideas most clearly, drawing upon ideas about the natural foundations of government established by Catholic scholastics in the School of Salamanca, and upon the artificiality of political subjection advanced by Vázquez. This position allowed him to defend limited monarchy as a lawful and viable form of civil government, one that increased parliamentary sovereignty over the king. But he also merged this political position with a traditional Reformed emphasis on the covenanted nation and the king's *cura religionis*. Since human beings created governments, they could recall their original power from a king who failed to uphold the covenants he entered into with both God and his subjects during his coronation, especially if he failed to defend the true religion appropriately. In contrast to royalist ideas about the civil state, the supposedly theocratic Covenanters thus infused the temporal kingdom with a greater amount of human activity by making the king accountable to inferior magistrates and to God.

However, these limits on the king's civil authority were not simply political in nature. The Covenanters' defence of limited monarchy and parliamentary sovereignty directly answered many of the ecclesiological concerns that had been raised by royalists, as discussed in previous chapters. Their political thought allowed them to defend their proposed religious settlement for Britain and protect the sovereignty of the church from royal interference, all while showing that Presbyterianism could complement limited monarchy (which was the best and most divinely ordained form of civil government). These political ideas confirmed their belief that Parliament held the authority to act independently of the king to secure Scotland's religious settlement, and that the king had no authority over the church.

But as the next chapter will show, these political ideas only worked when subjects and Parliament remained united to hold the king accountable. With the Engagement of 1647 and the resulting breakdown of any initial Covenanting consensus, these ideas produced drastically different, radicalised approaches to the duty of resistance, defence of the true religion, and the relationship between the church and Scotland's civic institutions.

Notes

1. Coffey, *Politics, Religion and the British Revolutions*, 146–87 (see introduction, n.54); John Coffey, 'George Buchanan and the Scottish Covenanters,' in Erskine and Mason, *George Buchanan*, 189–204 (see introduction, n. 52); John D. Ford, '*Lex, rex iusto posita:* Samuel Rutherford on the Origins of Government,' in Mason, *Scots and Britons*, 262–90 (see introduction, n. 37).
2. Shaun Alberto de Freitas, 'Law and Federal-Republicanism: Samuel Rutherford's Quest for a Constitutional Model' (PhD diss., University of the Free State, 2014).
3. De Freitas, 'Law and Federal-Republicanism,' 6.
4. Edward J. Cowan, 'The Political Ideas of a Covenanting Leader: Archibald Campbell, Marquis of Argyll, 1607–1661,' in Mason, *Scots and Britons*, 243–4.
5. Ian Michael Smart, 'The Political Ideas of the Scottish Covenanters. 1638–88,' *History of Political Thought* 1, no. 2 (1980): 167.
6. Smart, 'Political Ideas,' 181.
7. Karie Schultz, 'Catholic Political Thought and Calvinist Ecclesiology in Samuel Rutherford's *Lex, Rex* (1644),' *Journal of British Studies* 61, no. 1 (2022): 162–84; Simon J. G. Burton, 'The Scholastic and Conciliar Roots of Samuel Rutherford's Political Philosophy: The Influence of Jean Gerson, Jacques Almain, and John Mair,' in Broadie, *Scottish Philosophy*, 208–25 (see introduction, n. 50); Coffey, *Politics, Religion and the British Revolutions*, 146–87.
8. Anne O. Albert, *Jewish Politics in Spinoza's Amsterdam* (London: Liverpool University Press, 2022), especially 81–114.
9. Eric Nelson, *The Hebrew Republic: Jewish Sources and the Transformation of European Political Thought* (Cambridge, MA: Harvard University Press, 2010), 21–2.
10. Graeme Murdock, 'The Importance of Being Josiah: An Image of Calvinist Identity,' *Sixteenth Century Journal* 29, no. 4 (1998): 1,044.
11. Coffey, *Politics, Religion and the British Revolutions*, 80–1.
12. Salvatore Cipriano, 'Seminaries of Identity: The Universities of Scotland and Ireland in the Age of British Revolution,' (PhD diss., Fordham University, 2018); Steven J. Reid, '"Ane Uniformitie in Doctrine and good Order": The Scottish Universities in the Age of the Covenant, 1638–1649,' *History of Universities* 29, no. 2 (2017): 13–41.
13. Aaron Clay Denlinger, 'Swimming with the Reformed Tide: John Forbes of Corse (1593–1648) on Double Predestination and Particular Redemption,' *Journal of Ecclesiastical History* 66, no. 1 (2015): 67–89; Giovanni Gellera, 'Natural Philosophy in the Graduation Theses of the Scottish Universities of the First Half of the Seventeenth Century,' (PhD Diss., University of Glasgow, 2012); Reid, 'Reformed Scholasticism,' 149–78 (see introduction, n. 50).
14. 'Author Catalogue, Seventeenth Century,' IN1/ADS/LIB/1/Da.1.1, Records

of the University of Edinburgh, EUL; 'Press Catalogue, 1641,' IN1/ADS/LIB/2/Da.1.15, Records of the University of Edinburgh, EUL; 'Donations Lists, 1619–1644,' IN1/ADS/LIB/2/Da.1.29, Records of the University of Edinburgh, EUL; 'List of books in library, 1644–1649,' UYLY105/1, Muniments of the University of St Andrews, StAUL.

15. Brett, *Changes of State*, 62–89 (see introduction, n. 72).
16. Coffey, *Politics, Religion and the British Revolutions*, 74–5.
17. Laura Stewart has also recently argued against the label 'theocratic' to define the Covenanters. See Stewart, *Rethinking the Scottish Revolution*, 20 (see introduction, n. 3).
18. I. B. Cowan 'The Covenanters: A Revision Article,' *Scottish Historical Review* 47, no 143 (1968): 42. See also Andreas Pecar, *Macht der Schrift. Politischer Biblizismus in Schottland und England zwischen Reformation und Bürgerkrieg (1534–1642)* (Munich: Oldenbourg Wissenschaftsverlag, 2011); Crawford Gribben, 'Samuel Rutherford and the Liberty of Conscience,' *Westminster Theological Journal* 71, no. 2 (2009): 368–72; Margaret Steele, 'The "Politick Christian": The Theological Background to the National Covenant,' in Morrill, *Scottish National Covenant in its British Context*, 31–67 (see introduction, n. 24).
19. Richard A. Muller, *Divine Will and Human Choice: Freedom, Contingency, and Necessity in Early Modern Reformed Thought* (Grand Rapids, MI: Baker Academic, 2017).
20. Carl Friedrich, *Transcendent Justice: The Religious Dimension of Constitutionalism* (Durham, NC: Duke University Press, 1964); John F. H. New, *Anglican and Puritan: The Basis of Their Opposition, 1558–1640* (Stanford: Stanford University Press, 1964).
21. Coffey, *Politics, Religion and the British Revolutions*, 152, fn. 31.
22. Gillespie, *A dispute*, 197–8 (see chap. 2, n. 30).
23. Gillesipe, *A dispute*, 199.
24. Gillespie, *A dispute*, 200.
25. Gillespie, *A dispute*, 198.
26. Alexander Henderson, *A sermon preached before the right honourable House of Lords in the Abbey-church at Westminster, Wednesday the 28. Of May 1645. Being the day appointed for solemne and publick humiliation* (London, 1645), 6.
27. Samuel Rutherford, *Lex, Rex; or the law and the prince* (London, 1644), 1.
28. Samuel Rutherford, *The divine right of church-government and excommunication* (London, 1646), 75; For an analysis of Rutherford's views on the natural law and the Decalogue, see Coffey, *Politics*, 153.
29. For a useful overview of the current state of Rutherford studies, see Matthew Vogan, 'Fresh Directions in Rutherford Studies,' *Studies in Puritanism and Piety* 1, no. 1 (2019): 3–37.
30. Alexander Henderson, *The answeres of some brethren of the ministrie, to the replyes of the ministers and professours of divinite in Aberdene* (Aberdeen: Edward Raban, 1638), 10.
31. Henry Guthry, *Memoirs of Henry Guthry, late bishop of Dunkel, in Scotland: wherein the conspiracies and rebellion against King Charles I of blessed memory, to the time of the murther of that monarch, are briefly and faithfully related* (London, 1702), 139.
32. Coffey, *Politics, Religion and the British Revolutions*, 149.
33. Rutherford, *Lex, Rex*, 1–2.
34. Coffey, *Politics, Religion and the British Revolutions*, 152.

35. Rutherford, *Lex, Rex*, 2.
36. Gillespie, *A dispute*, 199.
37. Rutherford, *Lex, Rex*, 2.
38. Wariston, *Reasons against the rendering*, 1 (see chap. 2, n. 71).
39. Wariston, *Reasons against the rendering*.
40. Rutherford, *Lex, Rex*, 3.
41. Stefania Tutino, Introduction to *On temporal and spiritual authority; On laymen or secular people; On the temporal power of the Pope against William Barclay; On the primary duty of the Supreme Pontiff*, trans. And ed. Stefanio Tutino (Indianapolis: Liberty Fund, 2012), xiv.
42. Vitoria, 'On civil power (*De potestate civili*)' in *Vitoria: Political Writings*, at 9.
43. Vitoria, 'On civil power,' 9.
44. Suárez, *Selections from Three Works* (see chap. 3, n. 70); Molina, *De iustitia et iure*, Tract. II, Disp. 22 (see chap. 3, n. 74).
45. Brett, *Changes of State*, 69.
46. Harro Höpfl, *Jesuit Political Thought: The Society of Jesus and the State, c.1540–1630* (Cambridge: CUP, 2004), 204–8.
47. Suárez, 'A Treatise on Laws and God the Lawgiver,' in *Selections from Three Works*, 418.
48. Molina, *De iustitia et iure*, Tract II. Disp. 22.
49. Vitoria, 'On civil power,' 9.
50. Fernando Vázquez de Menchaca, *Controversiarum illustrium, aliarumque usu frequentium libri tres* (Frankfurt, 1572), Preface, no. 121: 'Nec dubium est, quin haec societas ac communio seu familiaritas soleat parere discordias ... Est enim ingenium humanum procliue ad dissentiendum.' [All translations mine].
51. Vázquez, *Controversarium illustrium*, Preface, no. 25: 'Unde regum creandorum originem ex iure gentium processisse bellorum calamitatibus iniuriam, rapinarum, violentiarum impetus, internecionum, seditionum, rixarumque vitandarum causa scripserunt.'
52. Vázquez, *Controversaarium illustrium*, Preface, no. 104: 'regnum non est proper regem, sed rex propter regnum, vel propter regni civiumve utilitatem.'
53. Rutherford, *Lex, Rex*, 92.
54. Rutherford, *Lex, Rex*, 3.
55. Rutherford, *Lex, Rex*, 93.
56. Rutherford, *Lex, Rex*, 93.
57. Rutherford, *Lex, Rex*, 3.
58. Rutherford, *Lex, Rex*, 5.
59. Rutherford, *Lex, Rex*, 385.
60. Rutherford, *Lex, Rex*, 385.
61. Rutherford, *Lex, Rex*, 387.
62. Rutherford, *Lex, Rex*, 177–8.
63. Rutherford, *Lex, Rex*, 76.
64. Rutherford, *Lex, Rex*, 5. This likely refers to: Diego de Covarruvias y Leyva, *Variarum ex Iure Pontificio, Regio, & Caesareo Resolutionum Libri III* (Salamanca, 1552); Domingo de Soto, *Libri Decem de Iustitia et Iure* (Lyons, 1569); Suárez, *Tractatus de legibus ac deo legislatore*.
65. Henderson, *A sermon preached*, 12.
66. Henderson, *A sermon preached*, 12.
67. Rutherford, *Lex, Rex*, 12.

68. Rutherford, *Lex, Rex*, 72.
69. Rutherford, *Lex, Rex*, 22.
70. Rutherford, *Lex, Rex*, 46.
71. Rutherford, *Lex, Rex*, 155.
72. Rutherford, *Lex, Rex*, 231.
73. Alexander Henderson, 'Instructions for defensive arms,' in *The History of the Church and State of Scotland, from the Accession of K. Charles I to the Restoration of K. Charles II*, ed. Andrew Stevenson (Edinburgh: Thomas Nelson, 1840), 358.
74. Johannes Althusius, *The politics of Johannes Althusius*, trans. and ed. Frederick S. Carney (London: Eyre & Spottiswoode, 1964), 117.
75. Althusius, *Politics*, 117.
76. Stephanus Junius Brutus, *Vindiciae, contra tyrannos: or, Concerning the Legitimate Power of a Prince over the People, and of the People over a Prince*, trans. and ed. George Garnett (Cambridge: CUP, 1994), 68.
77. Brutus, *Vindiciae, contra tyrannos* (ed. and trans. Garnett), 68.
78. Rutherford, *Lex, Rex*, 98.
79. Rutherford, *Lex, Rex*, 98. See also: 2 Kings 17:11; 2 Chronicles 33:17; Hosea 4:13.
80. Rutherford, *Lex, Rex*, 99. Here Rutherford referenced Jeremiah 15:4.
81. Coffey, 'England's Exodus,' 254–80 (see introduction, n. 71); G. Groenhuis, 'Calvinism and National Consciousness: The Dutch Republic as the New Israel,' in *Britain and the Netherlands. Vol. 7, Church and State since the Reformation*, eds A. C. Duke and C. A. Tamse (The Hague: Nijhoff, 1981), 118–34.
82. Murdock, 'Importance,' 1,044–7.
83. James B. Torrance, 'The Covenant Concept in Scottish Theology and Politics and its Legacy,' *Scottish Journal of Theology* 34, no. 3 (1981): 235.
84. Rutherford, *Lex, Rex*, 234.
85. Rutherford, *Lex, Rex*, 237.
86. Rutherford, *Lex, Rex*, 237.
87. Henderson, 'Instructions for defensive arms,' 359.

CHAPTER SIX

The Evolution of Resistance Theory

At the core of their political thought, Covenanter leaders defended parliamentary sovereignty over the king, the rule of law above the monarch's arbitrariness, and the duty of inferior magistrates to resist an ungodly ruler who harmed the true religion. These ideas were all predicated upon a symbiotic, harmonious relationship between Parliament and ecclesiastical authorities in the General Assembly. The effectiveness of these ideas required both institutions to remain unified in their mutual pursuit of defending the true religion from idolatrous royal interference. The two institutions had previously collaborated to secure Scotland's Protestant Reformation in 1560, while they coordinated their efforts to protect the kirk from Charles's ecclesiastical innovations after 1638. However, a series of complex, rapidly changing events after the conclusion of the first English civil war in 1646 challenged this relationship between the two governing institutions, resulting in the fracturing of the Covenanting movement and a drastic shifting of allegiances. These events included the failure of the highly controversial Engagement (1647), the emergence of the radical Kirk Party and the Act of Classes (1649), the execution of Charles I (1649) and the coronation of Charles II (1651). These incidents forced the Covenanters to continually reassess the political theories that they originally advanced, ones that depended upon parliamentary sovereignty and the support of inferior magistrates for the true religion, as the relationship between Parliament and General Assembly deteriorated. Societal divisions wrought by the Engagement and its aftereffects thus raised new questions about how ecclesiastical authorities should respond when they could no longer rely upon the parliamentary Estates to defend their vision of the 'godly commonwealth'.

This chapter analyses how the events of the latter half of the 1640s contributed to the evolution of Covenanting political theory, especially their legitimisations of resistance by inferior magistrates. It first examines the ideas that the Covenanting leadership advanced about resistance during the Bishops' Wars and the Solemn League and Covenant. At this time, many Covenanters agreed that they lawfully responded to Charles's military aggression out of self-defence, articulating widely accepted elements of the Reformed resistance theories circulating throughout Europe. In the early years of the Scottish Revolution, Covenanting resistance theory thus thoroughly aligned with broader Protestant intellectual traditions. However, this position became increasingly untenable when inferior magistrates in

Parliament, whom the Covenanting leadership had initially tasked with carrying out this military resistance, began to dismiss or exclude the General Assembly from decisions after the Engagement. The chapter concludes by analysing the Scottish reaction to the execution of Charles I and the crowning of his son Charles II, events that again forced Covenanters to confront the radical implications of their theories of resistance while developing a relationship with a new king who might persist in carrying out their religious goals across all three kingdoms. This chapter thus argues that tensions about the nature of the godly, covenanted nation (and the best means to secure it) drove the radicalisation of Covenanting theories of resistance in the latter half of the 1640s. Scots on both sides of the Engagement controversy viewed their own allegiances as the ones which best upheld the terms of the Solemn League and Covenant (thereby enacting God's will in politics), while accusing the other side of abandoning its aims. Ultimately, the period between 1646 and 1651 demonstrates the breakdown of any initial consensus among Scots about how to attain the godly commonwealth – one established through a covenant with God and protected through the force of arms – as Scotland's civic and ecclesiastical institutions diverged.

Scholarship on the latter half of the Scottish Revolution has predominantly focused on the institutional context of the Engagement, dividing society into moderate members of the nobility (those in Parliament) and radical ministers (those in the General Assembly). Scots who favoured the Engagement have been regarded as conservatives who favoured civil stability over prolonged warfare, whereas anti-Engagers have been labelled religious zealots in the kirk who continued to push for a Presbyterian settlement across the British Isles at any cost.[1] Laura Stewart challenged this institutional perspective, arguing that it demonstrates little 'understanding of how and in what terms arguments were constructed in order to address people within and beyond central governing institutions.'[2] She has shown that the public played a key role in debates surrounding the Engagement, for Engagers had to appeal to local governing elites to implement parliamentary policy and support the war effort, while anti-Engagers had to convince Scots to reject mobilisation. Salvatore Cipriano has also demonstrated that anti-Engagers aimed to exercise broader societal influence by purging the universities of their opponents. Indeed, by being 'well positioned to exert particular influence over the universities', anti-Engagers could conduct an effective 'crusade against the Engagement'.[3] By eradicating their opposition, anti-Engagers ensured that these educational institutions remained under the control of those ideologically committed to the same goals, and that they would produce sympathetic students who could later take up positions in the ministry and government. However, the events surrounding the Engagement were far from a strictly Scottish story. Kirsteen MacKenzie has compellingly drawn out the distinctively 'British' angle to events after 1646, especially regarding the development of a Covenanted interest. The

Engagement forced Presbyterians within the Covenanting leadership to compromise with Scottish royalists as they negotiated with the king, especially given the growing threat posed by the English Independents and the New Model Army. Interactions between royalists and Covenanters, including the shifting political allegiances that followed, therefore resulted in the breakdown of a unified Covenanted interest centred around the spread of Presbyterianism across the British Isles.[4]

This chapter presents a different interpretation of the events during the second half of the Scottish Revolution by focusing on the evolution of Covenanting theories of resistance, paying special attention to shifts in their ideas about inferior magistrates and parliamentary sovereignty in response to the practical challenges they faced after 1646. Studies of Calvinist resistance theory typically focus on a set of canonical printed works or authors, such as the *Vindiciae, contra tyrannos,* John Calvin's ideas about the Spartan ephors in the *Institutes*, or the works of Theodore Beza and Martin Bucer. These works do highlight distinctive, common elements of early modern resistance theory, such as the centrality of self-defence and the doctrine of inferior magistrates. But by focusing on resistance theories explicitly as *theories*, these ideas can appear static and unchanging. However, this chapter demonstrates that the Covenanters radicalised, evolved or even wholly abandoned their previous legitimisations of resistance when they believed that inferior magistrates in Parliament, especially the nobility, could no longer be trusted to institute a Presbyterian settlement and secure a godly commonwealth. Ultimately, while most of the Covenanting leadership remained firmly ensconced in a typical Reformed tradition of resistance thinking at the start of the Scottish Revolution, the events after 1646 caused a notable shift in their understanding of the proper relationship between civil and ecclesiastical institutions.

Scottish Theories of Resistance in a European Context, 1638–1646

When the First Bishops' War broke out in 1639, the Covenanting leadership immediately began to justify their military response for royalists and sceptics, both at home and in England.[5] They appealed to nature and divine revelation in markedly different ways than their royalist contemporaries to prove two key points: natural law permitted individuals to respond in self-defence against threats to their lives, while divine law commanded Christians to actively defend the true religion against idolatry and persecution. For many royalists, such as the Aberdeen Doctors, John Corbet, William Drummond of Hawthornden and John Maxwell, nature and scripture dictated that subjects must obey their authorities, even tyrants. God alone would punish and depose wicked rulers, while subjects had the highest duty of obedience. By contrast, Covenanters argued that God commanded militant action as He gave humans greater agency over political life. With few exceptions, Covenanters viewed resistance as a divinely mandated duty that God required inferior magistrates to carry out in the face of idolatry. To make this case, they appealed to standard elements of continental European Reformed resistance thinking, such as ideas about self-defence and inferior magistrates, while articulating their duty to protect the true religion if the king failed in his *cura religionis*.

As tensions with the king escalated into the military skirmishes of the Bishops' Wars, some Covenanters first argued that natural law permitted self-defence. They emphasised that Charles had taken up arms against them first, making a perceived threat against their lives. As a result, Scots were justified in reciprocating militarily based upon the instinct for self-preservation. In 1638 (prior to the onset of the First Bishops' War), Sir Archibald Johnston of Wariston authored a short treatise for English subjects in which he described the state of the kirk and the king's threats against the kingdom. He claimed that, after the Scottish Reformation, the kirk 'did by degrees attaine to as great perfection both in doctrine & discipline as any other reformed kirk in Europe.'[6] The Church of Scotland had always been Presbyterian, but this polity proved insufferable because it did not allow kings absolute control over the church. As a result, power-hungry bishops convinced the king to institute episcopacy in Scotland and secure absolute authority over its church, leading the Scots to respond through the National Covenant. After the signing of the Covenant, 'a ship arrived at the road of Leith, carrying a great deale of munition . . . to beate down Edinburgh, and force them to undergoe any thing should bee injoyned.'[7] Charles had already acted as the aggressor against Scotland, while the Covenanters only intended to preserve their religion as it had previously been established by Parliament. Wariston claimed that the Covenanters were therefore defending the kirk's historical precedents as codified in civil law and former confessions of faith.[8] There was no sense in which they usurped the sword for the violent propagation of religion. Wariston thus began laying foundations for Covenanting resistance theory when he portrayed the Scots as entirely defensive against Charles's aggression, interested in restoration rather than innovation.

Once military engagement with the king had occurred, Alexander Henderson wrote the 'Instructions for defensive arms' (1639) to defend the Covenanters' actions, drawing explicitly upon ideas about natural law and self-defence. According to Robert Baillie, Henderson had been selected to 'draw up somewhat for the common view' a work that defended the Scots' response in the Bishops' Wars.[9] Engaging with the Doctors' criticisms that the Covenanters waged an unjust civil war, Henderson framed the military skirmishes as exclusively defensive. Like Wariston, he emphasised that their military action was 'merely and simply about our own defence and safety.'[10] After outlining the various ways that Charles threatened the lives of his Scottish subjects, Henderson concluded that, '[I]t is lawful for us to take arms for our defence against such unjust violence.'[11] Since the king advanced armies first, natural law and the instinct of self-preservation permitted the Scots to respond in like manner. As he claimed, 'If a private man be found by the law of nature intitled to defend himself ... then, much more may the whole body defend themselves against all invasions whatsoever.'[12] Importantly, Henderson did not classify self-defence as a natural 'right' to protect one's life but as an action that God permitted through natural law. Nor was this a highly individualistic right to self-defence derived from a state of nature. Instead, Henderson's perspective on self-defence still required the involvement of inferior magistrates. He carefully noted that 'difference would be put between some private persons taking arms for resistance, and inferior magistrates ... standing to their own defence.'[13] By responding to the king's aggression, the Covenanters were not a group of subjects 'standing out against law and reason, that they may be freed from the yoke of their obedience.'[14] Instead, their actions were wholly permissible by natural law, constituting neither a rebellion nor an offensive war.

Crucially, Henderson also believed that self-defence applied to the protection of the true religion as established by law. While threatening his subjects' lives, Charles simultaneously attacked the true religion itself as 'a prince labouring by arms to introduce innovations in religion contrary to the laws.'[15] Henderson accordingly merged natural law arguments about self-defence with direct appeals to the Christian duty to defend the true religion. Charles had firstly failed to rule for the good of his subjects by arbitrarily transgressing the laws of the land and threatening their lives. Secondly, he had failed to protect the true religion as established in law. Since he had broken his covenants with both his subjects and with God respectively, he could no longer be considered a legitimate ruler. The Scots' military defence against him was therefore 'no disobedience to the magistrate, but obedience to God, who ... becometh their immediate superior.'[16] Charles had lost his status as a legitimate authority, and his subjects' obedience transferred to inferior magistrates whom God commanded to resist on their behalf. Henderson thus merged language about the natural law with divinely mandated duty, portraying the Covenanters' resistance as a twofold obligation to the laws of the kingdom and to God.

An anonymous sixteen-page manuscript on resistance from 1638 or 1639 also emphasised the Christian duty to defend the true religion with arms by incorporating large sections of unacknowledged borrowing from the *Vindiciae, contra tyrannos* (1579).[17] Although the manuscript is anonymous, it began with an exposition of Hosea 5:10–11 (the same verses which open the *Vindiciae*). According to Wariston's diary, ministers throughout Edinburgh had been preaching on various chapters of Hosea during the last few months of 1637.[18] On 8 December, Wariston recorded that, 'Foranoon I went to the West Kirk, heard Mr. James Bonner on 5 Hosea 11 v., "Ephraim is oppressed and brokin in judgment, because he willinglie walked after the commandement".'[19] The manuscript itself began with an exegesis of this very verse. Additionally, on 8 February 1638, Wariston recorded that, 'Al that week I was busie on the question of defence, and by Gods assistance I wryte out my reasons and epitomized Brutus for his reasons.'[20] Wariston thus documented his direct engagement with the *Vindiciae* around the same time that he actively listened to sermons on Hosea, two distinguishing features of this manuscript. Nevertheless, the hand is not immediately recognisable as Wariston's despite the general points of similarity.

Regardless of its potential authorship, the manuscript referenced the seventy elders of Israel as a model for inferior magistrates to resist idolatry, lest the entire commonwealth be punished for the sins of the king. It began with an exposition on Hosea 5:10–11, arguing that God explicitly required the nobility, as one of the parliamentary Estates, to remove a tyrant who threatened kirk and commonwealth.[21] The author suggested that God required Scottish subjects to resist all ungodly commands issued by their civil magistrate, not just disobey them and bear the resulting punishment (as royalists had argued). Additionally, members of the nobility were bound in a covenant with God to resist a prince who violated God's law by introducing idolatry. Much like the elders in Israel had authority to resist their kings, the Scottish nobility 'have power and right to resist their prince oppressing the subjectis, violating the lawes, and destroying the commonwealth.'[22]

Notably, resistance was not just permitted. Instead, God mandated the action to prevent Christian subjects from falling into idolatry and false religion. Whereas royalists maintained that God punished sinful communities with tyrants, this manuscript conversely argued that God would punish the people if they did not root out idolatry and resist ungodly commands. Indeed, the Israelites had been led into captivity precisely because they obeyed, rather than vehemently resisted, the evil commandment of Jeroboam that they should worship at Dan and Bethel (where the golden calves were erected).[23] The author concluded:

> the people of God ought not onlie to withstand a wicked prince goeing about to destroy religion, bot especallie to provyid and prevent, that nothing by his fault or negligence creipe in secretlie that by proces of tyme may corrupt the puritie of religioun.[24]

God therefore required his people to actively, not passively, fulfil their end of the covenant, eradicating idolatry and preventing the magistrate from leading the people astray.

The author also drew directly upon the *Vindiciae* to confirm a standard element of Reformed resistance theory: only inferior magistrates – or, in this case, the Scottish nobility – could take up arms.[25] The manuscript held that the officers who represented the Israelites shared in commandment with the king and were not unconditionally subject to his power. Much as Old Testament kings could not act without the advice of the seventy elders of Israel, contemporary kings could not act without the approval of the people's representatives.[26] As a result, 'the nobilitie and estaites who represent the haill people; The parliamentes and generall meitinges' had been tasked with defence of their subjects.[27] Furthermore, the Scottish nobility would be guilty of the same sin as the king if they did not intervene to stop his tyranny. The manuscript claimed that 'if the king destroy religioun or persecut the kirk, Israel is bund to resist, which if they doe not, they ar guyltie of the same cryme and lyable to the same punishment.'[28] This manuscript thus capitalised on the Scottish constitutional settlement, requiring Parliament and the nobility to act independently of royal authority to root out idolatry and enact religious reform at God's command.

Baillie also advanced similar ideas about resistance by inferior magistrates in a sermon that he delivered on Judges 11 sometime between 1637 and 1639, notes of which remain in manuscript form. In this sermon, Baillie told his congregation that, regarding taking up arms, 'privat men may no but a stat is not privat feloing ther laues.'[29] For Baillie, the state consisted of inferior magistrates in positions of political authority who were not classified as private citizens. If inferior magistrates resisted their superiors, they would not be committing private, individual acts of violence. As both the anonymous tract on resistance and Baillie's sermon suggest, between 1637 and 1639, supporters of the Covenanting agenda called upon the nobility and Estates of the parliament to fulfil their duty to carry out resistance on the people's behalf, either as an action permitted by natural law or as a duty directly commanded by God.

These elements of Covenanting resistance theory also reflected a mainstream Protestant position on the legitimacy of resistance developed in sixteenth- and seventeenth-century Europe, one based upon inferior magistrates and self-defence. There is substantial evidence that these Protestant theories directly informed the thought of individual Covenanters as they drew up their own justifications. For example, Wariston's diary revealed that he engaged with continental European debates about resistance, specifically regarding the Dutch Revolt and the French Wars of Religion. In his diary entry from 1 February 1638, he stated that he 'read out Phil. Pareus anuer to Ovens against D. Pareus on the 13 Rom' only weeks prior to drawing up the National Covenant.[30] David Pareus's commentary on Romans 13 included a section entitled *'De potestate civili'*, or 'On the civil power', in which he argued that superior civil powers could lawfully be resisted for religion based on the word of God.[31] Pastors or others in positions of ecclesiastical authority had a duty to correct superiors who went astray, while civil magistrates were subject to divine law and to the laws of the republic.[32] Religion was therefore a justifiable reason for correcting or resisting civil rulers.

However, Pareus held that the power to take up arms on behalf of the true religion was 'constituted in inferior magistrates, not in private citizens.'[33] He also listed specific conditions which must be met for inferior magistrates to resist. For example, inferior magistrates might challenge a superior who degenerated into tyranny by forcing his subjects into idolatry or blasphemy, an approach that Wariston recognised as informing his own resistance thinking.[34] Furthermore, on 27 January 1639, when drafting justifications for resistance to Charles, Wariston recorded that, 'I set on to work to exstract my remarques out of Knoxe and Buchanan for the hypothese, and to turne Althusius reasons and De Jure Majestatis in Inglisch.'[35] These authors had all legitimised resistance by inferior magistrates in defence of the true religion, much like Pareus. Wariston's diary entries thus indicate his engagement with a host of Protestant authors from France, Scotland and the German-speaking lands preceding the drafting of the National Covenant. He consequently imagined Scotland as part of this international Reformed tradition, enabling him to contextualise the Covenanters' actions as conforming to accepted standards for resistance.

While there was some commonality in the approaches taken by Henderson and Wariston, including their ideas about inferior magistrates and defence of the true religion, not all Covenanters supported the legitimacy of resistance to the same extent or for the same reasons. For example, Baillie demonstrated a different strand of resistance thinking within the Covenanting leadership. He initially hesitated on the question of its legitimacy, acknowledging that he had drunken in 'that slavish tenet, that all resistance to the Supreame Magistrat, in anie case, was simplie unlawfull.'[36] But on 12 February 1639, Baillie told his cousin, William Spang, that, 'I inclyne now to think otherwayes ... whereto I was brought, not by Paraeus, or Buchanan, or Junius Brutus, for their reasons and conclusions I yet scunner at: bot mainly by Bilsone de Subjectione.'[37]

Thomas Bilson (1547–1616), bishop of Worcester, generally upheld the divine right of kings, but he also believed that resistance to the monarch might be lawful in some cases. In 1585, he authored *The true difference betweene Christian subiection and unchristian rebellion*, a text that likely appealed to Baillie because it maintained that resistance should not be carried out for religious reasons alone. Bilson specifically criticised the Jesuits' belief that subjects might bear arms against their civil magistrate at the pope's command. He attacked this doctrine by arguing that the 'temporall and spirituall' were two 'distinct regiments' that the Jesuits conflated by instituting the pope as ruler over both.[38] According to Bilson, princes should for their own good observe the commandments of God and listen to His messengers. But the prince could not be deposed if he failed to do so, especially not by the pope.[39] Rulers who did not act in accordance with God's commands might be warned, but they could not lose their crowns at the urging of ecclesiastical authorities.

However, Bilson did distinguish between resistance by church officials or the pope, and resistance by nobles or the commons. According to Bilson, the church must not hold the prince accountable but 'if the Nobles and commons joyne togither to defend their aunctient & accustomed libertie, regiment and lawes, they may not well be counted rebels.'[40] Bilson thus justified resistance as a defence of liberties and laws, not as a defence of religion waged at the command of church officials. Ministers could not wield the sword, for this would conflate the boundaries of the spiritual and temporal kingdoms. Yet the nobility, as representatives of the subjects, could legitimately resist a king who led the commonwealth toward tyranny. This view of resistance, as opposed to alternative forms advanced by Pareus or in the *Vindiciae, contra tyrannos*, likely appealed to Baillie because it rejected war against the king as a religious endeavour and preserved a sharp distinction between the temporal and spiritual. It therefore reflected more of a legal-constitutional case for resistance, as opposed to the religiously infused interpretations that other Covenanters employed.

In Baillie's own justifications of the Scots' actions, however, he did touch upon cases of religion. As he stated, '[W]hen a handfull of wicked Prelats doe seduce a prince to destroy himselfe and whole kingdomes, that in that case it is lawfull for the nobles and states of a land to stand upon their guard.'[41] He also argued that the Covenanters took up arms because

> subjects defence of their Religion and liberties established by Law, against the violent usurpation of Papists, Praelets or Malignants, is not the planting of Religion by arms, much lesse is it the cutting of the throats of al Magistrats, who differ in any point of Religion.[42]

For Baillie, the Covenanters did not wage an aggressive religious operation against Charles to violently institute Presbyterianism. Instead, they simply defended and upheld the laws that had already established the true religion in Scotland through parliamentary sanction. Baillie thus aligned himself with theorists like Bilson when he argued that defending the kirk's polity and doctrine was permitted because it had been established by law, not as an active rooting out of idolatry as other Covenanters maintained.[43]

After the Solemn League and Covenant, Rutherford presented a similar interpretation of Scottish military engagement with the king, an endeavour now undertaken on behalf of the oppressed people of England. In *Lex, Rex*, he maintained that, based upon the 'bonds to our deare Brethren in England', the Scots were required 'not to suffer their innocent blood to be shed, but to defend them; when they against all law of God, of men, of state, of nations, are destroyed and killed.'[44] Indeed, the plight of their English brethren meant that it would have been 'a guiltinesse of blood upon Scotland, if we had not helped them, and risen in armes to defend our selves, and our innocent brethren.'[45] Even the extended title of the book suggested Rutherford's intention to provide justifications 'of the most necessary Defensive wars of the kingdom of Scotland, and of their expedition for the aid and help of their dear Brethren of England'. Rutherford therefore defended Scottish participation in the civil wars after 1643 by extending the lawfulness of self-defence to include English contemporaries who faced persecution by the crown. In doing so, the Scots simultaneously fulfilled their covenant with God to protect and advance the true religion by aiming for a Presbyterian settlement across the British Isles.

Nuances therefore existed in how various Covenanting leaders defended resistance in the early years of the Scottish Revolution, both as warranted by the natural law for self-defence, and as a divinely mandated duty to defend the true religion against idolatry. Many conceived of the legitimacy of resistance in such a way that their action became an active obligation, not a passive option. If the magistrate corrupted the true religion, inferior magistrates must resist, lest they and their subjects become guilty of the same sin. This position initially applied to the protection of Presbyterianism within Scotland, but it came to include the defence of English subjects who equally suffered under oppression, idolatry and false religion. In this sense, the Covenanters' view of human agency in the temporal kingdom was far more militant and demanding than the passive form articulated by royalists. They saw politics as imposing a duty to maintain the purity of the visible church and seek the formation of a godly commonwealth, even by the force of arms.

Debates about the Engagement, 1647–1649

The idea that the parliamentary Estates (especially the nobility) had a divinely mandated duty to resist a king who threatened his subjects' lives and imposed idolatry formed a central part of Covenanter resistance theory, one that aligned their thought with broader Protestant intellectual traditions. But the Engagement of 1647 called this element of their political theory into question when ministers could no longer trust inferior magistrates in Parliament to defend the true religion. Instead, the Scottish parliament and the General Assembly began to work in competition (rather than in cooperation) regarding the establishment of a Presbyterian settlement beyond Scotland's borders. Between January 1645 and July 1647, Covenanter commissioners negotiated with Charles in hopes of attaining a settlement favourable to Presbyterianism.[46] In early 1645, they presented Charles with the Uxbridge Treaty, which was jointly proposed by the English parliamentarians and the Covenanters amidst worsening relations between the two nations. The treaty comprised twenty-seven articles that required the king to swear the Solemn League and Covenant and impose it upon his subjects, to abolish episcopacy, and to allow the English and Scottish parliaments greater control over the military in their countries. Charles unsurprisingly refused these terms, especially as he believed that a royalist victory could still be attained. His rejection of the Uxbridge Treaty led to the abandonment of negotiations on 22 February 1645.

Following the defeat of the royalists in the first civil war, however, Charles surrendered to the Covenanters. In July 1646, the Scots offered the king the Propositions of Newcastle which required the king to sign the Solemn League and Covenant, to abolish episcopacy in Scotland while reforming the national churches of England and Ireland along Presbyterian lines, and to give Parliament control of the army for twenty years. Charles delayed in responding, hoping that the growing tensions between the Scots and the English parliamentarians would give him time to garner support from France and Ireland. But his inaction prompted the Scots to withdraw from England and hand him over to the parliamentarians in February 1647. The New Model Army ultimately seized him from Parliament later that summer. Alarmed that Charles had been taken by the radical Independents, many Covenanters began to fear the encroachment of the heresies of Independency on Scotland, advocating the rescue of the king to reach a compromise that would protect Presbyterianism. In October 1647, three Scottish Commissioners – John Campbell, 1st Earl of Loudon (1598–1662), William Hamilton, Earl of Lanark (1616–1651), and John Maitland, Earl of Lauderdale (1616–1682) – renewed negotiations with the king while he was held at Hampton Court. But Charles derailed these negotiations when he escaped captivity and fled to the Isle of Wight, remaining as a prisoner in Carisbrooke Castle from November 1647 until September 1648. The Scottish commissioners resumed negotiations with Charles during his captivity, reaching a secret military alliance known as the Engagement on 26 December 1647.

From its onset, the Engagement proved highly divisive among the Covenanting leadership. In return for the Scots' military assistance, the king agreed to institute Presbyterianism in England for only three years (while suppressing the rise of heresies in the country). He also agreed to confirm the Solemn League and Covenant in the English parliament. However, Charles still refused to subscribe the Covenant himself, nor would he compel his English subjects to do so against their consciences. Although the Scottish parliament authorised the Engagement in March 1648, the terms of this alliance significantly divided Covenanters within Scotland's primary institutions: Parliament, the army and the kirk. As Cipriano has argued, the Engagement was not simply an unpopular alliance brokered by a small minority of Covenanting nobles. Instead, this controversial treaty 'sowed the seeds of schism in the Kirk that would sunder the Covenanting movement entirely.'[47] The majority of ministers denounced the Engagement under the direction of Archibald Campbell, Marquis of Argyll (1607–1661), while Hamilton organised noble support for the treaty within Parliament.[48] As the rest of this section will show, core points of tension emerged between Parliament and the kirk over the validity of the alliance, eradicating any previous collaboration between the two institutions in seeking the godly commonwealth. This breakdown of consensus demonstrated a changing interpretation of what it meant to be a godly, covenanted nation, in addition to a radicalisation of previous theories of resistance, as reliance upon the nobility or inferior magistrates in Parliament became increasingly unstable.

One central point of dispute that emerged about the Engagement pertained to whether it upheld or betrayed the terms of the Solemn League and Covenant which had bound the Scots to both their English contemporaries and to God. According to the Covenant, the Scots had sworn to ardently pursue 'the reformation of religion in the kingdoms of England and Ireland, in doctrine, worship, discipline, and government, according to the Word of God, and the example of the best reformed Churches.'[49] Yet the Engagement included an alliance with royalists (who had not adhered to the Covenanters' definition of the 'true religion'), while it failed to provide sufficient provisions for Presbyterianism. The king's agreement to impose Presbyterianism for only three years, coupled with his previous refusal to abolish episcopacy, convinced many sceptics that the Engagement was an inadequate compromise that abandoned the original aim of securing the total reformation of all three kingdoms.

This question of whether the Engagement betrayed the terms of the Solemn League and Covenant generated rifts between commissioners of the kirk and Parliament. As Baillie told Spang in a letter on 27 March 1648, '[A]s yet our discords increase, and are ready to breake out in a fearfull rupture both of Church and State.'[50] In particular, as ministers deliberated the Engagement's legitimacy, they agreed 'to stand to our former principles and Covenant', which required that the king agree, by his oath and consent to a parliamentary Act, to establish religion according to the Covenant.[51] As a result, Baillie recorded that they 'stuck many days on that negative expression, "The King not to be restored till he had sworn the Covenant".'[52] Additionally, they found it troublesome that malignants who had not sworn the Covenant might be admitted into the army, both terms which seemed to renege on the aims of the Covenant itself.

In a letter to Zachary Boyd, Baillie also explained why the commissioners of the kirk deemed the Engagement unlawful on multiple grounds. First, the king had not guaranteed any security for Presbyterianism, still declaring himself an Episcopalian and refusing to swear the Covenant himself. Second, the management of the war effort would be undertaken by men who did not mind religion, meaning that military power would be removed from the hands of the truly godly men committed to the terms of the Covenant. As a result, the kirk could not support the Engagement, even though many had been

> most cordiall for a Warre, against the Sectaries of England and their adherents, for the vindication of our Covenant, for the delyverance of our oppressed brethren in England, for the rescuing of our King from his unjust imprisonment, and restoreing of him to the exercise of his royall power, upon his performance of these necessare duties which the Parliaments of both Kingdomes did require from him.[53]

The Commission of the General Assembly echoed Baillie's sentiments when they argued that the king had not made convincing guarantees for Presbyterianism, while agreeing to support Charles militarily

> before security had from him, yea before applications to be made to him by his Parliaments for settling Religion according to the Covenant,

wee conceive to be not only a postponing of Christs interest to the kings, but an apparent hazzard of the subvertion of all the Ends of the Covenant.[54]

Most problematic, however, was the apparent disregard for the advice and position of the General Assembly. In July 1648, the General Assembly issued a Declaration concerning the unlawful Engagement. It expressed frustration that the kirk's previously synergetic relationship with the parliamentary Estates had deteriorated surrounding the Engagement, especially as the kirk had been excluded from critical religious decisions. For example, the commissioners claimed that 'the liberties of the Kirk have been grievously encroached upon' in the early months of 1648.[55] Parliament and the Committee of Estates had issued multiple declarations 'containing severall things highly concerning religion, without the advice or consent of the Generall Assembly or their Commissioners, which was a ground of protestation to divers Members of Parliament, who have been most zealous and active in the cause.'[56] Furthermore, the kirk should have been included in any decisions about an alliance with the king, for 'The Coronation Oath doth also suppose the antecedent judgement of the Kirk, as the proper and competent judge who are enemies to true religion, and who are not.'[57] When Parliament secured the Engagement with the king, although seemingly a temporal alliance, they failed to recognise the kirk's role in ascertaining and confirming if he was 'godly magistrate' who could best protect and advance the true religion.

These grievances marked a critical turning point in relations between the two institutions as the commissioners of the General Assembly perceived their authority being subverted by Parliament and some nobility who no longer shared their commitment to the creation of a godly commonwealth through the terms of the Covenant. The parliament that met on 10 March 1648 – one which generally favoured the Engagement – appointed Robert Balfour, Sir Robert Innes and Sir Alexander Wedderburn to meet with the commissioners of the kirk and 'show them that it is the desire of the parliament that there might be a mutual correspondence between church and state in this great business so far as concerns religion.'[58] Nevertheless, the commissioners maintained that they had been omitted from critical decisions that directly affected Scotland's religious settlement and thus required the input of its ecclesiastical authorities. As they ultimately declared,

> The wars of God's people are called the wars of the Lord . . . But if the principall end of this present Engagement were for the glory of God, how comes it to passe, that not so much as one of the desires of the Kirk, for the safety and security of religion in the said Engagement, is to this day satisfied or granted?[59]

Knowing that they would need to convince sceptics to support the Engagement, on 11 April, the Scottish parliament passed an Act defending their proposed invasion of England and alliance with the king.[60] They described various breaches of the Covenant between England and Scotland and included a strict demand for reparations. The Act claimed that, in England, 'instead of reformation and defence of religion, that reformation by which the covenant ought to be endeavoured is resisted and hindered.'[61] It argued that the English Independents had preserved and tolerated prelacy and heresy rather than abolish these evils according to the Covenants' terms. It equally blamed the Independents for the proliferation of the 'most horrid blasphemies, heresies, and schisms' in the country, while they failed to maintain 'the rights and privileges of parliament and preserving of his majesty's person and authority in defence of the true religion and liberties of the kingdoms.'[62] As a result, members of the Scottish parliament declared that they 'do conceive religion, the king, monarchical government and the privileges of parliament to be eminently wronged and endangered, to be ruined' if the New Model Army prevailed, warranting their shift of allegiances and new alliance with the king.[63] David Stevenson has noted, however, that this Act served primarily as propaganda, intended to satisfy sceptical ministers by outlining how the English had broken the terms of the Covenant first and to justify military invasion of England following reparations that were unlikely to be met.[64] Nevertheless, it demonstrated how Engagers viewed themselves as the true interpreters of the Covenant, upholding its terms despite English transgressions.

Some Scottish ministers agreed with this assessment of the Engagement's legitimacy, especially given the threat that the English Independents now posed for religion in Scotland. For example, Baillie recognised that the English had not upheld their end of the Solemn League and Covenant and demonstrated initial support for the Engagement. As Chapter 4 showed, Baillie had little sympathy for Independents in the Westminster Assembly and disparaged their ideas about the liberty of conscience, including their radical implications for political authority. On 8 March 1648, Baillie wrote a letter to Sir Daniel Carmichael (who had been nominated treasurer depute by Parliament) in which he commented upon the validity of the Engagement in such terms.[65] He supported war against the English, claiming, 'The conclusion, that Scotland at this time hes a just cause of Warre against the Sectarian army in England, and their adherents, none of us doth question.'[66] By engaging in war against England, the Scots would be staying true to the Covenant's requirements for the reformation of religion beyond their own borders. As he argued, the justness of war derived from that 'faction of sectaries and hereticks, now prevalent in the Army and Parliament, who openly and obstinately doe tread under foote the whole and every part of our Covenant.'[67] Even though Baillie agreed that the English sectarians had broken the terms of the Covenant, he and his brethren in the ministry feared that the king would not protect Presbyterianism after a military success, meaning that 'the yoke of tyrannie in the state, of poperie and prelacie in the Church, is lyklie to be put upon our neck.'[68]

He then made a few stipulations on behalf of his brethren in the ministry to ensure long-term protection of the kirk through limits upon the king's power. First, he argued that the king must not be entrusted with full power until he had confirmed that he would settle religion in England according to the terms of the Solemn League and Covenant.[69] Second, the 'malignant partie of papists, prelates, and others opposite to our Covenant' should not be allowed to gain enough power 'to give us the law.'[70] Baillie, and the Scottish ministers whom he represented in this letter, therefore conceived of the Engagement as a just war in defence of Scotland's own religious traditions from the potential encroachment of the English Independents who now posed a worse threat than the king. Yet he did not give the king unlimited authority as a way to uphold the terms of the Covenant.

Baillie thus supported the Engagement at the outset, believing that its terms might be favourable to Presbyterianism and that a war against sectarians in the New Model Army was expedient.[71] However, his support for the Engagement also reflected his less ardent commitment to traditional theories of resistance than many of his Covenanting contemporaries. Although Baillie had come to legitimise resistance during the First Bishops' War by reading authors like Bilson, he demonstrated less certainty about its justifications from the earliest days of conflict. In *Ladensium autokatakrisis* (1640), written during the Bishops' Wars, Baillie already began to lament military conflicts with the king, urging his readers to compromise and protect the monarch lest their fighting build 'a bridge for the Spainyard or French to come over the Sea.'[72] In light of the Catholic threat, Baillie argued that 'Pietie would command us to put up all our homeward quarrels, though they were both great and manie.'[73] Already weary of fighting, Baillie viewed divisions amongst Protestants as an invitation for papist infiltration and likely saw an alliance with Charles as the most expedient end to the conflict. Additionally, he expressed concern for Charles's physical safety while the king was held captive by the New Model Army, demonstrating his respect for the monarch's life despite legitimising resistance.[74] Baillie likely sought to return to public peace and order by allying with the king against the more dangerous threat from England (rather than continue with prolonged fighting, violence and purging of Scotland's civic institutions).

While Baillie represented a more moderate strand of resistance-thinking after 1646, other Covenanters radicalised in their aims and justified purging Scotland's civic institutions to ensure that only committed, godly inferior magistrates remained in office. For example, Samuel Rutherford had been just as concerned about the growing threat of the English Independents and viewed their willingness to let heresy abound as a direct betrayal of the Solemn League and Covenant. His failure to establish Presbyterianism at the Westminster Assembly (which he left in November 1647) was a source of great frustration, as was the control that the Independents secured over the English government. He authored two treatises directed toward the English in which he demonstrated his sense of betrayal, in addition to his anger about the rise of heretical religious sects south of the border. In *A Survey of Spiritual Antichrist* (1648), Rutherford vehemently denounced the heresies circulating in England that pertained to the erroneous doctrine of liberty of conscience. He criticised the Independents for contributing to their proliferation, and for betraying the terms of the Covenant regarding the establishment of Presbyterianism. He argued that the Scots' brethren in England had sworn the Covenant without intending to keep it, and that they 'have endeavoured not to preserve but to destroy and extirpate the Reformed religion, doctrine, worship, discipline and government in Scotland, and persecuted us because we assert it.'[75] Simultaneously, the English malignants 'ingaged their faithfull and well-minded brethren in a blind cause to establish abominable liberty of conscience', a doctrine that produced a multitude of heresies, such as antinomianism and Socinianism. Similarly, in *A Free Disputation Against Pretended Liberty of Conscience* (1649), Rutherford scorned the rise of religious sects in England which advocated for liberty of conscience and toleration. Both theological treatises thus reflected his vehement opposition to the growth of sectarians and malignants in England, and his anger that the Independents spurned the Covenant by rejecting Presbyterianism.

Such frustration about the failure to establish Presbyterianism throughout the British Isles came to a head following Oliver Cromwell's defeat of the Engagers' army at Preston in August 1648. On 23 January 1649, the Scottish parliament passed the Act of Classes, a piece of legislation that banned all former royalists and Engagers from holding public office or taking up positions within the army.[76] Parliament justified the action by declaring that the Engagement had been undertaken 'contrary to God's word' and that it constituted 'a manifest breach of covenant and treaties as destructive to the cause and covenant, to religion, the king and these kingdoms.'[77] The Act also concluded that the failed Engagement 'is the cause of all the oppressions and miseries that has followed or may follow thereupon.'[78] For this reason, Parliament annulled all former Acts made in support of the Engagement and barred any of its 'authors or abettors' from holding public office 'without the consent of that kingdom against which their Engagement was.'[79] Consensus within the Covenanting movement about how to establish a godly commonwealth that properly advanced the true religion fractured, while an increasingly coercive state under the direction of a minority Kirk Party led by Argyll, Rutherford and Wariston emerged. By purging Parliament of previous Engagers and royalists, the Kirk Party eliminated their opposition and ensured that only inferior magistrates who confirmed and supported their agenda could hold office.

The events surrounding the failed Engagement, the Act of Classes and the emergence of the Kirk Party demonstrate a critical breakdown in the Covenanting consensus about how best to fulfil the terms of the Solemn League and Covenant. But it also resulted in a fundamental shift in both Covenanting resistance theory and ideas about the godly, covenanted nation. The desire to purge public offices of former Engagers was significantly motivated by fear that the Scots had failed to uphold the terms of the Covenant, and that they would be answerable to God for the progress of religious reformation in Britain and Ireland. Rutherford especially supported purging Parliament and the General Assembly of former Engagers, reflecting both his sense of betrayal and his continued zeal for a Presbyterian settlement across the British archipelago.[80]

But even prior to the Act of Classes, he doubted that the reformation of religion could be carried out properly through the apparatuses of the civil state (especially through the nobility in Parliament) as he had previously championed in *Lex, Rex*. Instead, Rutherford became increasingly committed to the idea that Scotland was a Covenanted nation that needed to fulfil God's will, even if that required transferring power over resistance and warfare from the parliamentary Estates to a purged, restricted group of the 'godly' in Scotland's civic institutions. As John Coffey has convincingly argued, Rutherford developed an increasingly apocalyptic mindset toward reformation of the three kingdoms of the British Isles after 1647, a mindset that forced him 'into a denial of the Scottish constitutionalism and natural-law theory that he had advocated in the mid-1640s.'[81] Rutherford ultimately jettisoned the political theory he developed in 1644 in favour of a radical commitment to attaining theological purity within Scotland's civic institutions.

Crucially, this shift in ideas about the parliamentary Estates and the establishment of the godly nation did not have precedents in canonical works of Reformed resistance theory – the works that the Covenanters had previously used to develop their own ideas during the Bishops' Wars. Instead, the Engagement controversy drastically narrowed the scope of who comprised the covenanted community tasked with carrying out God's reformation, even leading anti-Engagers to exclude the same inferior magistrates with whom they had previously worked to achieve their shared religious goals. The Engagement thus represented an important radicalisation of traditional Reformed resistance theory – a theory predicated upon the support of inferior magistrates in Parliament – toward the defence of purging, forced deposition, and a restricted definition of the true covenanted society.

The Execution of Charles I and Coronation of Charles II

Despite the internal divisions that the Engagement sowed within the Covenanting leadership, prompting the removal of former Engagers from civic and ecclesiastical offices, Scots equally had to confront the radical implications of their political theory when faced with the trial and execution of the king. On 30 January 1649, the English Rump Parliament executed Charles I, prompting the Scots to immediately respond by proclaiming Charles II King of Great Britain and Ireland (not just Scotland) on 5 February. They negotiated the Treaty of Breda with Charles II, according to which he agreed to guarantee Presbyterianism in Scotland and take the Covenant himself. But the regicide destroyed any remaining relations between the English and Scottish governments, as was evident when the English declared Charles II King of Scots only.[82] The Scots now seemed to threaten the stability of the new English Republic through their commitment to upholding monarchical power, leading Cromwell's New Model Army to defeat the Scots (led by David Leslie) at the Battle of Dunbar in September 1650 and take control of Edinburgh. Cromwell's invasion of Scotland resulted in another division among Scots as they debated whether to repeal the Act of Classes and allow 'malignants' back into offices and the military for their common defence. This challenge divided Covenanters further into the Protestors (those who favoured the malignants' continued exclusion) and Resolutioners (those who favoured their readmittance).

News of the execution of Charles I on 30 January 1649 was met with immediate outrage in Scotland, likely for a few reasons. First, the Scots had not been consulted before the Rump Parliament carried out the trial; the Scots only sought the correction of the king and the implementation of their religious agenda, not his beheading. Since the time of the National Covenant, they had been careful to reiterate their respect for the king's majesty, maintaining that they had no desire to threaten his life and that they engaged in military action exclusively out of self-defence. The Act of the General Assembly denouncing the Engagement also confirmed that the Scots had no 'disloyalty or undutifulnesse to the King's Majesty, to whom we heartily wish, and to his posterity after him, a happy reigne over these dominions.'[83] The Scots had also petitioned the Rump Parliament to protect the king's life while seeking guarantees of religious reform. In a letter authored on 6 January 1649 to William Lenthall (1591–1662), speaker of the House of Commons, Scottish commissioners requested that the English uphold the terms of the Solemn League and Covenant in their negotiations for a peace treaty with the king. They claimed that the Estates of the Scottish parliament believed the English would allow them to peacefully present their own propositions to Charles for establishing 'the Covenant and Presbyteriall government, the Confession of Faith, directory for worship, and catechisme.'[84] But when news of the execution emerged, they accused the English of 'proceeding against the king, to take away his life, and for changing the government of this kingdome', all while overturning 'the whole work of Reformation, to cast off the ministry, and introduce a toleration of all religions and formes of worship.'[85]

In articulating their earliest theories of resistance, the Covenanting leadership had been careful to portray their wars as just ones waged in defence of their lives, liberties and faith. They continually referred to their respect for the king's person and for the institution of monarchy itself (albeit limited rather than absolute). As the previous chapter demonstrated, Rutherford believed that inferior magistrates could hold the king accountable to his covenantal obligations, but that limited monarchy was the best form of government. Equally, Covenanters tended to portray their resistance as a corrective measure, not as a radical method for altering the type of civil government under which they lived. As a result, they had not attempted to justify the aggressive murder of kings, an action that went beyond a corrective or disciplinary power. Indeed, the Scottish parliament had reiterated in their defence of the Engagement that they 'have no intention to diminish his [the king's] just power and greatness'.[86] The Scots therefore viewed the regicide as a radical, unwarranted and populist uprising that they themselves had been careful to avoid.

While they denounced the execution of the king as a disgrace to monarchical government, the Covenanters also framed the action as an insult to religious reformation in the British Isles, one that contravened the terms of the Solemn League and Covenant. The Covenant had never sanctioned a change to the form of civil government, and Scots had maintained that monarchy was the best divinely approved form. Their appeal to the English parliament to negotiate a treaty favourable to religious reformation with Charles therefore reflected an intrinsic connection between religion and the form of civil government, as they requested that 'the rights and priviledges of Parliament may be preserved; That there may be no change of the fundamentall Government; And that there be no harme, injury or violence' carried out against the king.[87] They therefore expressed the interconnections between their religious concerns, as established in the Covenant, with limited monarchy, refusing to change the form of government according to the will of the Rump Parliament.

Although the Scots objected to the execution of the king and sought to maintain the institution of monarchy, they did not unequivocally accept Charles II either. Instead, their commitment to securing a godly magistrate who would enact Presbyterianism persisted throughout their new negotiations. On 27 April 1650, Baillie delivered a speech to King Charles II at The Hague, as the representative of the Scottish commissioners of the Church of Scotland. He lamented the execution, claiming that the Scots were filled with mournful sorrow for the

> tragick parricide which, though men on earth should passe over unquestioned, yet we nothing doubt but the great judge of the world will arise, and plead against every one, of what condition soevir who have been either authores or actors or consenters or approvers of that hardly expressible crime.[88]

He also claimed to represent 'all sorts of men in our land' who expressed great joy at the 'imediat filling of the vacant throne with your Ma[jes]ties most gracious and hopefull person', demonstrating his fundamental respect for the institution of monarchy.[89]

Following their return from The Hague in July 1650, the Scottish commissioners of the church presented a report to Parliament and the General

Assembly that contained papers exchanged with the king during their negotiations.[90] This report included the commissioners' letter to the king in which they had defended their integrity. The letter clarified that the kirk had good intentions 'towards Monarchicall Government, and the continuance thereof in your Majesties person and posterity', and that they utterly detested the 'abominable and unparalleld practises of some against the Person of your Majestie's Father, and their subverting the ancient and fundamentall Lawes and Government of these Kingdomes.'[91] The commissioners employed the same language of subversion of the laws of the land that they had previously used to challenge Charles's arbitrary rule, but they now applied it to the English parliament while remaining committed to upholding limited monarchy.

The desire of the Scots to both uphold monarchy as an institution but continue to pursue the protection of Presbyterianism appeared at the coronation of King Charles II on 1 January 1651. Robert Douglas, the moderator of the General Assembly, officiated the coronation of the new king at Scone. In his sermon, he returned to standard elements of Covenanting political thought about the mutual contract between king and subjects, in addition to their covenant with God. For example, he highlighted the obligations that the covenant (established through the coronation process) placed upon both kings and subjects. First and foremost, the king's crowning allowed him to 'renew a Covenant with God and His People, and to make a Covenant with the People.'[92] According to Douglas, 'When a King is Crowned, and received by the people, there is a Covenant or mutual contract between him and them, containing conditions mutually to be observed.'[93] These conditions included the king's subordination to three powers: God, laws and government. Douglas argued that the king had to obey divine law because God's power was superior to his own. If he did not rule as God's subordinate, he risked becoming an atheist or tyrant who exercised arbitrary power at his own will. Second, kings swore to govern according to the laws of the kingdom. Ruling contrary to these would constitute a breach of covenant, since the king was meant to uphold them for the common good of the people. Lastly, the king's power should be balanced by other members of government. Douglas observed that, 'The total Government is not upon a King. He hath Counsellors, a Parliament, or Estates in the Land, who share in the burthen of Government. No King should have the sole Government.'[94] According to Douglas, all three checks on the king's power came into being through the process of the coronation.

But this covenant also gave the king a very specific purpose: maintaining Reformed Protestantism through proper doctrine, worship, discipline and polity in the church. Douglas reaffirmed the king's *cura religionis* when he claimed that the king acted as the keeper of both tables of the Decalogue.[95] As a result, he had a duty to preserve the 'true religion according to the Word of God ... to see his Subjects observe both tables, and to punish the transgressors of the same.'[96] The king was bound to rid the kingdom of 'popery', heresy and blasphemy, especially following the events of the 1640s. He also needed to undertake a process of reformation throughout the kingdom that included personal reformation, reformation of his family and court, and reformation of the entire land.[97] Douglas similarly assigned specific duties to Christian subjects, such as maintaining the king's authority and the true religion to fulfil their end of the covenantal obligation.[98] The covenant therefore established a delicate balance of power between king and subjects. As Douglas maintained, 'A King should keep within the bounds of the Covenant made with the people ... And subjects should keep within the bounds of this Covenant, in regulating that Power.'[99] He needed to tread a fine line regarding when the covenant was broken, especially because he denounced Charles I's execution multiple times in the sermon. Instead, he sought to strike a balance of power that would not lead to drastic actions by the people and justify regicide, but that would not give Charles II license to rule arbitrarily against the true religion.

Conclusion

As this chapter has demonstrated, the events that occurred after 1646 eradicated any initial unity of the Covenanting movement, resulting in the development of new interests and power struggles pertaining to the nature of the 'covenanted nation'. While the political thought of the Covenanting leadership had previously been predicated upon a cooperative relationship between Parliament and General Assembly, according to which the General Assembly made religious decisions that Parliament codified into law, the Engagement raised new questions about the relationship between the aims and authorities of the two institutions when they came into conflict. Divisions within both institutions resulted in a radicalisation of many ministers in the General Assembly, leading them to justify purging Scotland's civic institutions – such as Parliament and the universities – to enforce their vision of the godly commonwealth, ensure theological purity and uphold their covenant with God. By contrast, others began to defend the unity of the commonwealth, opting to accommodate royalists and Engagers to secure temporal peace and counteract the greater threat of the English Independents. They prioritised civil stability above any zeal for theological purity within Scotland's governing institutions – much as royalists had done at the start of the Scottish Revolution. Covenanter political thought and ideas about resistance were therefore far from static, and they had to be continually negotiated in response to rapid political and religious developments across the British Isles after 1646. While the Covenanting leadership began from a shared, standard Reformed position on resistance through the first half of the 1640s, their thought radicalised or shifted as they sought to secure a continued symbiotic relationship with inferior magistrates who would carry out their vision of the godly commonwealth.

Notes

1. Macinnes, *British Revolution*, 152–92 (see introduction, n. 3); Stevenson, *Revolution and Counter-Revolution*, chs 3 and 4 (see introduction, n. 3).
2. Stewart, *Rethinking the Scottish Revolution*, 262 (see introduction, n. 3).
3. Salvatore Cipriano, 'The Engagement, the Universities and the Fracturing of the Covenanter Movement, 1647–51,' in Langley, *National Covenant in Scotland*, 148 (see introduction, n. 4).
4. Kirsteen MacKenzie, *The Solemn League and Covenant of the Three Kingdoms and the Cromwellian Union, 1643–1663* (London: Routledge, 2017), ch. 2.
5. Waurechen, 'Covenanter Propaganda,' 63–86 (see introduction, n. 63).
6. Archibald Johnston of Wariston, *A short relation of the state of the kirk of Scotland since the reformation of religion, to the present time for information, and advertisement to our brethren in the Kirk of England, by an hearty well-wisher to both kingdomes* (Edinburgh, 1638), sig. A2r.
7. Wariston, *A short relation*, sig. Cr.
8. Wariston, *A short relation*, sig. B4r.
9. Robert Baillie, *The Letters and Journals of Robert Baillie*, ed. David Laing (Edinburgh: Robert Ogle, 1841), 1: 189–90.
10. Henderson, 'Instructions for defensive arms,' 357 (see chap. 5, n. 73).
11. Henderson, 'Instructions for defensive arms,' 358.
12. Henderson, 'Instructions for defensive arms,' 359.
13. Henderson, 'Instructions for defensive arms,' 357.
14. Henderson, 'Instructions for defensive arms,' 357.
15. Henderson, 'Instructions for defensive arms,' 357.
16. Henderson, 'Instructions for defensive arms,' 358.
17. For a transcription and critical edition of this manuscript, see Karie Schultz, 'Essay on Resistance to Magistrates, c. 1637, 1638,' in *Miscellany of the Scottish History Society, volume XVII* (Woodbridge: Boydell, forthcoming 2024).
18. I am grateful to Matthew Vogan for bringing these observations from Wariston's diary regarding preaching on Hosea (and their implications for this manuscript's potential authorship) to my attention.
19. Sir Archibald Johnston of Wariston, *Diary of Sir Archibald Johnston of Wariston, 1632–1639*, ed. G. M. Paul (Edinburgh, 1911), 1: 283.
20. Wariston, *Diary*, 410.
21. Hosea 5:10: 'The princes of Judah were like them that remove the bound: therefore I will pour out my wrath upon them like water (KJV). This verse also opens the *Vindiciae, contra tyrannos*. See Brutus, *Vindiciae, contra tyrannos* (ed. and trans. Garnett), quest. 1, 14 (see chap. 5, n. 76).
22. NLS, Wodrow Folio XXIX, no. 15, fol. 39v.
23. 1 Kings 12:25–33.
24. Wodrow Folio XXIX, no. 15, fol. 39r.
25. Wodrow Folio XXIX, no. 15, fol. 41.
26. Wodrow Folio XXIX, no. 15, fol. 42.
27. Wodrow Folio XXIX, no. 15, fol. 39.
28. Wodrow Folio XXIX, no. 15, fol. 39r.
29. NLS, Advocates Manuscripts, Adv.20.6.4, fol. 105r.
30. Wariston, *Diary*, 1: 310. This was a debate engaged in by David Owen at Cambridge against David Pareus regarding whether subjects have the right

to resist their superiors. Owen had allegedly overheard a colleague discussing resistance in the staff common room, resulting in the latter's deposition. See David Owen, *Anti-Pareus: siue Determinatio de iuro region habita Cantabrigiae in scholis theologicis* (Cambridge, 1619). This text was translated into English in 1642.
31. David Pareus, *In divinam ad Romanos S. Pauli ap. espistolam commentarius* (Frankfurt, 1608), 1,380.
32. Pareus, *In divinam*, 1,381–2: 'Quia etiam superior magistratus est subiectus legibus divinis & suae reipublicae.' [All translations mine].
33. Pareus, *In divinam*, 1,381: 'Subditi non privati, sed in magistratu inferiori constituti, adversus superiorem magistratum se & rempub. & ecclesiam seu veram religionem etiam armis defendere iure possunt.'
34. Pareus, *In divinam*, '1. Cum superior magistratus degenerat in tyrannum. 2. Aut ad manifestam idololatriam atque blasphemias ipsos vel subditos alios vi vult cogere.'
35. Wariston, *Diary*, 1: 408. Likely Theodore Beza's *De jure magistratuum in subditos; et officio subditorum erga magistratus* (Lyon, 1574).
36. Baillie, *Letters and Journals*, 1: 189.
37. Baillie, *Letters and Journals*, 1: 116.
38. Thomas Bilson, *The true difference betweene Christian subiection and unchristian rebellion* (Oxford, 1585), 358.
39. Bilson, *True difference*, 359.
40. Bilson, *True difference*, 520. For an assessment of Bilson's thought within a wider context of resistance-thinking in seventeenth-century England, see Howard Nenner, 'Loyalty and the Law: The Meaning of Trust and the Right of Resistance in Seventeenth-Century England,' *Journal of British Studies* 48, no. 4 (2009): 859–870, at 862.
41. Baillie, *An historicall vindication*, 76 (see chap. 2, n. 68).
42. Baillie, *Review of Dr Bramble*, 90 (see chap. 4, n. 103).
43. Campbell, *Life and Works of Robert Baillie*, 67 (see introduction, n. 54).
44. Rutherford, *Lex, Rex*, 442 (see chap. 5, n. 27).
45. Rutherford, *Lex, Rex*, 442.
46. For a more detailed description of the negotiations that took place between 1645 and 1647, see MacKenzie, *The Solemn League*, 63–8.
47. Cipriano, 'The Engagement,' 146.
48. Campbell, *Life and Works of Robert Baillie*, 50.
49. 'Solemn League and Covenant,' 132 (see introduction, n. 32).
50. Baillie, *Letters and Journals*, 3: 33.
51. Baillie, *Letters and Journals*, 3: 33.
52. Baillie, *Letters and Journals*, 3: 33.
53. Baillie, *Letters and Journals*, 3: 42.
54. *A short information from the commission of the generall assembly, concerning the Declaration of the Hounourable Court of Parliament, lately emitted to the kingdom* (Edinburgh, 1648), 3.
55. 'Declaration of the Generall Assembly, concerning the present Dangers of Religion, and especially the unlawfull Engagement in War against the Kingdom of England,' in *Acts of the General Assembly of the Church of Scotland 1638–1842*, ed. Church Law Society (Edinburgh: Edinburgh Printing and Publishing Company, 1843), 173.

56. 'Declaration of the Generall Assembly,' 173.
57. 'Declaration of the Generall Assembly,' 174.
58. *RPS*, 1648/3/30 (accessed 24 July 2023).
59. 'Declaration of the Generall Assembly,' 174.
60. *RPS*, 1648/3/66 (accessed 24 July 2023).
61. *RPS*, 1648/3/66.
62. *RPS*, 1648/3/66.
63. *RPS*, 1648/3/66.
64. Stevenson, *Revolution and Counter-Revolution*, 104.
65. Baillie, *Letters and Journals*, 3: 24, fn. 8.
66. Baillie, *Letters and Journals*, 3: 25.
67. Baillie, *Letters and Journals*, 3: 26.
68. Baillie, *Letters and Journals*, 3: 28.
69. Baillie, *Letters and Journals*, 3: 28.
70. Baillie, *Letters and Journals*, 3: 28.
71. Campbell, *Life and Works of Robert Baillie*, 50–1.
72. Robert Baillie, *Ladensium autokatakrisis, the Canterburians self-conviction* (Amsterdam, 1640), p. A2.
73. Baillie, *Ladensium autokatakrisis*, sig. A3. Stewart, *Rethinking the Scottish Revolution*, 261 (see introduction, n. 3); Stevenson, *Revolution and Counter-Revolution*.
74. Campbell, *Life and Works of Robert Baillie*, 50.
75. Samuel Rutherford, *A survey of the spirituall antichrist* (London, 1648), sig A2.
76. *RPS*, 1649/1/43 (accessed 16 June 2023).
77. *RPS*, 1649/1/43.
78. *RPS*, 1649/1/43.
79. *RPS*, 1649/1/43.
80. Coffey, *Religion, Religion and the British Revolutions*, 247.
81. Coffey, *Religion, Religion and the British Revolutions*, 248.
82. Macinnes, *British Revolution*, 189.
83. 'Declaration of the Generall Assembly,' 172.
84. *A letter from the Commissioners of Scotland residing here at London* (London, 1649), 1.
85. *Letter from the Commissioners*, 1–2.
86. *RPS*, 1648/3/66.
87. *Letter from the Commissioners*, 5.
88. NLS, Wodrow Folio XXXI, fol. 92r. This speech is reproduced in Baillie, *Letters and Journals*, 3: 84–7.
89. Wodrow Folio XXXI, 92r.
90. *The proceedings of the Commissioners of the Church and Kingdom of Scotland with his Majestie at the Hague* (Edinburgh, 1649).
91. Baillie, *Letters and Journals*, 3: 511.
92. Robert Douglas, *The forme and order of the coronation of Charles the Second, King of Scotland, England, France, and Ireland* (Aberdeen, 1651), 11.
93. Douglas, *Forme and order*, 14.
94. Douglas, *Forme and order*, 14.
95. Douglas, *Forme and order*, 9.
96. Douglas, *Forme and order*, 9.
97. Douglas, *Forme and order*, 12–13.
98. Douglas, *Forme and order*, 12.
99. Douglas, *Forme and order*, 15.

Conclusion

Although the Scots crowned Charles II at Scone on 1 January 1651, they were defeated by the New Model Army at Worcester on 3 September 1651. This military loss presaged Scotland's incorporation into the Cromwellian Protectorate in February 1652. The kirk remained deeply divided, and the Covenanters' project of creating a uniform, godly commonwealth committed to Presbyterianism came to an end. Although the Covenanters' attempts to spread Presbyterianism and ensure religious purity in all three kingdoms failed, they developed a complex set of political and ecclesiological ideas during this decade that enabled the Scottish Revolution to take place. Yet they also encountered sustained intellectual opposition from a committed set of royalists – especially surrounding the National Covenant and the Bishops' Wars – who put forward equally sophisticated, competing theories about church and state. This book has compared the ideas that emerged within both intellectual traditions, situating them in a new cross-confessional and transnational context. It has shown how royalists and Covenanters drew upon and adapted Lutheran, Calvinist and Catholic scholastic debates to understand the problems they faced with Charles I's reign, and to defend their own political allegiances. In doing so, it has argued that ecclesiological ideas about the nature of the Reformed church in Scotland emerged in tandem with, and deeply informed, elements of Scottish political thought commonly associated with secularisation and the development of modernity.

As a result, this book has a few key implications, both for our understanding of Scottish intellectual culture, as well as for the relationship between early modern religion and politics more broadly. First, even though the Covenanting leadership purged Parliament, the General Assembly and the universities throughout the 1640s to ensure conformity to their agenda, Scottish intellectual culture was far from monolithic.[1] Royalism served as a critical intellectual antithesis to the Covenanting movement, but the political and ecclesiological ideas of Scottish royalists have only recently received sustained scholarly attention.[2] Unsurprisingly, Covenanting political theory has dominated the narrative of the civil wars, especially given that the leadership worked hard to legitimise resistance to the king, justify a Presbyterian settlement beyond Scotland's borders and defend parliamentary sovereignty. Yet Scottish royalism was an equally strong and complex intellectual force. Rather than being a minority movement restricted to the conservative northeast of Scotland, it extended across the nation and comprised individuals from a variety of professional and social backgrounds.[3] Additionally, royalists were just as intellectually innovative as their Covenanter contemporaries in the range of ideas that they advanced. They were not backwards, conservative or antiquated in their commitment to absolute monarchy and divine right theories of kingship. Rather, they defended absolute monarchy using a range of cutting-edge arguments drawn from nature, scripture and legal theory. They advanced these ideas to show that the temporal kingdom was a place for the preservation of peace and order above all else, while civil stability could only be attained through obedience to the hierarchy of nature and to absolute monarchy. The implication of this approach was that God had the highest, most immediate sovereignty over the temporal kingdom. Ecclesiastical authorities must not overextend their jurisdiction into the state by pretending to know God's will and urging resistance to an ungodly ruler. This position contrasted with the more active role that Covenanter leaders gave human beings over political life, one which included the creation of civil governments and the correction of magistrates who had gone astray, even in matters of religion. The intellectual history of Scottish royalism is thus a highly worthwhile area of enquiry for understanding the antithesis to Covenanter political theory and for revealing the multiple strands of Protestant intellectual culture that existed within Covenanted Scotland.

Second, this book has broadened our understanding of Scottish intellectual culture by redrawing the positions of Lutheran, Calvinist and Catholic intellectual traditions within royalist and Covenanter thought. Historians have frequently analysed Scottish political ideas as part of a national or 'British' story, one connected to key figures like George Buchanan, John Knox and Andrew Melville.[4] Others have interpreted the Covenanters as part of a Reformed intellectual tradition, noting their similarity to European authors, such as Johannes Althusius, Philippe de Mornay or David Pareus.[5] Yet Covenanters and royalists both engaged substantially with the political and legal categories developed by their Lutheran and Catholic scholastic contemporaries, an intellectual relationship that has been observed but not fully explored.[6] Protestants and Catholics did think differently about the purpose of politics, and their intellectual traditions both made valuable contributions to Scottish political thought.[7] Catholic scholastic political theory proved especially useful because it gave humans greater agency over the creation of civil governments. Catholics generally considered the natural world to be a space for the exercise of human reason and free will, an emphasis which did not exist to the same extent in orthodox Reformed political thought. As a result, Catholic ideas about human agency and rational political participation enabled the Covenanters to create a theory of elective limited monarchy that they directed to an ecclesiological end: the establishment of a *jure divino* presbyterian church settlement.

By exploring the cross-confessional nature of Covenanting political thought, especially its legal-constitutional elements, this book has challenged the claim that the Covenanters were religious militants who sought to impose a theocratic government in Britain and Ireland.[8] Instead, they also prioritised human reason as the basis for political participation and argued that God gave humans more freedom to create governments through their own agency. Subjects could choose a civil magistrate who would defend rather than persecute the church, making their political and ecclesiological ideas work hand in hand. The Covenanters developed this argument about the civil state by merging traditional Reformed emphases on the covenant between king, God and subjects with Catholic scholastic arguments about the natural origins of the civil state and the greater role that humans played in political life. Through an examination of multiple facets of Covenanting political thought, it is possible to challenge the perception that the Covenanters were strict biblical voluntarists who sought to impose a theocracy. Instead, they had a high respect for human rationality, rather than divine revelation alone, in determining the formation and function of the temporal kingdom.

Lastly, this book contributes most broadly to our understanding of the relationship between religion and politics in the early modern period. Even though Covenanter political ideas – such as consent of the governed, constitutionalism and the social contract – might be construed as secular when considered in isolation, they did not develop these arguments to distance the church from the state. Instead, they expressed their political ideas to help solve a crisis within the Protestant national church. Debates about church polity, the regulation of *adiaphora* and excommunication provided an essential intellectual framework for how royalists and Covenanters thought about the king's civil sovereignty and his relationship to Parliament. As the Covenanters sought to protect the church from royal interference and restore its traditional purity, they subjected the king to the rule of law and to Parliament. By contrast, in believing that civil magistrates should have a more active role in reforming the doctrines and ceremonies of the visible church, royalists extended the king's authority above that of civil law and inferior magistrates. An ecclesiological predicament, rather than the church's full marginalisation from the state, prompted royalists and Covenanters to reassess the nature of the king's civil sovereignty. As a result, Scots advanced languages of political legitimacy to settle a crisis about the doctrines, ceremonies and polity of their national church, reinserting ecclesiology into the development of early modern political theory.

Ultimately, although scholars have been prone to separate religious justifications for warfare from legal-constitutional ones in the early modern period, characterising the two as independent categories of thought, this book has shown that these approaches emerged concurrently and were far from antithetical. Scots did not simply wage 'religious wars' because they fought for a Presbyterian settlement in Britain and Ireland and believed they must defend the true religion to uphold their covenant with God. Equally, they did not intellectually defend a secular, political revolution based upon legal-constitutional grounds alone. Instead, a complex combination of arguments from law, nature, scripture and political theory informed how they reassessed the intrinsic connections between church and state.

Current interpretations of the 'Scottish Revolution' have correctly shown that religious tensions resulted in significant changes to the seat of political power within the kingdom.[9] These same religious disagreements precipitated increased political participation among previously disenfranchised individuals, allowing Scots to actively engage with the formation of the Covenanted state on a more popular level.[10] This book has contributed an intellectual history perspective to this growing historiographical debate, focusing specifically upon the range of ideas underlying Scotland's political developments during this period. I hope to have furthered our understanding of the Scottish Revolution (in some small part) by uncovering the diversity of the intellectual traditions that made this Revolution possible. Even as Covenanted Scotland became increasingly coercive through its leaders' pursuit of a godly, Reformed state, the justifications for these revolutionary changes depended upon an eclectic mixture of religious, legal and political ideas drawn from multiple schools of thought emerging across Europe. The 'Revolution' in Scotland may have occurred at the hands of a staunchly Reformed community for overtly religious purposes, distinguishing it from revolutions elsewhere, but the intellectual foundations upon which it was constructed were remarkably cross-confessional, interdisciplinary and transnational in nature.

Notes

1. Cipriano, 'The Engagement,' 145–60 (see chap. 6, n. 1); Cipriano, 'Scottish Universities and Opposition,' 12–37 (see introduction, n. 56).
2. Goatman and Lind, 'Glasgow and the National Covenant,' 39–52 (see chap. 3, n. 2); Lind, 'Royalism, Resistance,' 125–44 (see chap. 3, n. 3); Barry Robertson, *Royalists at War in Scotland and Ireland, 1638–1650* (Farnham: Ashgate, 2014).
3. Donaldson, 'Scotland's Conservative North,' 65–79 (see introduction, n. 55).
4. David George Mullan, 'A hotter sort of Protestantism? Comparisons between French and Scottish Calvinisms,' *Sixteenth Century Journal* 39, no. 1 (2008): 45–69; Ian Michael Smart, 'The Political Ideas of the Scottish Covenanters. 1638–88,' *History of Political Thought* 1, no. 2 (1980): 167–93.
5. Cowan, 'Political Ideas of a Covenanting Leader,' 241–61 (see chap. 5, n. 4); Ford, '*Lex, rex iusto posita*', 262–90 (see chap. 5, n. 1).
6. Simon J. G. Burton, 'Scholastic and Conciliar Roots,' 208–25 (see chap. 5, n. 7); Coffey, *Politics, Religion and the British Revolutions*, 146–87 (see introduction, n. 54); Stevenson, '"Letter on Sovereign Power",' 25–43 (see introduction, n. 64).
7. Mortimer, *Reformation* (see introduction, n. 69).
8. Cowan, 'Covenanters: A Revision Article,' 35–52 (see chap. 5, n. 18); Andreas Pecar, *Macht der Schrift. Politischer Biblizismus in Schottland und England zwis-*

chen Reformation und Bürgerkreig (1534–1642) (Munich: Oldenbourg Wissenschaftsverlag, 2011); Steele, 'The "Politick Christian",' 31–67 (see chap. 5, n. 18).
9. Stevenson, *Scottish Revolution*, 315–26 (see introduction, n. 3)
10. Stewart, *Rethinking the Scottish Revolution*, 16–22 (see introduction, n. 3).

Bibliography

I. MANUSCRIPT PRIMARY SOURCES

Aberdeen University Library (AUL)
MARISCHAL/5/1/3/4/1. 'Catalogue of Thomas Reid's Library, 1624'.
KINGS/5/1/1/2. 'List of books'.

Edinburgh University Library (EUL)
Dc.5.67. 'Robert Baillie, Treatises' (1643).
IN1/ADS/LIB/1/Da.1.1. 'Author Catalogue, Seventeenth Century'. Records of the University of Edinburgh.
IN1/ADS/LIB/2/Da.1.15. 'Press Catalogue, 1641'. Records of the University of Edinburgh.
IN1/ADS/LIB/2/Da.1.29. ''Donations Lists, 1619–1644'. Records of the University of Edinburgh.

Glasgow University Library (GUL)
MS Gen 1117. 'The lawfulness of the subscriptione to the covenant' (3 March 1638).
MS Gen 1239–1241. 'Robert Baillie. Letters and journals relating to affairs'.

National Library of Scotland (NLS)
Advocates' Manuscripts
Adv.20.6.4
Adv.MS.32.3.12
Rb.S.3013. William Guild, *To the Nobilitie, Gentrie, Burrowes, Ministers, and others of this late combination in Covenant, a friendly and faythfull advice* (Aberdeen: Edward Raban, 1639).
Wodrow Collection
Wodrow Folio XXIX
Wodrow Folio XLII
Wodrow Folio XLIII
Wodrow Octavo X
Wodrow Octavo XXVII
Wodrow Quarto XXV
Wodrow Quarto LX
Wodrow Quarto LXXVI

National Records of Scotland (NRS)
Correspondence of the Dukes of Hamilton, 1563–1712
GD406/1/432. John Forbes of Corse, Aberdeen to the laid of Leyes [Leyes], protesting that his previous remarks have been misunderstood and emphasizing his refusal to subscribe the Covenant', 3 August 1638.
GD406/1/446. 'Supplication of the ministers and professors of Aberdeen to the marquis of Huntly. Having heard of the coming assembly at Glasgow, they plead for "ane exemption from repairing to the said synod", as such as journey could do little good', 5 October 1638.
GD406/1/457. 'John Forbes of Corse to the marquis of Huntly, Aberdeen, informing him that, despite their former objections, he, Dr. Barron, and Dr. Sibbald intend to set out shortly for Glasgow', 6 November 1638.
GD406/1/664. The professors of Aberdeen to the marquis of Hamilton, thanking him for his kindness and hoping for his continued help', 20 September 1638.
GD406/1/667. 'The professors of Aberdeen to the marquis of Hamilton, informing him that they are at work on their reply to the covenanters' latest publication', 18 August 1638.

New College Library, University of Edinburgh (NCL)
MS BAILL 1   'Papers relating to Robert Baillie (1599–1661), Principal of Glasgow University'.
MS BAILL 2   'Letters and journals, 1637–62, copy dated 1701'.
MS BAILL 3   'Letters and journals, 1637–62, copy dated 1728'.
MS BAILL 4   'Letters and journals, 1637–62' (n.d).
MS BAILL 5   'Sermons from Jan. 1648 to Jan. 1652'.

St Andrews University Library (StAUL)
UYLY105/1. 'List of books in library, 1644–1649'. Muniments of the University of St Andrews.
Roy BX890.S8. 'Francisco Suárez, *Tractatus de legibus ac Deo legislatore*' (Antwerp, 1613).

II. PRINTED PRIMARY SOURCES

A letter from the Commissioners of Scotland residing here at London. London, 1649.
Althusius, Johannes. *The Politics of Johannes Althusius*. Edited and translated by Frederick S. Carney. London: Eyre & Spottiswoode, 1964.
Ane shorte and general confession of the trewe Christiane fayth and religion, according to Godis Word and actis of our Parliamentis. Edinburgh, 1581.
Aristotle. *The Politics*. Edited and translated by Ernest Barker and R. F. Stalley. Oxford: Oxford University Press, 1995.

Augustine. *Contra Faustum (Answer to Faustus, a Manichean)*. Translated by R. J. Teske. Hyde Park, NY: New City Press, 2007.
Augustine. *The City of God against the Pagans*. Edited and translated by R. W. Dyson. Cambridge: Cambridge University Press, 1998.
Baillie, Robert. *The Letters and Journals of Robert Baillie*. Edited by David Laing, 3 vols. Edinburgh: Robert Ogle, 1841.
Baillie, Robert. *A review of Doctor Bramble, late Bishop of Londonderry, his Faire warning against the Scotes discipline*. Delft, 1649.
Baillie, Robert. *Anabaptism, the true fountaine of Independency, Brownisme, Antinoy, Familisme, and the most of the other errours, which for the time doe trouble the Church of England, unsealed*. London, 1647.
Baillie, Robert. *An historicall vindication of the government of the Church of Scotland*. London: Samuel Gellibrand, 1646.
Baillie, Robert. *A dissuasive from the errours of the time*. London, 1645.
Baillie, Robert. *The unlawfulnesse and danger of limited episcopacie*. London, 1641.
Baillie, Robert. *Ladensium autokatakrisis, the Canterburians self-conviction*. Amsterdam, 1640.
Balcanquhall, Walter. *A large declaration concerning the late tumults in Scotland, from their first originals*. London, 1639.
Barclay, William. *De potestate papae; an & quaetenus in reges & principes seculars ius & imperium habeat*. Hanover, 1617.
Barclay, William. *De regno et regali potestate aduersus Buchananum, Brutum, Boucherium, & reliquos monarchomacos, libri sex*. Paris, 1600.
Bellarmine, Robert. *De laicis, or the Treatise on Civil Government*. Edited and translated by Kathleen E. Murphy. New York: Fordham Press, 1928.
Bellarmine, Robert. *On Temporal and Spiritual Authority: On Laymen or Secular People. On the Temporal Power of the Pope: Against William Barclay. On the Primary Duty of the Supreme Pontiff*. Edited and translated by Stefania Tutino. Indianapolis: Liberty Fund, 2012.
Bellarmine, Robert. *De laicis, or the treatise on civil government*. Edited and translated by Kathleen E. Murphy. New York: Fordham University Press, 1928.
Bellarmine, Robert. *Tractatus de potestate Summi Pontificis in rebus temporalibus, adversus Gulielmum Barclay*. Rome, 1610.
Beza, Theodore. *De jure magistratuum in subditos; et officio subditorum erga magistratus*. Lyon, 1574.
Bilson, Thomas. *The true difference betweene Christian subiection and unchristian rebellion*. Oxford, 1585.
Blackwood, Adam. *Adversus Georgii Buchanani dialogum, de iure regni apud scotos, pro regibus apologia*. Poitiers, 1581.
Blackwood, Adam. *De coniunctione religionis et imperii libri duo*. Paris, 1575.
Bodin, Jean. 'Book I, Chapter 8: On Sovereignty.' In *Bodin: On Sovereignty*. Edited by Julian H. Franklin, 1–45. Cambridge: Cambridge University Press, 2012.

Bodin, Jean. 'Book I, Chapter 10: On the True Marks of Sovereignty.' In *Bodin: On Sovereignty*, edited by Julian H. Franklin, 46–88. Cambridge: Cambridge University Press, 2012.

Bodin, Jean. *De republica libri sex.* Leiden, 1586.

Bodin, Jean. *Les six livres de la république.* Paris, 1576.

Bramhall, John. 'A faire warning to take heed of the Scotish discipline, as being of all others most injurious to the civil magistrate, most oppressive to the subject, most pernicious to both (1649).' In John Bramhall, *Three Treatises Concerning the Scotish Discipline*, 3–36. Hagh, 1661.

Brown, Keith M., Gillian H. Mackintosh, Alastair J. Mann, Pamela E. Ritchie, and Roland J. Tanner, eds. *Records of the Parliaments of Scotland to 1707.* St Andrews, 2007–2011. https://www.rps.ac.uk [accessed 2 August 2023].

Brutus, Stephanus Junius. *Vindiciae, contra tyrannos: or, Concerning the Legitimate Power of a Prince over the People, and of the People over a Prince.* Edited and translated by George Garnett. Cambridge: Cambridge University Press, 1994.

Brutus, Stephanus Junius. *Vindiciae, contra tyrannos: sive, de Principis in Populum, Populique in Principem, legitima potestate.* Edinburgh, 1579.

Buchanan, George. *A Dialogue on the Law of Kingship among the Scots: A Critical Edition and Translation of George Buchanan's De Iure Regni apud Scotos Dialogus.* Edited and translated by Roger A. Mason and Martin S. Smith. London: Routledge, 2004.

Calderwood, David. *The True History of the Church of Scotland.* Edinburgh, 1678.

Calderwood, David., *A re-examination of the Five Articles enacted at Perth anno 1618.* [Holland?], 1636.

Calderwood, David. *The altar of Damscus, or Patern of the English hierarchie and church policie obtruded upon the Church of Scotland.* Amsterdam, 1621.

Calderwood, David. *Perth Assembly.* Leiden, 1619.

Calvin, John. 'On Civil Government [*Institutio Christianae Religionis*, Book IV, chapter 20].' In Höpfl, *Luther and Calvin on Secular Authority*, 47–86. Cambridge: Cambridge University Press, 1991.

Calvin, John. *Commentaries on the Epistle of Paul the Apostle to the Romans.* Edited and translated by John Owen. Edinburgh: Calvin Translation Society, 1849.

Calvin, John. *Institutes of the Christian Religion.* Vol. 2. Translated by Henry Beveridge. Edinburgh: T. & T. Clark, 1863.

Calvin, John. *Institutio Christianae Religionis.* Geneva, 1559.

Cartwright, Thomas. *A replye to an ansvvere made of M. Doctor VVhitgifte Against the admonition to the Parliament.* n.p., 1573.

Church of Scotland. *Acts of the General Assembly of the Church of Scotland 1638–1842.* Edited by Church Law Society. Edinburgh: Edinburgh Printing & Publishing Co., 1843.

Church of Scotland. 'The Second Booke of Discipline.' In *The Doctrine and Discipline of the Kirke of Scotland*, 77–100. London, 1641.

Coleman, Thomas. *Hopes deferred and dashed*. London, 1645.

Confessio et apologia pastorum & reliquorum ministrorum Ecclesiae Magdeburgensis. Magdeburg, 1550.

Corbet, John [Lysimachus Nicanor]. *The epistle congratulatorie of Lysimachus Nicanor of the Societie of Jesu, to the Covenanters in Scotland*. London, 1640.

Corbet, John. *The ungirding of the Scottish armour*. Dublin, 1639.

Covarruvias, Diego de. *Variarum ex Iure Pontificio, Regio, & Caesareo Resolutionum Libri III*. Salamanca, 1552.

Daneau, Lambert. *Ethices christianae libri tres*. Geneva, 1577.

Davies, Sir John. *Discoverie of the true causes why Ireland was never entirely subdued, nor brought under obedience of the crowne of England, until the beginning of his maiesties happie raigne*. London, 1612.

'Declaration of the Generall Assembly, concerning the present Dangers of Religion, and especially the unlawfull Engagement in War against the Kingdom of England.' In *Acts of the General Assembly of the Church of Scotland 1638–1842*, edited by the Church Law Society, 171–81. Edinburgh: Edinburgh Printing and Publishing Company, 1843.

Douglas, Robert. *The forme and order of the coronation of Charles the Second, King of Scotland, England, France, and Ireland*. Aberdeen, 1651.

Drummond, William. 'Remora's for the National League between Scotland and England, 1642.' In Sage and Ruddiman, *Works of William Drummond*, 188–9.

Drummond, William. 'A speech (Which may be called A Prophecy) to the noblemen, barons, gentlemen, &c. who have leagu'd themselves for the defence of the Religion and Liberties of Scotland, 2 May 1639.' In Sage and Ruddiman, *Works of William Drummond*, 179–82.

Drummond, William. 'Irene: a remonstrance for concord, amity and love, amongst his majesty's subjects; written after his declaration publish'd at Edinburgh, 22nd of September, 1638.' In Sage and Ruddiman, *Works of William Drummond*, 163–73.

Duplyes of the Ministers and Professors of Aberdene to second Answers of some Reverend Brethren, Concerning the Late Covenant. Aberdeen: Edward Raban, 1638.

Dury, John. *A petition to the honourable House of Commons in England now assembled whereunto are added certaine considerations showing the necessity of a correspondencie in spiritual matters betwixt all Protestant churches*. London, 1642.

Dury, John. *A memoriall concerning peace ecclesiasticall amongst Protestants*. London, 1641.

Dury, John. *A summary discourse concerning the work of peace ecclesiastical, how it may concurre with the aim of a civill confederation amongst Protestants*. Cambridge, 1641.

Erastus, Thomas. *A treatise of excommunication wherein 'tis fully, learnedly, and *modestly demonstrated that there is no warrant . . . for excommunicating any persons . . . whilst they make an outward profession of the true Christian faith.* London, 1682.

Forbes, John. *The First Book of the Irenicum of John Forbes of Corse.* Edited and translated by Edward Gordon Selwyn. Cambridge: The University Press, 1923.

Forbes, John. *Irenicum Amatoribus Veritatis et Pacis in Ecclesia Scoticana.* Aberdeen, 1629.

Forbes, John. *A peaceable warning, to the subjects in Scotland.* Aberdeen, 1638.

Generall demands, concerning the late covenant propounded by the ministers and professsors of divinitie in Aberdene. Aberdeen: Edward Raban, 1638.

Gillespie, George. *Aaron's rod blossoming; or, the divine ordinance of church-government vindicated.* London, 1646.

Gillespie, George. *An assertion of the government of the Church of Scotland.* Edinburgh, 1641.

Gillespie, George. *A dispute against the English-popish ceremonies, obtruded upon the Church of Scotland.* Leiden, 1637.

Goodman, Christopher. *How superior powers oght to be obeyd of their subjects.* Geneva, 1558.

Gordon, James. *History of Scots affairs, from 1637 to 1641.* Edited by Joseph Robertson and George Grub. Vol. 3. Aberdeen: Spalding Club, 1841.

Grotius, Hugo. *De jure belli ac pacis libri tres.* Paris, 1625.

Guild, William. *To the Nobilitie, Gentrie, Burrowes, Ministers, and others of this late combination in Covenant, a friendly and faythfull advice.* Aberdeen, 1639.

Guthry, Henry. *Memoirs of Henry Guthry, late bishop of Dunkel, in Scotland: wherein the conspiracies and rebellion against King Charles I of blessed memory, to the time of the murther of that monarch, are briefly and faithfully related.* London, 1702.

Hall, Joseph. *Episcopacie by divine right asserted.* London, 1640.

Henderson, Alexander. *A sermon preached before the right honourable House of Lords in the Abbey-church at Westminster, Wednesday the 28. of May 1645. Being the day appointed for solemne and publick humiliation.* London, 1645.

Henderson, Alexander. 'Instructions for defensive arms.' In *The History of the Church and State of Scotland, from the Accession of K. Charles I to the Restoration of K. Charles II*, edited by Andrew Stevenson, 356–60. Edinburgh: Thomas Nelson, 1840.

Henderson, Alexander. *The answeres of some brethren of the ministrie, to the replyes of the ministers and professours of divinite in Aberdene.* Aberdeen: Edward Raban, 1638.

Höpfl, Harro, ed. and trans. *Luther and Calvin on Secular Authority.* Cambridge: Cambridge University Press, 1991.

James VI and I. *King James VI and I: Political Writings.* Edited by Johann P. Sommerville. Cambridge: Cambridge University Press, 1995.

James VI and I. *An apologie for the oath of allegiance* [*Apologia pro iuramento fidelitatis*]. London, 1607.
James VI. *Basilikon doron. Devided into three bookes.* Edinburgh, 1599.
James VI. *The True Lawe of Free Monarchies.* Edinburgh, 1598.
Keckermann, Bartholomäus. *Systema disciplinae politicae.* Frankfurt, 1625.
Kerr, James, ed. *The Covenants and the Covenanters: Covenants, Sermons, and Documents of the Covenanted Reformation.* Edinburgh: R. Hunter, 1895.
Kirk, James, ed. *The Second Book of Discipline.* Edinburgh: Saint Andrew Press, 1980.
Knox, John. *The History of the Reformation of Religion within the Realm of Scotland.* London, 1587.
Knox, John. *The First Blast of the Trumpet against the Montrous Regiment of Women.* Geneva, 1558.
Laud, William. 'Canons and Constitvtions Ecclesiasticall, Gathered and put in forme, for the Government of the Church of Scotland.' In *The Works of the Most Reverend Father in God, William Laud, D. D*, Vol. 5, 583–606. Oxford: John Henry Parker, 1853.
Luther, Martin. 'Against the Robbing and Murdering Hordes of Peasants (1525).' In *The Essential Luther*, edited and translated by Tryntje Helfferich, 163–8. Cambridge: Hackett, 2018.
Luther, Martin. *Warnunge D. Martini Luther an seine lieben Deudschen.* Wittenberg, 1531.
Luther, Martin. *Widder die Mordischen und Reubischen Rotten der Bawren.* Leipzig, 1525.
Luther, Martin. *Von weltlicher uberkeyt wie weyt man yhr gehorsam schuldig sey.* [Augsburg], 1523.
Luther, Martin. *An den Christlichen Adel deutscher Nation.* Wittenberg, 1520.
Luther, Martin. 'On Secular Authority: How Far Does the Obedience Owed to it Extend? [*Von Weltlicher Oberkeit*].' In Höpfl, *Luther and Calvin on Secular Authority*, 3–43.
Mair, John. 'Disputatio de authoritate concilii, supra pontificem maximum.' In Jean Gerson, *Opera omnia, novo ordine digesta, & in V. Tomos distributa.* Edited by Ellies Du Pin, Vol. 2, 1,131–45. Antwerp, 1702.
Maxwell, John. *The burthen of Issachar: or, the tyrannicall power and practises of the presbyteriall government in Scotland.* London, 1646.
Maxwell, John. *Sacro-sancta regum majestas, or, the sacred and royal prerogative of Christian kings.* Oxford, 1644.
Melanchthon, Philip. 'Locus 20: Civil Rulers and the Validity of Governmental Matters.' In *Loci Communes, 1543*, translated by Jacob A. O. Preus, 211–27. St Louis: Concordia Publishing House, 1992.
Molina, Luis de. *De iustitia et iure tractatus: qui est de iustitia commutativa circa bona corporis, personarumque nobis coiunctarum.* Venice, 1611.
'The National Covenant or, the Confession of Faith (1638).' In Kerr, *Covenants and the Covenanters*, 39–51.

Owen, David. *Anti-Pareus: siue Determinatio de iuro region habita Cantabrigiae in scholis theologicis.* Cambridge, 1619.
Pareus, David. *Irenicum sive de unione et synodo evangelicorum concilianda liber votivus.* Heidelberg, 1614.
Pareus, David. *In divinam ad Romanos S. Pauli ap. espistolam commentarius.* Frankfurt, 1608.
Pareus, David. 'Commentary on the Divine Epistle to the Romans of St Paul the Apostle (1608).' In Campbell and Verhaart, *Protestant Politics Beyond Calvin*, 156–75.
Peterkin, Alexander, ed. *Records of the Kirk of Scotland, containing the Acts and Proceedings of the General Assemblies.* Vol. 1. Edinburgh: John Sutherland, 1838.
Ponet, John. *A shorte treatise of politike pouuer and of the true obedience which subiectes owe to kynges and other civile governours.* Strasbourg, 1556.
Proceedings of the Commissioners of the Church and Kingdom of Scotland with his Majestie at the Hague. Edinburgh, 1649.
Rivet, André. *Jesuita vapulans.* Lyon, 1635.
Rutherford, Samuel. *A survey of the spirituall antichrist.* London, 1648.
Rutherford, Samuel. *The divine right of church government and excommunication.* London, 1646.
Rutherford, Samuel. *The due right of presbyteries; or, a peaceable plea, for the government of the Church of Scotland.* London, 1644.
Rutherford, Samuel. *Lex, Rex; or the law and the prince.* London, 1644.
'The Solemn League and Covenant.' In Kerr, *Covenants and the Covenanters*, 131–5.
John Sage and Thomas Ruddiman, eds. *Works of William Drummond of Hawthornden.* Edinburgh: James Watson, 1711.
Soto, Domingo de. *Libri Decem de Iustitia et Iure.* Lyons, 1569.
Spalding, John. *History of the Troubles and Memorable Transactions in Scotland, from 1624–1645.* Aberdeen: John Rettie, 1830.
Spottiswoode, John. *History of the Church and State of Scotland.* London, 1677.
Spottiswoode, John. *De pace inter Evangelicos procuranda, eminentiorum in Ecclesia Scoticana theologorum sententiae.* Frankfurt, 1643.
Stephen, William, ed. *Register of the Consultations of the Ministers of Edinburgh and some other Brethren in the Ministry.* Vol. 1. Edinburgh: T. & A. Constable, 1921.
Suárez, Francisco. *Tractatus de legibus ac deo legislatore: in decem libros distributes.* Antwerp, 1613.
Suárez, Francisco. *Defensio fidei Catholociae et Apistolicae adversus Anglicanae Sectae Errores.* Coimbra, 1613.
Suárez, Francisco. *Selections from Three Works: A Treatise on Laws and God the Lawgiver; A Defence of the Catholic and Apostolic Faith; A Work on the Three Theological Virtues: Faith, Hope, and Charity.* Edited by Thomas Pink and translated by Gwladys L. Williams, Ammi Brown, and John Waldron. Indianapolis: Liberty Fund, 2015.

Thomson, T., and C. Innes, ed. *The Acts of the Parliament of Scotland.* Edinburgh, 1814–1872.

Van Dixhoorn, Chad, ed. *The Minutes and Papers of the Westminster Assembly 1643–1652. Vol. 2, Minutes, Sessions 45–119, 155–198 (1643–1644).* Oxford: Oxford University Press, 2012.

Vázquez Fernando, *Controversiarum illustrium, aliarumque usu frequentium libri tres.* Frankfurt, 1572.

Von Amsdorff, Nicolaus. *Confessio et Apologia Pastorum & reliquorum ministrorum Ecclesiae Magdeburgensis.* Magdeburg, 1550.

Vermigli, Peter Martyr. *Loci communes.* London, 1576.

Vitoria, Francisco de. 'De potestate ecclesiae prior: on the power of the Church.' In *Vitoria: Political Writings*, edited by Anthony Pagden and translated by Jeremy Lawrance, 45–152. Cambridge: Cambridge University Press, 1991.

Vitoria, Francisco de. 'On civil power (*De potestate civili*).' In *Vitoria: Political Writings*, edited by Anthony Pagden and translated by Jeremy Lawrance, 1–44. Cambridge: Cambridge University Press, 1991.

Wariston, Archibald Johnston of. *Diary of Sir Archibald Johnston of Wariston.* Edited by George Morison Paul. 3 vols. Edinburgh: Edinburgh Constable, 1911.

Wariston, Archibald Johnston of. *Reasons against the rendering of our sworne and subscribed confession of faith.* Edinburgh, 1638.

Wariston, Archibald Johnston of. *A short relation of the state of the Kirk of Scotland since the reformation of religion, to the present time for information, and advertisement to our brethren in the Kirk of England, by an hearty well-wisher to both kingdoms.* Edinburgh, 1638.

Whitgift, John. 'The Defence of the Answer to the Admonition, Against the Reply of Thomas Cartwright: Tractates I–VI.' In *The Works of John Whitgift, D.D.*, edited by John Ayre, Vol. 1. Cambridge: Cambridge University Press, 1851.

III. SECONDARY SOURCES

Adams, Sharon and Julian Goodare, eds. *Scotland in the Age of Two Revolutions.* Woodbridge: Boydell, 2014.

Adamson, John. Introduction to *The English Civil War: Conflicts and Contexts*, edited by John Adamson, 7–18. Basingstoke: Palgrave Macmillan, 2007.

Albert, Anne O. *Jewish Politics in Spinoza's Amsterdam.* London: Liverpool University Press, 2022.

Armstrong, Robert. *Protestant War: The 'British' of Ireland and the Wars of the Three Kingdoms.* Manchester: Manchester University Press, 2005.

Bainton, Roland H. *Christian Attitudes towards War and Peace: A Historical Survey and Critical Re-Evaluation.* New York: Abingdon, 1960.

Ballor, Jordan J. 'Church Discipline and Excommunication: Peter Martyr

Vermigli among the Disciplinarians and the Magistraticals.' *Reformation & Renaissance Review* 15, no. 1 (2013): 99–110.

Barth, Karl. *Eine Schweizer Stimme: 1938–1945*. Zürich: Evangelischer Verlag, 1948.

Becker, Michael. *Kriegsrecht im frühneuzeitlichen Protestantismus: Eine Untersuchung zum Beitrag Lutherischer und Reformierter Theologen, Juristen und anderer Gelehrter zur Kriegsrechtsliteratur im 16. und 17. Jahrhundert*. Tübingen: Mohr Siebeck, 2017.

Beeke, Jonathon D. *Duplex Regnum Christi: Christ's Twofold Kingdom in Reformed Theology*. Leiden: Brill, 2021.

Bornkamm, Heinrich. *Luther's Doctrine of the Two Kingdoms in the Context of His Theology*. Translated by Karl H. Hertz. Philadelphia: Fortress Press, 1966.

Bowie, Karin. *Public Opinion in Early Modern Scotland. c. 1560–1707*. Cambridge: Cambridge University Press, 2020.

Braddick, Michael J., ed. *The Oxford Handbook of the English Revolution*. Oxford: Oxford University Press, 2015.

Brett, Annabel. *Changes of State: Nature and the Limits of the City in Early Modern Natural Law*. Princeton, NJ: Princeton University Press, 2011.

Broadie, Alexander, ed. *Scottish Philosophy in the Seventeenth Century*. Oxford: Oxford University Press, 2020.

Brown, Keith M. 'Early Modern Scottish History – A Survey.' *Scottish Historical Review* 92, no. 234 (2013): 5–24.

Brown, Keith M. *Noble Power in Scotland from the Reformation to the Revolution*. Edinburgh: Edinburgh University Press, 2011.

Brown, Keith M. and Alan R. MacDonald, eds. *The History of the Scottish Parliament: Parliament in Context, 1235–1707*. Edinburgh: Edinburgh University Press, 2010.

Brown, Keith M. *Kingdom or Province?: Scotland and the Regal Union, 1603–1715*. Basingstoke: Palgrave Macmillan, 1992.

Brown, Keith M. 'Courtiers and Cavaliers: Service, Anglicisation and Loyalty among the Royalist Nobility.' In Morrill, *Scottish National Covenant in Its British Context*, 155–92.

Brown, Keith M. 'In Search of the Godly Magistrate in Reformation Scotland.' *Journal of Ecclesiastical History* 40, no. 4 (1989): 553–81.

Burgess, Glenn. 'Religion and the Historiography of the English Civil War.' In Prior and Burgess, *England's Wars of Religion, Revisited*, 1–25.

Burgess, Glenn. 'Political Obedience.' In *The Oxford Handbook of the Protestant Reformations*, edited by Ulinka Rublack, 83–102. Oxford: Oxford University Press, 2017.

Burgess, Glenn. *British Political Thought, 1500–1660: The Politics of the Post-Reformation*. Basingstoke: Palgrave Macmillan, 2009.

Burgess, Glenn. 'Scottish or British? Politics and Political Thought in Scotland, c. 1500–1707.' *Historical Journal* 41, no. 2 (1998): 579–90.

Burgess, Glenn. 'Was the English Civil War a War of Religion? The Evidence

of Political Propaganda.' *Huntington Library Quarterly* 61, no. 2 (1998): 173–201.
Burgess, Glenn. 'The Divine Right of Kings Reconsidered.' *English Historical Review* 107, no. 425 (1992): 837–61.
Burns, James H. 'Political Ideas and Parliament.' In Brown and MacDonald, *History of the Scottish Parliament*, 216–43.
Burns, J. H. *The True Law of Kingship: Concepts of Monarchy in Early-Modern Scotland*. Oxford: Clarendon Press, 1996.
Burns, J. H. and Mark Goldie, eds. *The Cambridge History of Political Thought, 1450–1700*. Cambridge: Cambridge University Press, 1991.
Burton, Simon J.G. 'The Scholastic and Conciliar Roots of Samuel Rutherford's Political Philosophy: The Influence of Jean Gerson, Jacques Almain, and John Mair.' In Broadie, *Scottish Philosophy in the Seventeenth Century*, 208–25.
Burton, Simon J. G. 'Disputing Providence in Seventeenth-Century Scottish Universities: The Conflict Between Samuel Rutherford and the Aberdeen Doctors and it Repercussions.' *History of Universities* 29, no. 2 (2017): 121–42.
Cameron, James K. 'Some Scottish Students and Teachers at the University of Leiden in the Late 16th and Early 17th Centuries.' In *Scotland and the Low Countries, 1124–1994*, edited by Grant G. Simpson, 122–35. East Linton: Tuckwell Press, 1996.
Cameron, James K. 'The Conciliarism of John Mair: A Note on the *Disputation on the Authority of a Council.*' *Studies in Church History Subsidia* 9 (1991): 429–35.
Campbell, Alexander D. *The Life and Works of Robert Baillie (1602–1662): Politics, Religion and Record-Keeping in the British Civil Wars*. Woodbridge: Boydell Press, 2017.
Campbell, Alexander D. 'Episcopacy in the Mind of Robert Baillie, 1637–1662.' *Scottish Historical Review* 93, no. 1 (2014): 29–55.
Campbell, Ian and Floris Verhaart, eds. *Protestant Politics Beyond Calvin: Reformed Theologians on War in the Sixteenth and Seventeenth Centuries*. London: Routledge, 2022.
Campbell, Ian W. S. 'Aristotelian Ancient Constitution and Anti-Aristotelian Sovereignty in Stuart Ireland.' *Historical Journal* 53, no. 3 (2010): 573–91.
Catterall, Douglas. *Community without Borders: Scots Migrants and the Changing Face of Power in the Dutch Republic, c. 1600–1700*. Leiden: Brill, 2002.
Chapman, Alister, John Coffey and Brad S. Gregory, eds. *Seeing Things Their Way: Intellectual History and the Return of Religion*. South Bend, IN: University of Notre Dame Press, 2009.
Cipriano, Salvatore. 'The Engagement, the Universities and the Fracturing of the Covenanter Movement, 1647–1651.' In Langley, *National Covenant in Scotland*, 145–60.
Cipriano, Salvatore. 'The Scottish Universities and Opposition to the

National Covenant, 1638.' *Scottish Historical Review* 97, no. 1 (2018): 12–37.
Coffey, John. 'The Language of Liberty in Calvinist Political Thought.' In *Freedom and the Construction of Europe: Volume 1, Religious and Constitutional Liberties*, edited by Quentin Skinner and Martin van Gelderen, 296–316. Cambridge: Cambridge University Press, 2013.
Coffey, John. 'George Buchanan and the Scottish Covenanters,' In Erskine and Mason, *George Buchanan*, 189–203.
Coffey, John. 'England's Exodus: The Civil War as a War of Deliverance.' In Prior and Burgess, *England's Wars of Religion, Revisited*, 254–80.
Coffey, John. 'Quentin Skinner and the Religious Dimension of Early Modern Political Thought.' In Chapman, Coffey and Gregory, *Seeing Things Their Way*, 46–74.
Coffey, John. 'Puritanism and Liberty Revisited: The Case for Toleration in the English Revolution.' *Historical Journal* 41, no. 4 (1998): 961–85.
Coffey, John. *Politics, Religion and the British Revolutions: The Mind of Samuel Rutherford*. Cambridge: Cambridge University Press, 1997.
Cowan, Edward J. 'The Political Ideas of a Covenanting Leader: Archibald Campbell, Marquis of Argyll 1607–1661.' In Mason, *Scots and Britons*, 241–61.
Cowan, Edward J. 'The Making of the National Covenant.' In Morrill, *Scottish National Covenant in Its British Context*, 68–89.
Cowan, Edward J. *Montrose: For Covenant and King*. London: Weidenfeld and Nicolson, 1977.
Cowan, I. B. 'The Covenanters: A Revision Article.' *Scottish Historical Review* 47, no 143 (1968): 35–52.
Cunningham, Jack. *James Ussher and John Bramhall: The Theology and Politics of Two Irish Ecclesiastics of the Seventeenth Century*. Aldershot: Ashgate, 2007.
Cunningham, William. 'The Political Philosophy of the Marquis of Montrose.' *Scottish Historical Review* 14, no. 56 (1917): 354–69.
Cust, Richard and Ann Hughes, eds. *The English Civil War*. London: Arnold, 1997.
Daly, James. 'Cosmic Harmony and Political Thinking in Early Stuart England.' *Transactions of the American Philosophical Society* 69, no. 7 (1979): 1–41.
Dauber, Noah. 'Political Thought.' In *Interpreting Early Modern Europe*, edited by C. Scott Dixon and Beat Kümin, 388–414. London: Routledge, 2020.
De Freitas, Shaun and Andries Raath. 'Samuel Rutherford and the Protection of Religious Freedom in Early Seventeenth-Century Scotland.' *Westminster Theological Journal* 78 (2016): 231–48.
De Freitas, Shaun and Andries Raath. 'A Reply to John Coffey's Analysis of Samuel Rutherford's Theology and Political Theory.' *Journal for Christian Scholarship* (2015): 69–84.

De Groot, Jerome. *Royalist Identities*. Basingstoke: Palgrave Macmillan, 2004.
Denlinger, Aaron Clay. 'The Aberdeen Doctors (c. 1620–1641) on Tolerable and Intolerable Tolerance.' *Global Intellectual History* 5, no. 2 (2020): 137–51.
Denlinger, Aaron Clay. 'The Aberdeen Doctors and Henry Scougal.' In *The History of Scottish Theology, Vol. 1: Celtic Origins to Reformed Orthodoxy*, edited by David Fergusson and Mark W. Elliott, 279–95. Oxford: Oxford University Press, 2019.
Denlinger, Aaron Clay. 'Swimming with the Reformed Tide: John Forbes of Corse (1593–1648) on Double Predestination and Particular Redemption.' *Journal of Ecclesiastical History* 66, no. 1 (2015): 67–89.
Denlinger, Aaron Clay. '"Men of Gallio's Naughty Faith?": The Aberdeen Doctors on Reformed and Lutheran Concord.' *Church History and Religious Culture* 92, no. 1 (2012): 57–83.
Devine, T. M. *Scotland's Empire, 1600–1815*. London: Penguin, 2003.
Donagan, Barbara. 'Varieties of Royalism.' In McElligott and Smith, *Royalists and Royalism*, 66–88.
Donald, Peter. *An Uncounselled King: Charles I and the Scottish Troubles, 1637–1641*. Cambridge: Cambridge University Press, 1990.
Donaldson, Gordon. 'Scotland's Conservative North in the Sixteenth and Seventeenth Centuries.' *Transactions of the Royal Historical Society* 16 (1966): 65–79.
Donaldson, Gordon. *Scotland: James V – James VIII*. Edinburgh: Mercat Press, 1987.
Donaldson, Gordon. *Scottish Church History*. Edinburgh: Scottish Academic, 1985.
Donaldson, Gordon. 'Scotland's Conservative North in the Sixteenth and Seventeenth Centuries.' *Transactions of the Royal Historical Society* 16 (1966): 65–79.
Donaldson, Gordon. *The Scottish Reformation*. Cambridge: Cambridge University Press, 1960.
Eire, Carlos M. N. *War against the Idols: The Reformation of Worship from Erasmus to Calvin*. Cambridge: Cambridge University Press, 1986.
Erskine, Caroline. 'The Political Thought of the Restoration Covenanters.' In Adams and Goodare, *Scotland in the Age of Two Revolutions*, 155–72.
Erskine, Caroline and Roger A. Mason, eds. *George Buchanan: Political Thought in Early Modern Britain and Europe*. London: Routledge, 2012.
Estes, James. *Peace, Order and the Glory of God: Secular Authority and the Church in the Thought of Luther and Melanchthon, 1518–1559*. Leiden: Brill, 2005.
Estes, James M. 'Luther on the Role of Secular Authority in the Reformation.' *Lutheran Quarterly* 17, no. 2 (2003): 199–225.

Estes, James M. 'Erastus, Melanchthon, and the Office of the Christian Magistrate.' *Erasmus of Rotterdam Society Yearbook* 18 (1998): 21–39.
Estes, James M. 'The Role of Godly Magistrates in the Church: Melanchthon as Luther's Interpreter and Collaborator.' *Church History* 67, no. 3 (1998): 463–84.
Figgis, John Neville. *The Political Aspects of S. Augustine's 'City of God'*. London: Longmans, Green and Co., 1921.
Figgis, John Neville. *The Divine Right of Kings*. 2nd ed. Cambridge: Cambridge University Press, 1914.
Ford, John D. 'Conformity in Conscience: The Structure of the Perth Articles Debate in Scotland, 1618–1638.' *Journal of Ecclesiastical History* 46, no. 2 (1995): 256–77.
Ford, John D. 'The Lawful Bonds of Scottish Society: The Five Articles of Perth, the Negative Confession and the National Covenant.' *Historical Journal* 37, no.1 (1994): 45–64.
Ford, John D. '*Lex, rex iusto posita*: Samuel Rutherford on the Origins of Government.' In Mason, *Scots and Britons*, 262–90.
Fradkin, Jeremy. 'Protestant Unity and Anti-Catholicism: The Irenicism and Philo-Semitism of John Dury in Context.' *Journal of British Studies* 56 (2007): 273–94.
Franklin, Julian H. 'Sovereignty and the Mixed Constitution: Bodin and His Critics.' In Burns and Goldie, *Cambridge History of Political Thought*, Vol. 3, 298–328.
Friedrich, Carl. *Transcendent Justice: The Religious Dimension of Constitutionalism*. Durham, NC: Duke University Press, 1964.
Friedrich, Markus. 'Orthodoxy and Variation: The Role of Adiaphorism in Early Modern Protestantism.' In *Orthodoxies and Heterodoxies in Early Modern German Culture*, edited by Randolph C. Head and Daniel Christensen, 45–68. Leiden: Brill, 2007.
Gellera, Giovanni. 'Reformed Scholastic Philosophy in Seventeenth-Century Scottish Universities.' In Broadie, *Scottish Philosophy in the Seventeenth Century*, 94–110.
Gellera, Giovanni. 'The Reception of Descartes in the Seventeenth-Century Scottish Universities: Metaphysics and Natural Philosophy (1650–1680).' *Journal of Scottish Philosophy* 13, no. 3 (2015): 179–201.
Goatman, Paul R. 'The National Covenant, 1638: Religion and Politics.' In Hazlett, *Companion to the Reformation in Scotland*, 630–59.
Goatman, Paul R. and Andrew Lind. 'Glasgow and the National Covenant in 1638: Revolution, Royalism and Civic Reform.' In Langley, *National Covenant in Scotland*, 39–52.
Goodare, Julian. 'The Rise of the Covenanters, 1637–1644.' In Braddick, *Oxford Handbook of the English Revolution*, 43–59.
Goodare, Julian. *The Government of Scotland, 1560–1625*. Oxford: Oxford University Press, 2004.

Goodare, Julian. *State and Society in Early Modern Scotland*. Oxford: Oxford University Press, 1999.

Graham, Michael F. *The Uses of Reform: 'Godly Discipline' and Popular Behaviour in Scotland and Beyond, 1560–1610*. Leiden: Brill, 1996.

Greenspan, Nicole. 'Charles II, Exile, and the Problem of Allegiance.' *Historical Journal* 54, no. 1 (2011): 73–103.

Gribben, Crawford. 'Samuel Rutherford and the Liberty of Conscience.' *Westminster Theological Journal* 71, no. 2 (2009): 355–73.

Grosjean, Alexia and Steve Murdoch, eds. *Scottish Communities Abroad in the Early Modern Period*. Leiden: Brill, 2005.

Grosjean, Alexia. *An Unofficial Alliance: Scotland and Sweden, 1569–1654*. Leiden: Brill, 2003.

Harris, Tim. 'Revisiting the Causes of the English Civil War.' *Huntington Library Quarterly* 78, no. 4 (2015): 615–35.

Hazlett, William Ian P., ed. *A Companion to the Reformation in Scotland, ca. 1525–1638: Frameworks of Change and Development*. Leiden: Brill, 2022.

Heckel, Johannes. *Lex Charitatis: A Juristic Disquisition on Law in the Theology of Martin Luther*. Translated and edited by Gottfried G. Krodel. Grand Rapids: Eerdmans, 2010.

Henderson, G. D. *The Burning Bush: Studies in Scottish Church History*. Edinburgh: Saint Andrew Press, 1957.

Henreckson, David P. *The Immortal Commonwealth: Covenant, Community, and Political Resistance in Early Reformed Thought*. Cambridge: Cambridge University Press, 2019.

Hill, Christopher. *The Intellectual Origins of the English Revolution – Revisited*. Oxford: Oxford University Press, 1997.

Höpfl, Harro. *Jesuit Political Thought: The Society of Jesus and the State, c.1540–1630*. Cambridge: Cambridge University Press, 2004.

Hotson, Howard. 'Irenicism and Dogmatics in the Confessional Age: Pareus and Comenius in Heidelberg, 1614.' *Journal of Ecclesiastical History* 46, no. 3 (1995): 432–56.

Jackson, Clare. *Restoration Scotland, 1660–1690. Royalist Politics, Religion and Ideas*. Woodbridge: Boydell, 2003.

James, Leonie. *'This Great Firebrand': William Laud and Scotland, 1617–1645*. Woodbridge: Boydell, 2017.

Johnson, James T. *Ideology, Reason, and the Limitation of War: Religious and Secular Concepts, 1200–1740*. Princeton, NJ: Princeton University Press, 1975.

Killeen, Kevin. *The Political Bible in Early Modern England*. Cambridge: Cambridge University Press, 2017.

Kingdon, Robert M. 'Calvinism and Resistance Theory, 1550–1580. In Burns and Goldie, *Cambridge History of Political Thought*, 193–218.

Kingdon, Robert. 'The Political Resistance of the Calvinists in France and the Low Countries.' *Church History* 27, no. 3 (1958): 220–33.

Kornahrens, Douglas. 'Praying for the Christian Departed: A Brief View of the Doctrine and Practice in Scottish Episcopacy.' *Theology in Scotland* 18, no. 2 (2011): 47–79.

Kirk, James. *Patterns of Reform. Continuity and Change in the Reformation Kirk.* Edinburgh: T. & T. Clark, 1989.

Lake, Peter. 'Introduction: Puritanism, Arminianism and Nicholas Tyacke.' In *Religious Politics in Post-Reformation England*, edited by Kenneth Fincham and Peter Lake, 1–15. Woodbridge: Boydell, 2006.

Lake, Peter. *Anglicans and Puritans? Presbyterianism and English Conformist Thought from Whitgift to Hooker.* London: Unwin Hyman, 1988.

Langley, Chris R., ed. *The National Covenant in Scotland, 1638–1689.* Woodbridge: Boydell, 2020.

Langley, Chris R. *Worship, Civil War and Community, 1638–1660.* London: Routledge, 2016.

Lazareth, William H. *Christians in Society: Luther, the Bible, and Social Ethics.* Minneapolis: Fortress Press, 2001.

Lee, Maurice Jr. 'Scotland, the Union and the Idea of a "General Crisis."' In Mason, *Scots and Britons*, 41–57.

Lee, Maurice Jr. 'Scotland and the "General Crisis" of the Seventeenth Century.' *Scottish Historical Review* 63, no. 176 (1984): 136–54.

Lee, Maurice. *Government by Pen: Scotland Under James VI and I.* London: University of Illinois Press, 1980.

Lee, Maurice. 'James VI and the Revival of Episcopacy in Scotland, 1596–1600.' *Church History* 43, no. 1 (1974): 50–64.

Lind, Andrew. 'Royalism, Resistance and the Scottish Clergy, c. 1638–41.' In Langley, *National Covenant in Scotland*, 125–44.

Lind, Andrew. '"You may take my head from my shoulders, but not my heart from my soveraigne": Understanding Scottish Royalist Allegiance During the British Civil Wars, 1639–1651.' In *Loyalty to the Monarchy in Late Medieval and Early Modern Britain, c. 1400–1688*, edited by Matthew Ward and Matthew Hefferan, 211–30. Cham: Palgrave, 2020.

Lloyd, Howell A. 'The Political Thought of Adam Blackwood.' *Historical Journal* 43, no. 4 (2000): 915–35.

Lyall, Francis. *Church and State in Scotland: Developing Law.* Abingdon: Routledge, 2016.

Lyall, Francis. *Of Presbyters and Kings: Church and State in the Law of Scotland.* Aberdeen: Aberdeen University Press, 1980.

McAlister, Kirsty F. and Roland J. Tanner. 'The First Estate: Parliament and the Church.' In Brown and MacDonald, *History of the Scottish Parliament*, 31–66.

McCafferty, John. *The Reconstruction of the Church of Ireland: Bishop Bramhall and the Laudian Reforms, 1633–1641.* Cambridge: Cambridge University Press, 2007.

McCallum, John, ed. *Scotland's Long Reformation: New Perspectives on Scottish Religion, c. 1500–c.1660.* Leiden: Brill, 2016.

MacCallum, John, ed. *Scotland's Long Reformation: New Perspectives on Scottish Religion, c. 1500–c.1660*. Leiden: Brill, 2016.

M'Crie, Thomas. 'The Life of Andrew Melville.' In *The Works of Thomas M'Crie*, edited by Thomas M'Crie. Edinburgh: William Blackwood, 1856.

MacDonald, Alan R. 'Church and State in Scotland from the Reformation to the Covenanting Revolution.' In Hazlett, *Companion to the Reformation in Scotland*, 607–29.

MacDonald, Alan R. *The Burghs and Parliament in Scotland, circa 1550–1651*. London: Routledge, 2016.

MacDonald, Alan R. 'James VI and I, the Church of Scotland, and British Ecclesiastical Convergence.' *Historical Journal* 48, no. 4 (2005): 885–903.

MacDonald, Alan R. 'Ecclesiastical Representation in Parliament in Post-Reformation Scotland: The Two Kingdoms Theory in Practice.' *Journal of Ecclesiastical History* 50, no. 1 (1999): 38–61.

MacDonald, Alan R. *The Jacobean Kirk, 1567–1625: Sovereignty, Polity and Liturgy*. Aldershot: Ashgate, 1998.

MacDonald, Alan R. 'The Subscription Crisis and Church-State Relations, 1584–1586.' *Records of the Scottish Church History Society* (1994): 222–55.

McDougall, Jamie. 'Episcopacy and the National Covenant.' *Scottish Church History* 47, no. 1 (2019): 3–30.

McElligott, Jason and David L. Smith, eds. *Royalists and Royalism During the English Civil Wars*. Cambridge: Cambridge University Press, 2007.

McElligott, Jason. *Royalism, Print and Censorship in Revolutionary England*. Woodbridge: Boydell, 2007.

McGrath, Alister E. *Reformation Thought: An Introduction*. 2nd ed. Oxford: Blackwell, 1993.

Macinnes, Allan I., Patricia Barton and Kieran German, eds. *Scottish Liturgical Traditions and Religious Politics: From Reformers to Jacobites, 1540–1764*. Edinburgh: Edinburgh University Press, 2021.

Macinnes, Allan I. *The British Confederate: Archibald Campbell, Marquess of Argyll, c. 1607–1661*. Edinburgh: John Donald, 2011.

Macinnes, Allan I. *The British Revolution, 1629–1660*. Basingstoke: Palgrave Macmillan, 2005.

Macinnes, Allan I. 'Covenanting Ideology in Seventeenth-Century Scotland.' In *Political Thought in Seventeenth-Century Ireland*. Edited by Jane H. Ohlmeyer, 191–220. Cambridge: Cambridge University Press, 2000.

Macinnes, Allan I. *The British Revolution, 1629–1660: A Political and Constitutional Analysis*. Edinburgh: John Donald, 1996.

Macinnes, Allan I. *Clanship, Commerce and the House of Stuart, 1603–1788*. East Linton: Tuckwell Press, 1996.

Macinnes, Allan I. *Charles I and the Making of the Covenanting Movement, 1625–1641*. Edinburgh: John Donald, 1991.

McIntyre, Neil and Alison Cathcart, eds. *Scotland and the Wider World: Essays in Honour of Allan I. Macinnes.* Woodbridge: Boydell, 2022.

McKay, W. D. J. *An Ecclesiastical Republic: Church Government in the Writings of George Gillespie.* Carlisle: Paternoster Press, 1997.

MacKenzie, Kirsteen M. *The Solemn League and Covenant of the Three Kingdoms and the Cromwellian Union, 1643–1664.* London: Routledge, 2018.

Macmillan, Donald. *The Aberdeen Doctors: A Notable Group of Scottish Theologians of the First Episcopal Period, 1610–1638 and the Bearing of Their Teaching on Some Questions of the Present Time.* London: Hodder and Stoughton, 1909.

Marshall, Peter. 'Quentin Skinner and the Secularization of Political Thought.' *Studies in Political Thought* 2 (1993): 87–104.

Mason, Roger A. and Steven J. Reid, eds. *Andrew Melville (1545–1622): Writings, Reception, and Reputation.* Farnham: Ashgate, 2014.

Mason, Roger A. and Martin S. Smith, eds. *A Dialogue on the Law of Kingship among the Scots: A Critical Edition and Translation of George Buchanan's De Iure Regni apud Scotos Dialogus.* London: Routledge, 2004.

Mason, Roger A. 'Imagining Scotland: Scottish Political Thought and the Problem of Britain, 1560–1650.' In Mason, *Scots and Britons*, 3–14.

Mason, Roger A., ed. *Scots and Britons: Scottish Political Thought and the Union of 1603.* Cambridge: Cambridge University Press, 1994.

Mijers, Esther. '"Addicted to Puritanism": Philosophical and Theological Relations between Scotland and the United Provinces in the First Half of the Seventeenth Century.' *History of Universities* 29, no. 2 (2017): 69–95.

Millstone, Noah. *Manuscript Circulation and the Invention of Politics in Early Stuart England.* Cambridge: Cambridge University Press, 2016.

Milton, Anthony. *Laudian and Royalist Polemic in Seventeenth-Century England: The Career and Writings of Peter Heylyn.* Manchester: Manchester University Press, 2017.

Milton, Anthony. '"The Universal Peacemaker"? John Dury and the Politics of Irenicism in England.' In *Samuel Hartlib and Universal Reformation*, edited by Mark Greengrass, Michael Leslie, and Timothy Raylor, 1–25. Cambridge: Cambridge University Press, 1994.

Mitchell, Joshua. *Not by Reason Alone: Religion, History, and Identity in Early Modern Political Thought.* Chicago: University of Chicago Press, 1993.

Morrill, John. 'A British Patriarchy? Ecclesiastical Imperialism Under the Early Stuarts.' In *Religion, Culture and Society in Early Modern Britain*, edited by Anthony Fletcher and Peter Roberts, 209–37. Cambridge: Cambridge University Press, 1994.

Morrill, John. *The Nature of the English Revolution.* London: Longman, 1993.

Morrill, John. 'The National Covenant in its British Context.' In Morrill, *Scottish National Covenant in Its British Context*, 1–30.

Morrill, John, ed. *The Scottish National Covenant in Its British Context, 1638–51*. Edinburgh: Edinburgh University Press, 1990.

Morrill, John. 'The Religious Context of the English Civil War.' *Transactions of the Royal Historical Society* 34 (1984): 155–78.

Mortimer, Sarah. *Reformation, Resistance and Reason of State (1517–1625)*. Oxford: Oxford University Press, 2021.

Mullan, David G. 'Revolution, Consensus, and Controversy: Reformation Thought in Scotland.' In Hazlett, *Companion to the Reformation in Scotland*, 149–76.

Mullan, David G. 'A Hotter Sort of Protestantism? Comparisons Between French and Scottish Calvinisms.' *Sixteenth Century Journal* 39, no. 1 (2008): 45–69.

Mullan, David G. *Scottish Puritanism, 1590–1638*. Oxford: Oxford University Press, 2000.

Mullan, David G. '"Uniformity in Religion": The Solemn League and Covenant (1643) and the Presbyterian Vision.' In *Later Calvinism: International Perspectives*, edited by W. Fred Graham, 249–66. Kirksville, MO: Sixteenth Century Journal Publishers, 1994.

Mullan, David G. *Episcopacy in Scotland: The History of an Idea, 1560–1638*. Edinburgh: John Donald, 1986.

Muller, Richard A. *Divine Will and Human Choice: Freedom, Contingency, and Necessity in Early Modern Reformed Thought*. Grand Rapids, MI: Baker Academic, 2017.

Muller, Richard A. *After Calvin: Studies in the Development of a Theological Tradition*. Oxford: Oxford University Press, 2003.

Murdock, Graeme. 'The Importance of Being Josiah: An Image of Calvinist Identity.' *Sixteenth Century Journal* 29, no. 4 (1998): 1,043–59.

Murdoch, Steve. *Network North: Scottish Kin, Commercial and Covert Associations in Northern Europe, 1603–1746*. Leiden: Brill, 2006.

Murdoch, Steve. *Britain, Denmark-Norway and the House of Stuart, 1603–1660. A Diplomatic and Military Alliance*. East Linton: Tuckwell Press, 2003.

Nelson, Eric. *The Hebrew Republic: Jewish Sources and the Transformation of European Political Thought*. Cambridge, MA: Harvard University Press, 2010.

Nenner, Howard. 'Loyalty and the Law: The Meaning of Trust and the Right of Resistance in Seventeenth-Century England.' *Journal of British Studies* 48, no. 4 (2009): 859–70.

New, John F. H. *Anglican and Puritan: The Basis of Their Opposition, 1558–1640*. Stanford: Stanford University Press, 1964.

Newton, Russell. 'United Opposition? The Aberdeen Doctors and the National Covenant.' In Langley, *National Covenant in Scotland*, 53–70.

Niebuhr, Reinhold. *Christ and Culture*. New York: Harper & Row, 1975.

Niebuhr, Reinhold. *The Nature and Destiny of Man: A Christian Interpretation. Vol. 2, Human Destiny*. New York: Charles Scribner's Sons, 1964.

Oakely, Francis. *The Conciliarist Tradition: Constitutionalism in the Catholic Church, 1300–1870*. Oxford: Oxford University Press, 2003.
Oakley, Francis. '"Anxieties of Influence": Skinner, Figgis, Conciliarism and Early Modern Constitutionalism.' *Past & Present*, no. 151 (1996): 60–110.
Oakley, Francis. *Omnipotence, Covenant and Order: An Excursion in the History of Ideas from Abelard to Leibniz*. Ithaca, NY: Cornell University Press, 1984.
Oakley, Francis. 'On the Road from Constance to 1688: The Political Thought of John Major and George Buchanan.' *Journal of British Studies* 1, no. 2 (1962): 1–31.
Peacey, Jason. *Print and Public Politics in the English Revolution*. Cambridge: Cambridge University Press, 2013.
Peacey, Jason. *Politicians and Pamphleteers: Propaganda during the English Civil Wars and Interregnum*. Burlington, VT: Ashgate, 2004.
Pecar, Andreas. *Macht der Schrift. Politischer Biblizismus in Schottland und England zwischen Reformation und Bürgerkrieg (1534–1642)*. Munich: Oldenbourg Wissenschaftsverlag, 2011.
Pocock, J. G. A. 'Two Kingdoms and Three Histories? Political Thought in British Contexts.' In Mason, *Scots and Britons*, 293–312.
Pocock, J. G. A. 'The Limits and Divisions of British History: In Search of the Unknown Subject.' *American Historical Review* 87, no. 2 (1982): 311–36.
Powell, Hunter. *The Crisis of British Protestantism: Church Power in the Puritan Revolution, 1638–44*. Manchester: Manchester University Press, 2015.
Prior, Charles W. A. and Glenn Burgess, eds. *England's Wars of Religion, Revisited*. Farnham: Ashgate, 2011.
Prior, Charles W. A. 'Ecclesiology and Political Thought in England, 1580–c.1630.' *Historical Journal* 48, no. 4 (2005): 855–84.
Raath, Andries and Shaun de Freitas. 'Covenant and the Consolidated Christian Community: The Covenantal Roots of Theologico-Political Federalism in Samuel Rutherford's *Respublica Christiana*.' *In die Skriflig/ In Luce Verbi* 50, no. 1 (2016): 1–9.
Raffe, Alasdair. 'Intellectual Change before the Enlightenment: Scotland, the Netherlands and the Reception of Cartesian Thought, 1650–1700.' *Scottish Historical Review* 94, no. 1 (2015): 24–47.
Raffe, Alasdair. *The Culture of Controversy: Religious Arguments in Scotland, 1660–1714*. Woodbridge: Boydell Press, 2012.
Raffe, Alasdair. 'Scottish State Oaths and the Revolution of 1688–90.' In Adams and Goodare, *Scotland in the Age of Two Revolutions*, 173–91.
Raymond, Joad. *Pamphlets and Pamphleteering in Early Modern Britain*. Cambridge: Cambridge University Press, 2003.
Reid, Steven J. 'Cultures of Calvinism in Early Modern Scotland.' In *The Oxford Handbook of Calvin and Calvinism*. Edited by Bruce Gordon and Carl R. Trueman, 220–36. Oxford: Oxford University Press, 2021.

Reid, Steven J. "'Ane Uniformitie in Doctrine and good Order': The Scottish Universities in the Age of the Covenant, 1638–1649." *History of Universities* 29, no. 2 (2017): 13–41.

Reid, Steven J. 'Reformed Scholasticism, Proto-Empiricism and the Intellectual "Long Reformation" in Scotland: The Philosophy of the "Aberdeen Doctors," c.1619–c.1641.' In McCallum, *Scotland's Long Reformation*, 149–78.

Reid, Steven J. 'Andrew Melville and the Law of Kingship.' In Mason and Reid, *Andrew Melville*, 47–74.

Reid, Steven J. *Humanism and Calvinism: Andrew Melville and the Universities of Scotland, 1560–1625* (Farnham: Ashgate, 2011).

Robertson, Barry. *Royalists at War in Scotland and Ireland, 1638–1650*. London: Routledge, 2016.

Robertson, Barry. 'The Covenanting North of Scotland, 1638–1647.' *Innes Review* 61 (2010): 24–51.

Rose, Jacqueline. 'The Debate over Authority: *Adiaphora*, the Civil Magistrate, and the Settlement of Religion.' In *'Settling the Peace of the Church': 1662 Revisited*, edited by N. H. Keeble, 29–56. Oxford: Oxford University Press, 2014.

Rose, Jacqueline. 'John Locke, "Matters Indifferent", and the Restoration of the Church of England,' *Historical Journal* 48, no. 3 (2005): 601–21.

Russell, Conrad. *The Causes of the English Civil War: The Ford Lectures Delivered in the University of Oxford, 1987–1988*. Oxford: Clarendon Press, 1990.

Russell, Conrad. 'The British Problem and the English Civil War.' *History* 72, no. 236 (1987): 395–415.

Sanderson, John. *'But the People's Creatures': The Philosophical Basis of the English Civil War*. Manchester: Manchester University Press, 1989.

Scally, John. 'Counsel in Crisis: James, third Marquis of Hamilton and the Bishops' Wars, 1638–1640.' In *Celtic Dimensions of the British Civil Wars*, edited by John R. Young, 18–29. Edinburgh: John Donald, 1977.

Schultz, Karie. 'Catholic Political Thought and Calvinist Ecclesiology in Samuel Rutherford's *Lex, Rex* (1644).' *Journal of British Studies* 61, no. 1 (2022): 162–84.

Schultz, Karie. 'Protestant Intellectual Culture and Political Ideas in the Scottish Universities, ca. 1600–50.' *Journal of the History of Ideas* 83, no. 1 (2022): 41–62.

Shoenberger, Cynthia Grant. 'The Development of the Lutheran Theory of Resistance: 1523–1530.' *The Sixteenth Century Journal* 8, no. 1 (1977): 61–76.

Skinner, Quentin. 'The Origins of the Calvinist Theory of Revolution.' In *After the Reformation: Essays in Honor of J. H. Hexter*, edited by Barbara C. Malament, 309–30. Manchester: Manchester University Press, 1980.

Skinner, Quentin. *The Foundations of Modern Political Thought*. 2 vols. Cambridge: Cambridge University Press, 1978.

Smart, Ian Michael. 'The Political Ideas of the Scottish Covenanters. 1638–88.' *History of Political Thought* 1, no. 2 (1980): 167–93.
Smith, David Baird. 'William Barclay.' *Scottish Historical Review* 11, no. 42 (1914): 136–63.
Smith, David L. *Constitutional Royalism and the Search for Settlement, c. 1640–1649.* Cambridge: Cambridge University Press, 1994.
Smith, Haig Z. 'John Durie [Dury] (1596–1680).' In *Lives in Transit in Early Modern England: Identity and Belonging*, edited by Nandini Das, 94–9. Amsterdam: Amsterdam University Press, 2022.
Sommerville, J. P. 'Conscience, Law, and Things Indifferent: Arguments on Toleration from the Vestiarian Controversy to Hobbes and Locke.' In *Conscience and the Early Modern World, 1500–1700*, edited by Edward Vallance and Harold Braun, 166–179. Basingstoke: Palgrave Macmillan, 2002.
Sommerville, J. P. *Royalists and Patriots: Politics and Ideology in England, 1603–1640.* London: Longman, 1986.
Sommerville, J. P. 'The Royal Supremacy and Episcopacy "Jure Divino", 1603–1640.' *Journal of Ecclesiastical History* 34, no. 4 (1983): 548–58.
Spurlock, R. Scott. 'Polity, Discipline and Theology: The Importance of the Covenant in Scottish Presbyterianism, 1560–c.1700.' In Vernon and Powell, *Church Polity and Politics*, 80–103.
Spurlock, R. Scott. 'State, Politics and Society in Scotland, 1647–1662.' In Braddick, *Oxford Handbook of the English Revolution*, 363–78.
Steele, Margaret. 'The "Politick Christian": The Theological Background to the National Covenant.' In Morrill, *Scottish National Covenant in Its British Context*, 31–67. Edinburgh: Edinburgh University Press, 1990.
Stevenson, David. *The Scottish Revolution, 1637–1644: The Triumph of the Covenanters.* 2nd ed. Edinburgh: John Donald, 2003.
Stevenson, David. 'The "Letter on Sovereign Power" and the Influence of Jean Bodin on Political Thought in Scotland.' *Scottish Historical Review* 61, no. 171 (1982): 25–43.
Stevenson, David. *Revolution and Counter-Revolution in Scotland, 1644–1651.* London: Royal Historical Society, 1977.
Stewart, David. 'The "Aberdeen Doctors" and the Covenanters.' *Records of the Scottish Church History Society* 22 (1984): 35–44.
Stewart, Laura A. M. *Rethinking the Scottish Revolution: Covenanted Scotland, 1637–1651.* Oxford: Oxford University Press, 2016.
Stewart, Laura A. M. 'The Political Repercussions of the Five Articles of Perth: A Reassessment of James VI and I's Religious Policies in Scotland.' *Sixteenth Century Journal* 38, no. 4 (2007): 1,013–36.
Stewart, Laura A. M. '"Brothers in treuth": Propaganda, Public Opinion and the Perth Articles Debate in Scotland.' In *James VI and I: Ideas, Authority, and Government*, edited by Ralph Houlbrooke, 151–68. London: Routledge, 2006.
Strohm, Christoph. 'Melanchthon-Rezeption in der Ethik des frühen

Calvinismus.' In *Melanchthon und der Calvinismus*, edited by Günter Frank and Herman J. Selderhuis, 135–57. Stuttgart: Frommann-Holzboog, 2005.
Strohm, Christoph. *Ethik im frühen Calvinismus*. Berlin: De Gruyter, 1996.
Todd, Margo. *The Culture of Protestantism in Early Modern Scotland*. New Haven, CT: Yale University Press, 2002.
Torrance, Thomas F. *Scottish Theology: From John Knox to John Macleod Campbell*. Edinburgh: T. & T. Clark, 1996.
Torrance, James B. 'The Covenant Concept in Scottish Theology and Politics and its Legacy.' *Scottish Journal of Theology* 34, no. 3 (1981): 225–43.
Troeltsch, Ernst. *The Social Teaching of the Christian Churches*. 2 Vols, translated by Olive Wyon. London: George Allen & Unwin, 1931.
Tuininga, Matthew J. *Calvin's Political Theology and the Public Engagement of the Church: Christ's Two Kingdoms*. Cambridge: Cambridge University Press, 2017.
Tutino, Stefania. Introduction to *On Temporal and Spiritual Authority; On Laymen or Secular People; On the Temporal Power of the Pope against William Barclay; On the Primary Duty of the Supreme Pontiff*, edited and translated by Stefanio Tutino, viii–xxi. Indianapolis: Liberty Fund, 2012.
Tyacke, Nicholas. *Anti-Calvinists: The Rise of English Arminianism, c. 1590–1640*. Oxford: Clarendon, 1990.
Tyacke, Nicholas. 'Puritanism, Arminianism and Counter-Revolution.' In *The Origins of the English Civil War*, edited by Conrad Russell, 119–43. London: Palgrave Macmillan, 1973.
Vallance, Edward. 'Preaching to the Converted: Religious Justifications for the English Civil War.' *Huntington Library Quarterly* 65, no. 3/4 (2002): 395–419.
Van Dixhoorn, Chad. 'Presbyterian Ecclesiologies at the Westminster Assembly.' In Vernon and Powell, *Church Polity and Politics*, 104–29.
Van Dixhoorn, Chad. 'Scottish Influence on the Westminster Assembly: A Study of the Synod's Summoning Ordinance and the Solemn League and Covenant.' *Scottish Church History* 37, no. 1 (2007): 55–88.
Van Drunen, David. *Natural Law and the Two Kingdoms: A Study in the Development of Reformed Social Thought*. Grand Rapids, MI: Eerdmans, 2010.
Van Drunen, David. 'The Two Kingdoms Doctrine and the Relationship of Church and State in the Early Reformed Tradition.' *Journal of Church and State* 49 (2007): 743–63.
Vernon, Elliot and Hunter Powell, eds. *Church Polity and Politics in the British Atlantic World, c. 1635–66*. Manchester: Manchester University Press, 2020.
Vogan, Matthew. 'Fresh Directions in Rutherford Studies.' *Studies in Puritanism and Piety* 1, no. 1 (2019): 3–37.
Von Friedeburg, Robert. 'Ecclesiology and the English State: Luther and Melanchthon on the Independence of the Church in English

Translations of the 1570s.' *Archiv für Reformationsgeschichte* 101, no. 1 (2013): 138–63.

Von Friedeburg, Robert. 'Buchanan and the German Monarchomachs.' In Erskine and Mason, *George Buchanan*, 131–50.

Walzer, Michael. *The Revolution of the Saints: A Study in the Origins of Radical Politics.* London: Harvard University Press, 1965.

Walzer, Michael. 'War and Revolution in Puritan Thought.' *Political Studies* 12, no. 2 (1964): 220–9.

Waurechen, Sarah. 'Covenanter Propaganda and Conceptualizations of the Public during the Bishops' Wars, 1638–1640.' *Historical Journal* 52, no. 1 (2009): 63–86.

Weithman, Paul J. 'Augustine and Aquinas on Original Sin and the Function of Political Authority.' *Journal of the History of Philosophy* 30, no. 3 (1992): 353–76.

Wengert, Timothy. *Human Freedom: Christian Righteousness: Philip Melanchthon's Exegetical Dispute with Erasmus of Rotterdam.* Oxford: Oxford University Press, 1998.

Whitford, David M. *Tyranny and Resistance: the Magdeburg Confession and the Lutheran Tradition.* St Louis: Concordia Publishing House, 2014.

Whitford, David M. '*Cura Religionis* or Two Kingdoms: The Late Luther on Religion and the State in the Lectures on Genesis.' *Church History* 73, no. 1 (2004): 41–62.

Witte, John. 'Rights, Resistance, and Revolution in the Western Tradition: Early Protestant Foundations.' *Law and History Review* 26, no. 3 (2008): 545–70.

Witte, John. *The Reformation of Rights: Law, Religion, and Human Rights in Early Modern Calvinism.* Cambridge: Cambridge University Press, 2007.

Witte, John. 'Between Sanctity and Depravity: Law and Human Nature in Martin Luther's Two Kingdoms.' *Villanova Law Review* 48 (2003): 727–62.

Witte, John. *Law and Protestantism: The Legal Teachings of the Lutheran Reformation.* Cambridge: Cambridge University Press, 2002.

Wootton, David. 'The Fear of God in Early Modern Political Theory.' *Historical Papers/Communications Historiques* 18, no. 1 (1983): 56–80.

Wormald, Jenny. *Court, Kirk, and Community: Scotland, 1470–1625.* London: Edward Arnold, 1981.

Worthington, David. *British and Irish Emigrants and Exiles in Europe, 1603–1688.* Leiden: Brill, 2010.

Worthington, David. *Scots in Habsburg Service, 1618–1648.* Leiden: Brill, 2003.

Wright, William. *Martin Luther's Understanding of God's Two Kingdoms: A Response to the Challenge of Skepticism.* Grand Rapids, MI: Baker Academic, 2010.

Young, John R. 'The Covenanters and the Scottish Parliament, 1639–51:

The Rule of the Godly and the "Second Scottish Reformation."' In *Enforcing Reformation in Ireland and Scotland, 1550–1700*, edited by Elizabethanne Boran and Crawford Gribben, 131–58. Farnham: Ashgate, 2006.

Young, John R. *The Scottish Parliament, 1639–1661: A Political and Constitutional Analysis.* Edinburgh: John Donald, 1996.

IV. UNPUBLISHED PHD THESES

Benert, Richard. 'Inferior Magistrates in Sixteenth-Century Political and Legal Thought.' PhD diss., University of Minnesota, 1967.

Cipriano, Salvatore. 'Seminaries of Identity: The Universities of Scotland and Ireland in the Age of British Revolution.' PhD diss., Fordham University, 2018.

Culberson, James Kevin. '"For Reformation and Uniformity": George Gillespie (1613–1648) and the Scottish Covenanter Revolution.' PhD Diss., University of North Texas, 2003.

De Freitas, Shaun Alberto. 'Law and Federal-Republicanism: Samuel Rutherford's Quest for a Constitutional Model.' PhD diss., University of the Free State, 2014.

Gellera, Giovanni. 'Natural Philosophy in the Graduation Theses of the Scottish Universities of the First Half of the Seventeenth Century.' PhD Diss., University of Glasgow, 2012.

Lind, Andrew. '"Bad and Evill Patriotts"?: Royalism in Scotland During the British Civil Wars, c. 1638–1651.' PhD diss., University of Glasgow, 2020.

McDougall, Jamie Murdoch. 'Covenants and Covenanters in Scotland 1638–1679. PhD Diss, University of Glasgow, 2018.

Scally, John J. 'The Political Career of James, Third Marquis and First Duke of Hamilton (1606–1649) to 1643.' PhD diss., University of Cambridge, 1992.

Index

Aaron's rod blossoming (Gillespie), 40–1, 107–8
Aberdeen Doctors
  on hierarchy of nature, 71
  members of, 54–5
  on obedience to magistrates, 69–73, 139, 140
  rejection of banding tradition, 70
  response to the National Covenant, 54–8
  two-kingdoms theology, 38
  views on irenicism, 55–8, 72, 76
absolute monarchy
  Catholic views on, 80–3
  and constitutional royalism, 87
  Covenanter opposition to, 102, 107, 122, 125, 126, 127, 132
  and episcopacy, 93, 105
  James VI and I's support for, 6, 50–1
  and king's sovereignty over law, 80–5, 87–8, 129
  royalist support for, 68, 74, 76, 77–9, 83–4, 87–8, 96, 98, 99, 111, 162
  see also monarchy
adiaphora
  and church government, 96, 103
  and church reform, 15–16, 51–4, 59, 63, 101
  and civil government, 16, 46–7, 50
  definition of, 50–1
  and Five Articles of Perth, 51–2, 58
  indifferent/indifferency, 46, 49–54, 59
  and Leipzig Interim, 50
  and opposition to Charles I's church reforms, 52–4
  royal supremacy, development of, 1560–1640, 47–9
  and support for Charles I's church reforms, 54, 57–9
  as tool for toleration, 50
Adversus Georgii Buchanani (Blackwood), 83

agency
  divine over politics, 16, 78, 79–80, 85, 88, 118, 127
  human over politics, 9, 14, 17, 88, 104, 116, 118, 121, 126, 129, 130, 132, 146, 162, 163
  mediate/immediate, 78, 79, 80, 85, 88, 96, 99–100, 123, 126–7, 130
Almain, Jacques, 99
Althusius, Johannes
  federalism, 81, 117
  reception in Scotland, 144, 162
  sovereignty, definition of, 129
  symbiotic view of politics, 129
Anabaptists/Anabaptism, 26, 27, 30–1, 56, 78
anti-Engagers, 7, 138, 153
Antichrist, 52, 54
antinomianism, 152
Aquinas, Thomas, 13, 80, 120
aristocracy, 82, 126
Aristotle
  on civil government, 121, 122, 123, 129–30
  concept of *eudaimonia*, 24
  on human nature, 117, 121, 122, 123
  on *societas perfecta*, 80, 81
Arminianism, 15
Assertion of the government of the Church of Scotland (Gillespie), 102, 103
Augsburg Interim, 31–2, 50
Augustine, Saint
  City of Man and City of God, 27
  on civil government, 27, 33, 78–9, 121–3
  on human depravity, 27, 33
  just war theory, 70–1
authority
  civil, 16, 47, 48, 51, 58, 87, 102, 104, 128, 130, 132
  ecclesiastical, 8, 36, 39, 101, 103, 107, 108, 143
  see also inferior magistrates

Baillie, Robert
  on church polity, 101, 102, 104–5
  on church reform, 60
  commissioner to Westminster Assembly, 94
  on Engagement, 148, 150–1
  on excommunication, 109–10
  on Independents, 104
  on parliamentary sovereignty, 60, 105
  resistance-thinking, 143, 144–5, 151
  speech to Charles II, 155
  two-kingdoms theology, 101, 105
Bainton, Roland, 3
Balfour, Robert, 149
Barclay, William
  engagement with Buchanan, 82–3
  on king's relationship to law, 83
  on papal deposing power, 84, 97–8
  reception in Maxwell, 81, 83–4, 131
  theory of absolute sovereignty, 82–3
Baron, Robert, 55
Basilikon doron (James VI, King), 50–1
Bellarmine, Robert
  on absolute monarchy, 80–1
  on papal deposing power, 97–8
  reception in Scotland, 79, 104, 118
Berwick, Treaty of (1639), 49
Beza, Theodore, 32, 106, 139
Bilson, Thomas, 144–5, 151
Bishops' Wars (1639–1640), 2, 6, 49, 75, 137, 139, 140–1, 151, 161
Blackwood, Adam
  absolute sovereignty, theory of, 83
  engagement with Buchanan, 82–3
  reception in Maxwell, 81, 83–4, 131
blasphemy, 28, 29, 31, 39, 53, 105, 144, 157
Bodin, Jean
  absolute sovereignty, theory of, 81–2, 129, 131
  reception in Maxwell, 83–4
  use in Scottish constitutional royalism, 85–7
Book of Discipline
  First, 35
  Second, 35, 36–7, 48, 95
Bramhall, John, 109–10
Breda, Treaty of (1650), 7, 154
Brett, Annabel, 15, 124
Brown, Keith, 34
Bucer, Martin, 36, 139

Buchanan, George
  on elective kingship, 82, 131
  on king's relationship to law, 82, 83
  on limited monarchy, 11, 72, 83
  on resistance, 71, 144
  and Scottish intellectual tradition, 10, 122, 162
Burgess, Glenn, 5
Burns, J. H., 9–10

Calderwood, David, 68, 96
Calvin, John
  on conscience, 57–8
  'disciplinarian' model and excommunication, 106
  resistance and obedience, 57–8, 72, 139
  two-kingdoms theology, 30–1, 39
  views on *cura religionis*, 31
Calvinism/Calvinist
  confessional concord with Lutherans, 55–7
  as distinct Reformed intellectual tradition, 9, 13–14, 17, 72, 117, 119, 129–30, 139, 144, 161, 162
  doctrine of total depravity, 119
  resistance theory, 3–4, 139
  as revolutionary ideology, 2–4
  theological-political covenant, 16, 117, 130–1
Campbell, Alexander, 68, 94, 104
Campbell, Archibald, Marquis of Argyll, 10, 147, 152
Campbell, Ian, 4, 84
Campbell, John, 1st Earl of Loudon, 147
Canons, Book of, 1, 6, 75
Carisbrooke Castle, 147
Cartwright, Thomas, 97
Catholic scholastic political ideas
  absolute monarchy, 82
  covenant and contract, 79
  as distinct intellectual tradition, 2, 9, 12, 14, 15, 17, 119, 161, 162
  legal theory, 16, 118
  liberty and equality, 116, 124, 129
  origins of government, 116, 118, 122–4, 127, 128–9, 132, 163
  purpose of politics, 24, 25, 31, 33, 78, 121, 128, 162
  reception in Reformed thought, 13–14, 16–17, 116, 117
  and Scottish universities, 118
  societas perfecta, 80–1

see also conciliarism; papal deposing power
Catholicism
  as distinct intellectual tradition, 9, 12, 17, 119
  idolatry, 52, 54
  liturgical practices and ceremonies, 31–2, 52
  threat to Protestantism, 52, 54, 55, 57, 59, 70, 72–3, 76, 151
  see also Catholic scholastic political ideas
Charles I, King
  arbitrary rule, 1, 7, 61, 156
  coronation of, 74
  ecclesiastical reforms, 1, 6–7, 46, 51–4, 58–9, 60, 75, 96, 120, 137
  and Engagement, 146–8
  execution of, 137, 138, 153–5, 157
  and nobility, 7, 11
  response to the National Covenant, 49
  see also royal prerogative
Charles II, King
  coronation of, 156–7
  endorsement of Presbyterianism, 7
  negotiations with Covenanters, 153–4, 155–6
  proclaimed king, 7
Charles V, Holy Roman Emperor, 31–2, 50
church government/polity
  authority to determine, 61–2
  debates about, 93–115
  and political allegiances, 68
  relation to civil government, 9, 95
  and Solemn League and Covenant, 6, 94
  see also Episcopalianism; Presbyterianism
Church of England, 1, 6, 47, 48, 50, 96, 97
Cipriano, Salvatore, 138, 147
civil law
  origin of, 60, 83
  purpose of, 25, 27, 40, 77–8
  relationship to church, 63, 104, 140
  relationship to magistrates, 87, 163
Coffey, John, 14, 36, 94, 101, 104, 117, 118, 120, 122, 153
Coleman, Thomas, 107
Common Prayer, Book of, 1, 6, 13, 46, 51, 52, 54, 60, 62, 75
communion, kneeling at, 6, 48, 53, 57, 59

conciliarism/conciliarists, 16, 24, 93, 96–7, 100–1
confessionalisation, 24
Confessions
  Confession of Faith (1560), 47
  Negative Confession (1581), 53, 54, 61, 69
congregationalism, 94, 101, 102, 104–5
conscience
  liberty of, 104–5, 150, 152
  and obedience to laws, 57–8, 63
  and rejection of Charles I's church reforms, 54
  and two kingdoms theology, 30–1, 39, 77
Constance, Council of (1414–1418), 100
constitutional royalism, 68, 85–7
Controversiarum illustrium, aliarumque usu frequentium, libri tres (Vázquez), 124–5
Corbet, John
  absolute monarchy, 75–6, 98–9, 131
  on *cura religionis*, 37–8
  obedience to magistrates, 139
  on papal deposing power, 98–9
  on Presbyterian threat to state, 97, 99, 100
Corinthians, Book of, 102, 108
coronation oath, 116, 131–2, 149
Covenanters
  and coronation of Charles II, 130–2, 156
  exportation of Presbyterianism, 6, 62, 77, 93–4
  limitations of the term, 13
  National Covenant subscription campaign, 1–2, 10, 49, 55, 69, 73–4
  as theocrats, 34, 37, 69, 88, 118–19, 130, 132, 163
  see also Covenanting political thought; resistance theory
Covenanting political thought
  holy war theories, 5, 9, 17
  human rationality, 119–21
  ideas about theological-political covenant, 16, 163
  legitimisations of resistance, 137–46
  liberty and equality, 121–30
  limited monarchy, 17, 97, 116
  natural law, 119–21
  parliamentary sovereignty, 59–60
  two-kingdoms theology, 33–4, 67, 101
Cowan, Edward, 117

Cowan, I. B., 118–19
Cromwell, Oliver, 56, 152, 154, 161
cura religionis
   definition of, 24
   in early Protestant thought, 24–5, 27–33, 36–7, 87
   Scottish debates about, 40–1, 46, 53–4, 59, 102, 105, 140, 156

Daneau, Lambert, 129
Davies, Sir John, 84
De coniunctione religionis et imperii libri duo (Blackwood), 83
De Jure Regni apud Scotos (Buchanan), 72, 82, 122
De potestate papae (Barclay), 97–8
De regno Christi (Bucer), 36
De regno et regali potestate (Barclay), 83–4
De republica libri sex (Bodin), 81–2
Decalogue
   definition of, 27–8, 49
   first table of, 29, 40
   knowledge of, 121
   magistrate's protection of, 31, 33, 35, 37–8, 40–1, 46, 105, 156
   second table of, 41
Denlinger, Aaron Clay, 56
depravity, of human beings
   Augustinian views of, 27, 33, 78, 121
   Calvinist doctrine of, 119–20
   Covenanter interpretations of, 120–1
A Dispute against the English-Popish Ceremonies (Gillespie), 53–4, 101, 120
A Dissuasive from the errours of the time (Baillie), 104–5
divine law
   and absolute monarchy, 77, 79, 122, 126
   adiaphora and silence of, 50, 57
   and church polity, 101
   definition of, 83, 120–1
   and godly commonwealth, 24
   relationship to magistrates, 40, 82, 143, 156
   and resistance, 32, 139
Divine right of church government and excommunication (Rutherford), 39–40, 103
divine right theory of kingship
   Covenanters' rejection of, 123, 125, 127, 128
   definition of, 11–12
   James VI and I's views on, 48
   precedents in Catholic thought, 82–3
   royalist support for, 11, 68, 79, 83–4, 85, 162
Dixhoorn, Chad Van, 94
doctrines, fundamental and secondary, 56, 104
Donaldson, Gordon, 34, 95
Douglas, Robert, 156–7
Drummond, William, of Hawthornden, 74–5, 76, 77, 139
Due Right of Presbyteries (Rutherford), 103
Duplyes of the ministers and professors of Aberdene (Aberdeen Doctors), 58
Dury, John, 55–6
Dutch Republic, 130
Dutch Revolt (ca. 1566–1648), 3, 31, 129, 143

Ecclesiastes, Book Of, 70
Edinburgh, 1, 55, 62, 122, 140, 141, 154
Eisermann, Johannes, 29
Engagement, The
   divisions wrought by, 138–9
   failure of, 17, 133, 137
   Scottish debates about, 146–54
Episcopalianism/episcopacy
   and absolute monarchy, 6, 10, 37, 67, 93, 105
   and church reform, 61
   Covenanter rejections of, 52–3
   General Assembly's rejection of, 61, 96
   James VI and I's imposition of, 48
   and *jure divino* church polity debates, 96, 101, 102, 104
   and National Covenant, 61
   and negotiations with Charles I (1645–1647), 146, 148
   rift with Presbyterianism, 68, 93, 110
   within Scottish royalism, 38, 55, 74, 76, 87, 93
Erastasians/ Erastianism, 39, 106–8
Erastus, Thomas, 107
Estates of Parliament
   abolition of clerical Estate, 8
   authority of, 63, 72, 142, 143, 146, 156
   supremacy over king, 82
   tensions with kirk, 137, 149, 153
   see also inferior magistrates
excommunication
   defences of, 16, 35, 40, 107–9
   definition of, 106–7

and Erastianism, 106–7
rejection of, 48, 97–8, 109–10
see also papal deposing power
expediency, 58, 59

Faire Warning for England (Bramhall), 110
Five Articles of Perth (1618)
   and Charles I's reforms, 49, 52–4, 55, 57–8, 96
   contemporary debates about, 38, 46, 57
   introduction of, 6, 48, 51
Forbes, John of Corse
   on *adiaphora*, 57–8, 96
   and Charles I's reforms, 96
   defence of Five Articles of Perth, 38, 57, 96
   religious irenicism, 54–7
   views on *cura religionis*, 38
   see also Aberdeen Doctors
Ford, John, 51
France, 52, 55, 81, 82, 96, 144, 147
Free Disputation against Pretended Liberty of Conscience (Rutherford), 152
Freitas, Shaun de, 116–17
French Wars of Religion (1562–1598), 3, 31, 81, 143
Friedeburg, Robert von, 50
Friedrich, Carl, 119

General Assembly
   Act denouncing Engagement, 154
   Acts related to church reform, 61, 62, 95
   authority of, 6, 59, 60, 62, 63, 77, 98–9, 109
   and Court of High Commission, 48
   at Glasgow (1638), 37, 39, 49, 62, 96
   and papal deposing power, 98–9, 109
   purging of, 7, 153, 161
   ratification of Five Articles of Perth, 48
   tensions with parliament, 17, 137–8, 146, 148–9, 157
   see also Kirk, Commission of
Generall demands concerning the late covenant (Aberdeen Doctors), 58
Genesis, Book of, 79
Germany, 26, 52, 55
Gerson, Jean, 99
Gillespie, George
   on civil government, 40
   as commissioner to Westminster Assembly, 94, 104
   on excommunication, 106, 107–8
   on natural law, 120–1, 122–3
   opposition to Charles I's church reforms, 53–4
   two-kingdoms theology, 40–1, 108, 120–1
   views on authority over church, 60, 103
   views on church government, 101–3, 104, 105
Glasgow, 67; *see also* General Assembly; universities
'Golden Act' (1592), 95
Goodman, Christopher, 71
Gordon, George, 2nd Marquis of Huntly, 55
grace
   common, 25, 121
   divine, 29, 40, 123, 125
   special, 25
Graham, James, Marquis of Montrose, 10, 86
Greenspan, Nicole, 11
Gregory of Valencia, 131
Gregory VII, Pope, 97
Guild, William, 55, 75
Guthry, Henry, 122

Hague, the, 155
Hall, Joseph, 102
Hamilton, James, 1st Duke of Hamilton, 49
Hamilton, William, Earl of Lanark, 147
Harrington, James, 117
Hartlib circle, 55
Hartlib, Samuel, 55–6
Hebraic patriotism, 117
Hebrew Republic, 117
Heidelberg, University of, 56, 107
Henderson, Alexander
   as commissioner to Westminster Assembly, 94
   defence of resistance, 128, 131–2, 140–1, 144
   on limited monarchy, 127–8
   on natural law, 120–1, 122
Henreckson, David, 14
Henry, Duke of Rothesay, 51
Henry VIII, King, 47
heresy
   of English Independents, 150, 151
   against first table of Decalogue, 29

heresy (*cont.*)
  punishable by civil sword, 15, 17, 25, 28, 39, 40, 46, 105, 120–1, 122, 157
High Commission, Court of, 48, 108
Hill, Christopher, 4
Historicall vindication of the government of the Church of Scotland (Baillie), 109
Hobbes, Thomas, 117
holy war *see* warfare
Höpfl, Harro, 124
Hosea, Book of, 141–2

idolatry
  and Charles I's church reforms, 51–4, 61, 63, 67
  eradication as justification for warfare, 5, 17, 32, 57, 58, 139–40, 142–3, 156
  punishable by civil sword, 29, 31, 38, 130
  within Roman Catholicism, 60
  see also blasphemy; heresy
Independents/Independency
  heresies of, 150, 152
  seizure of Charles I, 147
  threats posed to Scotland by, 6, 17, 104–5, 139, 151, 157
  at Westminster Assembly, 39, 94, 151
  see also congregationalism
indifferent/indifferency *see adiaphora*
inferior magistrates
  definition of, 32
  duty to resist superiors, 17, 57, 118, 130, 131, 132, 139–43, 144, 146, 154–5
  failure to carry out duties, 147, 151–3, 157
  obligation to obey superiors, 71, 72, 83, 85, 96, 163
  within Reformed resistance theory, 31, 32, 57, 100, 137–8, 143
Innes, Sir Robert, 149
Institutes of the Christian Religion (Calvin), 30–1, 139
'Instructions for defensive arms' (Henderson), 131–2, 140–1
irenicism, 55–8, 72–3; *see also* Aberdeen Doctors
Irenicum Amatoribus Veritatis et Pacis in Ecclesia Scoticana (Forbes), 38, 57
Irenicum sine de unione et sinodo evangelicorum liber votivus (Pareus), 56–7

Isle of Wight, 7, 147
Israel/Israelites, 85, 107, 117, 119, 127, 130, 142–3

James VI and I, King
  and Five Articles of Perth, 48–9, 51
  ideas about *adiaphora*, 50–1, 59
  political thought, 10, 11, 50–1
  prohibition of bands/bonds, 70
  reintroduction of episcopacy, 6, 48, 95
  royal supremacy, 33, 36, 48, 95, 108
  see also divine right theory of kingship
Jesuita vapulans (Rivet), 71
Jesuits
  politically subversive nature of, 13–14, 71
  political theory of, 79, 80, 124, 126, 144
  see also Catholic scholastic political ideas; papal deposing power
Johnson, James Turner, 3
Judges, Book of, 126, 143
just war theory *see* warfare

Killeen, Kevin, 14
kingship *see* monarchy
Kirk, Commission of, 148–9, 155–6
Kirk, James, 34, 36, 95
'Kirk Party', 7, 137, 152
Kirkcudbrightshire, 39
Knox, John, 10, 47, 71, 144, 162

Ladensium autokatakrisis (Baillie), 151
Laud, Archbishop William, 1, 62, 74
Laudianism, 62, 74
law
  ecclesiastical law, 60, 62, 63, 84
  Mosaic law, 30
  of nations (*jus gentium*), 14, 125
  Scots law, 60–1, 68, 71
  see also civil law; divine law; natural law
law of nature *see* natural law
Lee, Maurice, 7
Leiden, 53
Leipzig Interim (1548), 50
Leith, 140
Lenthall, William, 154
Leslie, William, 55
Lex, Rex (Rutherford), 77, 117, 118, 121, 122–4, 125–8, 145, 153
Lind, Andrew, 67, 68
Loci Communes (Melanchthon), 29–30
London, Treaty of (1641), 49

Luther, Martin
  and Augustinianism, 27, 33
  development of two-kingdoms
    theology, 26–9, 40, 121
  reaction to Peasants' War, 28
  views on remit of *cura religionis*, 28, 31
Lutheranism/Lutheran
  adiaphora debates, 50
  confessional concord with Calvinism,
    55–6
  as distinct intellectual tradition, 2, 9,
    13, 17, 161, 162
  Magdeburg Confession (1550), 32
  resistance theory, 31–2
Lyall, Francis, 34, 47

MacDonald, Alan, 34, 48, 95
Macinnes, Allan, 7
Mackay, Donald, Lord Reay, 10
McKay, W. D. J., 106
MacKenzie, Kirsteen, 138–9
Magdeburg Confession (1550), 32
Mair, John, 100
Maitland, John, Earl of Lauderdale, 94,
  147
malignants, 145, 148, 151, 152, 154
Mary, Queen of Scots, 47
Mason, Roger, 9–10
Matthew, Book of, 102, 106
Maxwell, John
  criticisms of Presbyterianism, 99–101,
    109
  defence of absolute monarchy, 87, 125
  defence of absolute sovereignty, 80–4,
    128, 131
  on obedience to magistrates, 84–5, 139
  on origins of government, 77–80
  support for episcopacy, 96
  use of Catholic legal theory, 81–4, 86,
    97, 129, 131
  views on church reform, 62–3, 131
Melanchthon, Philip, 29–30, 32, 39, 50
Melville, Andrew, 10, 36–7, 39, 55, 95,
  162
Molina, Luis de, 80, 123, 124
monarchy
  constitutional monarchy, 117
  elective monarchy, 11, 117
  limited monarchy, 16, 76, 77, 87, 102,
    111, 116, 121–2, 132, 155, 156, 162
  see also absolute monarchy; divine right
    theory of kingship; royal supremacy

Mornay, Philippe de, 32, 129, 162; *see also*
  Vindiciae, contra tyrannos
Morrill, John, 4, 5
Mortimer, Sarah, 14–15, 24, 28
Mullan, David George, 94
Muller, Richard, 119
Murdock, Graeme, 117, 130

Napier, Archibald, 1st Lord Napier, 86
National Covenant (1638)
  Aberdeen Doctors' rejection of, 55, 58,
    71–2
  and authority over church reform,
    60–1
  and bands/bonds, 70
  and Five Articles of Perth debates, 46,
    51, 57
  and ideas about *adiaphora*, 54, 59
  as reaffirmation of Negative Confession
    (1581), 16, 140
  revolutionary nature of, 1–2, 7, 8, 117
  royalist resistance to, 70–4, 76–7, 93,
    161
  subscription campaign, 1–2, 11, 49
natural law/law of nature
  in Catholic political thought, 14, 118
  Covenanter views on, 116, 119–21,
    122–3, 153
  and duties of magistrates, 25, 27, 32
  knowledge provided by, 120
  and legitimacy of self-defence, 139–41,
    143, 146
  relation to divine law, 121
  as a source of political power, 24, 40,
    122–3, 125, 126
  whether binding on kings, 11, 82, 83,
    86
Nelson, Eric, 14
neo-Thomists, 117
New, John F. H., 119
New Model Army, 139, 147, 150, 151, 154,
  161
Newcastle, 49
Newcastle, Propositions of (1646), 146–7
Newton, Russell, 55
Nicanor, Lysimachus *see* Corbet, John
Ninety-Five Theses (Luther), 26

Oakley, Francis, 100
obedience
  as advancement of God's glory, 33
  and constitutional royalism, 86–7

obedience (*cont.*)
  as divinely mandated duty, 11, 16, 58, 59, 69, 80, 84, 85, 139
  to inferior magistrates, 141
  limitations on subject's duty of, 32
  necessity for temporal peace, 57, 63, 69–76, 78, 85
  Presbyterians' subversion of, 96, 98, 99, 100, 141
  scriptural warrants for, 57
  to supreme magistrates, 29, 38, 53, 82, 124
Ockham, William of, 99
Old Testament, 31, 85, 117, 127, 130, 142
Oldendorp, Johann, 29
On Secular Authority (Luther), 26–9

Pagden, Anthony, 123
papal deposing power, 16, 93, 96–9, 100, 109
Pareus, David, 56–7, 143–4, 145, 162
Parliament, English
  Act of Supremacy (1534), 47
  breach of Solemn League and Covenant, 155
  execution of Charles I, 7, 153–4, 155–6
  negotiations with Charles I, 146–7
  Rump Parliament, 7, 153–4, 155
  Scots' alliance with, 6, 56, 76
Parliament, Scottish
  abolition of clerical Estate, 35
  Act defending invasion of England (1648), 149–50
  Act of Classes (1649), 17, 137, 152, 153, 154
  Act prohibiting banding (1585), 70, 72
  authority over church reform, 6, 16, 46, 59–63, 140, 143
  and Engagement, 137–9, 146–53
  purging of, 7, 152–3
  ratification of Five Articles of Perth, 48
  relationship to kirk, 137–9, 146–53, 157
  and Scottish Reformation, 47
  sovereignty, 17, 116, 121–2, 126, 132, 137, 139, 161
  see also Estates of Parliament; inferior magistrates; 'Kirk Party'
Peasants' War (1524–1525), 2, 26, 28
persecution, 14, 31, 32, 72, 139, 145
Peter, Book of, 70
Poland-Lithuania, 55
polis, 80, 129

Politica Methodice Digesta (Althusius), 129
'popery'/'popish', 6, 14, 48, 53, 59, 61, 110, 118, 157
potestas coactiva/coactive power, 84, 98, 99, 131
potestas directiva/directive power, 98, 131
Powell, Hunter, 94
Prayer Book riots, 1
Presbyterianism/Presbyterians
  dismantling of, 6, 48, 95–6
  and Engagement, 7, 138–9, 146–53
  established by Parliament, 61–2, 140
  and excommunication, 106, 107–9
  jure divino nature of, 39, 77, 83, 93–4, 96, 101–5, 107, 122, 126, 132, 162
  and limited monarchy, 132
  negotiations with Charles II, 7, 154–5
  royal supremacy, 39–40, 41
  royalist criticisms of, 62, 77, 96–101, 109–10
  and Scottish Reformation, 33–7, 95, 140
  Solemn League and Covenant (1643), 5, 6, 77, 116, 145
  and theocracy, 34–5, 37, 118–19
  as threat to state, 16, 39, 70, 84, 93, 96–101, 109–10
  two-kingdoms theology, 34–5
Prior, Charles W. A., 50
privy council, Scottish, 48, 53
Protestantism
  and the purpose of politics, 24–5
  as a revolutionary ideology, 2–5
  see also Calvinism; Lutheranism/Lutheran
Protestors, 154
Prussia, 55
Puritanism/Puritans, 3, 4, 50, 107, 119

Raid of Ruthven, 70
reason/rationality
  and end of politics, 24, 162–3
  and human activity in politics, 25, 104, 119–21, 123, 127, 132
  and worship, 104
rebellion, 5, 28, 69, 70, 87, 98, 99, 141
Reformation, Scottish, 5–6, 9, 33–7, 46, 47, 59–60, 62, 63, 68, 70, 95, 101, 117, 137, 140
Reformations, Protestant, 2–3, 4, 8, 25, 26, 50, 58, 100, 118
Reformed tradition *see* Calvinism

Index

Reid, Steven, 36
resistance theory
   Covenanters' defence of, 117, 137, 139–46
   and Engagement, 146–53
   and execution of Charles I, 153–5
   Reformed tradition of, 57, 139, 143–6
   see also inferior magistrates; self-defence
Resolutioners, 154
Review of Dr Bramble (Baillie), 110
Revolution, English, 4, 8
Revolution, Scottish
   as conservative movement, 7
   intellectual culture of, 2, 17–18, 161
   as label, 7–8, 164
Rivet, André, 71–2
Robertson, Barry, 11
Romans, Book of, 28, 29, 32, 57, 102, 143
Rose, Jaqueline, 15, 50
Ross, Alexander, 55
royal prerogative, 1, 6, 46, 52, 59, 60, 61
royal supremacy
   and Charles I's church reforms, 49, 60, 63
   development of doctrine in Scotland, 46–9, 95
   Presbyterian challenges to, 36, 40, 41
royalism, Scottish
   diverse nature of, 10, 67, 68
   as intellectual tradition, 67–8, 161
   limitations of term, 11
   see also constitutional royalism; royalist political thought
royalist political thought
   absolute legal sovereignty, 80–5, 87–8
   hierarchy of nature, 67–9, 71, 72–3, 75, 161–2
   natural subjection, 78–9
   prioritisation of temporal peace, 69–76, 161–2
   see also absolute monarchy; constitutional royalism; obedience
Rump Parliament *see* Parliament, English
Rutherford, Samuel
   on *cura religionis*, 40, 41
   election of kings and limited monarchy, 77, 126–8, 129
   excommunication, 106, 108–9
   jure divino Presbyterianism, 101, 102, 103–4, 105
   on liberty and equality, 124–6
   on origins of government, 122–4

   on political-theological covenant, 130–2, 154–5
   resistance theory, 145, 154–5
   response to Engagement, 151–3
   within tradition of Reformed thought, 117
   two-kingdoms theology, 39–40
   use of Catholic political ideas, 118, 123–4, 127
   views on ancient Israel, 117
   views on natural law, 121

Sacro-sancta regum majestas (Maxwell), 77–80, 83–5, 99–101
St Andrews, 56; see also universities
salvation, 25, 50, 51, 54, 56, 57, 59
Schmalkaldic Wars, 2, 50
School of Salamanca, 14, 80, 117, 121, 122, 123, 124, 132
Scone, 74, 156, 161
Scotus, John Duns, 104
Scroggie, Alexander, 55
secular
   authorities, 8, 25, 27, 98, 107
   end of the state, 3–4, 25, 26, 28
   political ideas, 5, 14, 18, 72, 111, 119, 121, 163, 164
   see also warfare
secularisation, 2, 3, 4, 17, 119, 161
sedition, 69, 70, 73, 99, 125
Selden, John, 117
self-defence
   as justification for resistance, 118, 137, 140–1, 145, 154
   as natural right, 128
   in Reformed thought, 14, 139, 143
   warranted by natural law, 120, 139, 146
Sibbald, James, 55
Skinner, Quentin, 3–4, 14, 81
Smart, Ian Michael, 117
Smith, David Baird, 83
societas perfecta see Aristotle
Solemn League and Covenant (1643)
   and Charles I, 146–8
   and Charles II, 153–4
   Covenanter justifications of, 145
   and Engagement, 138, 147–8
   English breach of, 150–4, 155
   and exportation of Presbyterianism, 94–5
   royalist opposition to, 76–7
   terms of, 6, 94

Soto, Domingo de, 123, 131
sovereignty *see* absolute monarchy;
    Parliament, Scottish
Spottiswoode, John, 56, 68
Spurlock, Scott, 106
Stevenson, David, 7–8, 81, 83–4, 86, 150
Stewart, Laura, 8, 138
Strang, John, 74
Suárez, Francisco, 79, 104, 118, 123, 124
A Survey of Spiritual Antichrist (Rutherford), 152
Sweden, 55

Ten Commandments *see* Decalogue
theocracy, 34, 35, 36, 37, 118–19, 127, 163
Thirty Years War (1618–1648), 3, 9, 31
Timothy, Book of, 102
toleration, 50, 54, 56, 94, 152
treason
    against God, 82, 99
    against king, 49, 67, 70, 71, 73, 98
True difference between Christian subiection and unchristian rebellion (Bilson), 144–5
Tutino, Stefania, 123
two-kingdoms theology/theory, 25–33, 34, 36, 95, 121
Tyacke, Nicholas, 15

Ungirding of the Scottish Armour (Corbet), 37–8
Union of Crowns (1603), 6, 48
universities
    Cambridge, 97
    curriculum and methodologies, 9, 117–18
    Edinburgh, 9, 39, 74, 118
    Glasgow, 9, 74
    King's College, Aberdeen, 9, 38, 55
    Marischal College, Aberdeen, 9, 55
    purging of, 138, 157, 161
    royalism within, 10, 68, 73
    St Andrews, 9, 39, 62, 73, 118
Uxbridge, Treaty of (1645), 146

Vallance, Edward, 5
Vázquez de Menchaca, Fernando
    Althusius's use of, 129
    on artificiality of government, 124–5, 132
    on king's relation to law, 131
    Rutherford's use of, 123, 125–6, 128
    and School of Salamanca, 124
    views on liberty and equality, 124–5
Vernon, Elliot, 95
Vindiciae, contra tyrannos (1579), 32, 129, 139, 141–3, 145
Vitoria, Francisco de, 80, 118, 123, 124

Walzer, Michael, 3
warfare
    holy war, 3, 5, 9, 17
    just war theory, 3, 70, 71, 85, 150–1
    legal-constitutional justifications for, 5, 9, 17, 119, 145, 162, 163
    secular justifications for
Wariston, Sir Archibald Johnston of
    appeals to Scots law, 60–1
    assistance with *Lex, Rex*, 122
    commissioner to Westminster Assembly, 94
    contributions to National Covenant, 60–1
    on formation of societies, 123
    'Kirk Party' member, 152
    on resistance and self-defence, 122, 140, 141–2, 143, 144
    views on church government, 140
    views on legal provisions for kirk, 140
Wars of the Three Kingdoms (1639–1653), 2, 4, 10, 13
Wedderburn, Sir Alexander, 149
Westminster Assembly (1643–1653)
    debates about church polity, 94–5, 101, 103, 104, 105
    English Independents at, 150, 151–2
    Scottish commissioners to, 6, 39, 40, 93, 94, 110
Whig historiographical tradition, 11–12, 68
Whitgift, John, 102–3
Withers, George, 107
Witte, John, 29

Young, John, 106

EU representative:
Easy Access System Europe
Mustamäe tee 50, 10621 Tallinn, Estonia
Gpsr.requests@easproject.com

www.ingramcontent.com/pod-product-compliance
Lightning Source LLC
Chambersburg PA
CBHW051125160426
43195CB00014B/2347